Studies
in
First
Corinthians 15

Studies in First Corinthians 15

Life in a Risen Savior

Robert S. Candlish
Foreword by Cyril J. Barber

KREGEL PUBLICATIONS
Grand Rapids, Michigan 49501

Studies in First Corinthians 15: Life in a Risen Savior, by Robert
S. Candlish. Foreword by Cyril J. Barber. © 1989 by Kregel
Publications, a division of Kregel, Inc. P. O. Box 2607, Grand
Rapids, MI 49501. All rights reserved.

Cover Design: Don Ellens

Library of Congress Cataloging-in-Publication Data

Candlish, Robert S., 1806-1873.
  [Life in a Risen Savior]
  Studies in first Corinthians 15: life in a risen Savior / by
Robert S. Candlish; foreword by Cyril J. Barber.
        p.   cm.
  Reprint. Originally published: Life in a risen Savior. Ed-
inburgh: Adam and Charles Black, 1863.

  1. Bible. N.T. Corinthians, 1st, XV—Sermons. 2. Jesus
Christ—Resurrection—Sermons. 3. Mystical union—
Sermons. I. Title.
BS2675.C35   1989   227'.206—dc20   89-2564
                                                       CIP

ISBN   0-8254-2331-7 (pbk.)

            1 2 3 4 5 Printing/Year 93 92 91 90 89

            Printed in the United States of America

CONTENTS

6 • Contents

Practical Implications

PART TWO

The Nature of the Future Body

Practical Implications

SUPPLEMENTARY DISCOURSES

FOREWORD

Of all the men who illumined the galaxy of the Free Church of Scotland, few can rival Robert Smith Candlish! Born in Edinburgh in 1806, Robert Candlish was blessed with a godly home. His father was a medical teacher in the university, and his mother was a woman "of great excellence and force of character, who, through the narrowest of circumstances (for her husband died, leaving her to rear their three children) contrived to give her two sons university." In this she succeeded. James became a surgeon, while Robert entered the ministry.

Young Robert was prepared academically for entrance into the University of Glasgow by his mother, sister, and brother. The significance of this fact is heightened when we realize that he never had the opportunity to attend school. He passed the entrance exams and distinguished himself as a student. Following graduation he became a tutor at Eton, and two years later returned to Glasgow to enter a pastorate.

In his late twenties (about 1833) and following a successful pastorate near Loch Lomond, Candlish was invited back to Edinburgh and appointed Assistant Minister in the Church of Saint George—one of the most influential congregations in that city. On the passing of the senior minister, Candlish was asked to take his place, and for the next four or five years devoted himself almost exclusively to the duties of the pastorate. Many of his sermons later appeared in book form, and his well-known exposition on *Genesis**, his discourse on *First John**, as well as the present volume, date from this period of his ministry.

In 1839 an event took place which was to have a far-reaching effect on Robert Candlish's life and rocket him from relative obscurity to national prominence. The civil

---

* Published by Kregel Publications.

authorities refused the people of Scotland the right to appoint their own ministers. Candlish, as a young member of the General Assembly, rose from the back benches to deliver a speech that drew into sharp relief the essence of the problem. The principles which Candlish advocated are not new to us, but they were revolutionary in his day. He championed: a) the right of the people to an effective voice in the appointment of their ministers, and b) the separation of church and state. Candlish's speech set in motion the machinery which ultimately led to a group of ministers withdrawing from the Church of Scotland; however, this did not happen for another five years.

The tensions which had been developing within the Church of Scotland did not lead to a parting of the ways immediately. They did attract attention overseas where Candlish's evangelical stand was greatly appreciated. This led, in 1841, to his being honored with the Doctor of Divinity degree from the College of New Jersey (later Princeton University).

Candlish continued to give leadership to the church until, in 1843, the evangelicals withdrew and founded the Free Church of Scotland. From this time on Dr. Candlish became engrossed in the controversies which raged back and forth. He constantly aided those involved with his counsel, and such was his oratory that his exposition of the cardinal tenets of the faith delighted the citizens of Scotland and contributed to the popularity of the cause.

At one time Robert Candlish was offered the professorship in Biblical Criticism at the University of Edinburgh. His appointment, however, was denounced by those who remembered his previous opposition to civil authority, and the offer was withdrawn.

While engaging in all kinds of activities to strengthen the fledgling Free Church, Dr. Candlish continued as pastor of the Church of St. George, and in due time had Dr. Alexander Whyte as his assistant. In 1861 he became moderator of the General Assembly, and when, in 1862, another of Scotland's great men, Dr. Thomas Chalmers, passed on to his eternal reward, Dr. Candlish was offered the chair of Divinity in the New College at Edinburgh. He declined the appointment, but in 1862 became principal of the College and administered the affairs of the school in addition to his pastoral duties.

With many changes having taken place in Scotland since 1839, and with many in the established church having belatedly realized the wisdom of Dr. Candlish's convictions, the University of Edinburgh honored Candlish in 1865 with the same degree previously conferred on him by Princeton.

Within a few years, Dr. Candlish's strength began to fail, and in 1875 he died, leaving behind him a legacy of books, pamphlets, speeches, sermons, and other addresses. One biographer stated of him that "in life and in death he showed how he not only held but was held and moved by his theology, and derived from it courage and hope with which he seemed to be inspired."

It is a tribute to the forsight of the present publisher that they are making Robert Candlish's works available again. *Studies in First Corinthians 15: Life in a Risen Savior* is a particularly appropriate book to reprint. May its release kindle fires of evangelical fervor in the hearts of those who read it.

CYRIL J. BARBER

PREFACE

In the preface to the first edition, I stated that my object was not so much to expound the chapter exegetically, as to illustrate the line of argument pursued in it. It is not an argument about the Resurrection in general. It has respect to one particular view of the Resurrection: its bearing on the believer's spiritual and eternal life. In that view, I have sought to trace the thread of thought which gives unity and coherence to the apostle's reasoning. My idea of the general outline of the argument is indicated in the table of contents.

In an additional note to the second edition, I entered into explanation as to some questionable points that some critics had noticed in the first edition. It is not necessary to retain any more of the explanation than what refers to the nature of the primitive corporeity of the human race.

Adverting to the difference between the popish doctrine of an original tendency to sin in man, "restrained and held under subjection only by a supernatural gift," and the opinion that the bodily nature in man, in respect of its origin and its original constitution, was fitted primarily for the functions of the animal life, rather than for the uses of spiritual and divine life, I mentioned the following:

"Of course, if anyone maintains that the constitution and condition of man in paradise were the *ne plus ultra* of his possible attainment—that even if he had fulfilled the covenant, he never would have received a better constitution, or reached a better condition— I have nothing to say. My view and his are incapable of reconciliation.

"But if I maintain that man's constitution and condition were thoroughly perfect, 'very good' in the view of the probation which he was to undergo; that no sinful tendency adhered to any part of his nature, and no adverse circumstance made his state unfavorable to the maintenance of his innocency; am I heretical if I also believe that his original position was not what would have been his ultimate perfection; that had he stood his trial he would pass from a state of probation to one of confirmed acceptance; that his soul or spirit would then become even more God-like than at first; and that his body would cease to be a body fitted for animal functions, and would become, like our risen Lord's, a spiritual body, fitted wholly and exclusively for the spiritual life?

"There is nothing in all this that detracts from the perfect harmony of all the parts of man's constitution, as he was originally made. My only object is to show that, whereas the corporeity which we derive from the first Adam is allied to that of the inferior animals, and to the earth whence both sprint, there is another sort of corporeity awaiting us: a corporeity that is to be like that of our risen Savior. The former sort of corporeity was that best suited to man in his original state of probation; the latter is to be his in his ultimate and everlasting state of perfection."

My attempt to solve the difficulty as to reconciling verse 50, "Flesh and blood cannot inherit the kingdom of God," with our Lord's appeal (Luke 24:39) "A spirit hath not flesh and bones, as ye see me have," has been scouted in some places. I would like any objector to say he prefers my solution, or if he can suggest a better one.

I am more than ever impressed with the vast importance of 1 Corinthians 15, as an isolated and self-contained structure, in which the whole gospel is, like Jerusalem of old, "builded as a city that is compact together" (Psalm 122:3). If treated as one complete whole, which is its true character, I do not see how it can be otherwise interpreted than as a personal immortality. The oneness of Christ and his believing people is the pervading element which harmonizes all.

ROBERT S. CANDLISH

INTRODUCTION

CHAPTERS 1—3

THE opening portion of this chapter (verses 1-11) may be regarded as introductory to the argument. The apostle, with admirable tact, prepares the way for his close and faithful dealing with the Corinthians on the subject of their unsteadfastness in one article of the Christian faith, by a touching appeal to them on the subject of that faith as a whole.

The appeal turns upon his own personal relation to them, as the preacher and apostle who had been the chief instrument in introducing the gospel among them. How he was accustomed to present the truth to their acceptance, and what acceptance they were accustomed to give to the truth as he presented it ; how sure and satisfying, how sufficient and saving, they as well as he had experimentally found it to be ; what its substance was as he preached it, and what the evidence and authority on which he always rested it —the evidence and authority of his own apostolic testimony and the unanimous voice of the whole apostolic college of which he was a member ;—these are the topics on which Paul dwells in this exordium or opening address. They were the topics best fitted to win for his argument a favourable consideration, by recalling the past with all its tender associations of fellowship and brotherhood, and awakening a salutary jealousy of whatever novelties might tend to break up so blessed a harmony.

To the consideration, accordingly, of these topics, and of the manner in which Paul so handles them as to make them conducive to his object of obtaining a fair hearing for his subsequent pleading for the resurrection, our first three discourses are devoted. The subject of the first is the consistency of Paul's preaching and its acceptance. That of the second is the substance or subject-matter of the preaching. That of the third is the evidence of apostolic testimony, and authority on which the apostle rested his preaching.

1

THE CONSISTENCY OF PAUL'S PREACHING AND ITS ACCEPTANCE

Moreover, brethren, I declare unto you the gospel which I preached unto you, which also you received, and wherein ye stand; by which also ye are saved, if ye keep in memory what I preached unto you, unless ye have believed in vain.
—1 Corinthians 15:1, 2

THE first sentence in this chapter, taken in connection with the closing verse of the chapter before it, seems to mark the relief which the apostle feels in passing from the discussion about spiritual gifts, now beginning to be irksome, to a more congenial and welcome theme. He dismisses, almost impatiently, the former topic. One way or other let there be an end of it. Let us have no more trouble about these questions as to the conduct of your gifted men and women in your assemblies. Only "let all things be done decently and in order" (xiv. 40). And now let us turn to what is far more vital. Let me remind you of "the gospel which I preached unto you, which also ye have received."

What the substance of that gospel was, appears

from the summary of its facts or doctrines afterwards given. In the meanwhile, and as preliminary to that summary, the apostle describes the treatment which it got at the hands of the Corinthians when he first preached it to them—the treatment which he is entitled to presume that it gets, and will get, at their hands still. He puts them in remembrance of what it once was to them. He points out what it must still be to them, if they are not to stultify or falsify their whole Christian profession. And he does so, that he may found upon their own past, if not present, esteem of the gospel, a protest against their listening to any doctrine that would damage or disparage it. He appeals to their own better judgment regarding it, against that startling corruption of it which he is about to expose—that denial of the resurrection of the dead which cuts up by the roots its whole significancy and value. He would bring them back, at the very outset of the discussion on which he is entering, to the first freshness of their early trust in Christ, and the sure hold which they had of his great salvation. The gospel which I declare to you, of which I remind you, and which I would have you to keep pure, is the very gospel which I preached to you from the first, and all along,—the very gospel which you once received, standing fast in it, and hoping to be saved by it. It is the gospel which surely you retain and grasp firmly still, unless the entire fabric of your faith is to be levelled with the dust.

I. "I declare unto you the gospel which I preached unto you, which also ye have received" (verse 1).

I declare it as the gospel which I preached, and which you received. I have nothing new to tell on the subject to which it relates—the subject of your peace with God, and your walk with God. It is to the old gospel that I would bring you always back—to the gospel which I used to preach to you in all simplicity, and which in all simplicity you were wont to receive.

There is an affecting allusion here to past times. There is a touch of tenderness, as the apostle delicately recals his own early ministry among the Corinthians, and their reception of it.

"I marvel that ye are so soon removed from him that called you into the grace of Christ unto another gospel." So Paul somewhat indignantly remonstrates with another church (Gal. i. 6). So he virtually addresses the Corinthians here. I would have you to remember what sort of reception you once gave to the gospel which I preached to you. It is the same gospel that I declare to you still. The change, if there be any, is not in it but in you. If it is not to you now what it was then, may it not be good for you to look back and ask yourselves how I preached it then, and how you then received it?

There are occasions in Christian experience when such a retrospect may be most seasonable and profitable ; when it may be most useful to remind Christians of the kind of welcome which they were accustomed to give to the gospel in days gone by.

1. I am subjected, in some spiritual trial, to the temptation of having novelties in doctrine or in practice urged on my acceptance. It is proposed to me that I should contemplate the matter of which the gospel treats in a new light I am to look from a new point of view on the old question of my reconciliation to God, and the settlement of my peace with God. The righting of my state in relation to him and the renewing of my nature in conformity to his image—these, my essential and indispensable wants, are somehow to be met upon a new plan. Some new aspect of the Divine character—some new ideal of the Divine government—seems to flash on me, so as to fascinate and charm me. I feel as if I had made a fresh and great discovery as to what God is to me, and what he would have me to be to him.

Am I summarily to discard the new suggestions of my inquiring spirit, and shut my eyes to the new light which I think has dawned on me ? Surely no. But just as surely I do well, at such a crisis, to call to mind the Lord's former dealings with my soul, and my own experience under them. I am not rashly to set aside as fallacious or fictitious the whole of Paul's preaching of the gospel to me, as if it were a "song of the olden time," and the whole of my believing reception of the gospel which he preached, as if it had been all a delusion and a dream. The doctrine of the resurrection, or any other doctrine touching the life of the soul and the destiny of the race, may be presented to me in a new light. It may commend itself, or be commended to me, in the form of a sort of improved edition of the original message issuing from the cross, the grave, the opened heavens. And the new edition of it may appear to furnish a more satisfactory solution of difficulties, and a shorter and more royal road to faith, than the old system, encumbered as it is with ideas of guilt and wrath; sin and condemnation; eternal punishment; vicarious suffering; an imputed justifying righteousness; a lost world; an elect people; a redemption; a renewal; an adoption; a bodily rising from the dead; a real and local inheritance of glory. There may be, there is, risk and danger in our being solicited to put such "new wine" into our "old bottles." Surely, before we yield to the temptation, we may well be exhorted to consider what sort of gospel once satisfied us; what sort of gospel we once received. "No man, having drunk old wine, straightway desireth new; for he saith, The old is better" (Luke v. 39).

2. Again, apart from any suggestion of novelties, I find my heart becoming cold, my conscience callous,

my mind listless, in going through the routine of my customary religious exercises, and reading or hearing the commonplaces of ordinary religious instruction. Sacred duties, devotions, discourses, studies, all begin to pall upon me ; to become "weary, stale, flat, and unprofitable." Somehow the plain gospel, setting forth man's utter ruin and helplessness, and God's free and full salvation, fails to impress me ; it is felt to be trite and tiresome. I am conscious, when I am brought into contact with it, of a languid and lethargic sort of apathy, which I feel as if I could not shake off. I become morbid and gloomy. It seems as if it were all in vain for me to try to believe, or have peace, or be at liberty, on the terms of that mere free and sovereign grace whose offer is so constantly dinned in my ears. It "contents me not." And having nothing else to look to, I am driven almost to dark and blank despair.

May it not be good for me, in that extremity, to bethink me of what once, at least, appeared to meet my case, and satisfy the cravings of my anxious and awakened soul ;—to be reminded of the gospel which Paul once preached to me, and which I once received? Was I in a worse frame then than now for appreciating its real evidence, power, and value ? Nay, were there not circumstances in my state, and elements in my experience then—perhaps largely wanting now— that did conduce to a right estimate of Christ, and of his suitableness to my case, and of his free gift of himself to me? Was it not a time when there was less room than there is now for refining and objecting, —for starting scruples and making difficulties? Was there not more of straightforward singleness of eye? There was no dallying or hesitating then. There was an urgent necessity for prompt decision. And whatever I may think of the opportunities of calm reflection which prolonged leisure and comparative security have given me, was not the instinct of my first alarm when the terror of the Lord flashed upon me,—was not the fresh fervour of my first faith and love in my eager closing with his offered mercy,—as trustworthy, at least, as any of my more recent questionings and speculations? Let me "ask for the old paths, where is the good way." Let me try again, if "walking therein I may find rest for my soul" (Jer. vi. 16).

Surely, it may be good for us, when our confidence and affection are beginning to fail, and we are tempted to throw the blame of the failure on the gospel as preached to us in the old fashion, fancying that it might tell on us more in a new dress,—to go back to the old time, and recall our warm welcome of it in the days of our soul's spiritual birth,—our "life's morning march when our bosom was young." Let us hear the Lord's voice—"I have somewhat against thee, because thou hast left thy first love.

Remember, therefore, from whence thou art fallen, and repent, and do the first works" (Rev. ii. 4, 5). And let us be sure, that with reference to our believing now, as well as with reference to our believing at first, his saying holds true—" If they hear not Moses and the prophets, neither will they be persuaded though one rose from the dead" (Luke xvi. 31).

II.—" And wherein ye stand" (verse 1).

The gospel which I declare unto you is the gospel in which you have got a standing. This the apostle urges as another recommendation of that old gospel which some among the Corinthians would now, it seems, amend and improve upon. It commanded your assent and consent once ; your close embrace and cordial acceptance ; at a time, too, when you were in the best possible frame for appreciating its glorious excellency as a revelation of the character and will of God, and its gracious adaptation to your case, as guilty, lost, miserable sinners. And it might well do so ; you might well be willing to receive it as you did. For in it you have now a position which you never otherwise could reach ; a position of secure, stable, settled righteousness and peace ; a strong position ; a sure habitation ;—" Our feet shall stand within thy gates, O Jerusalem" (Psalm cxxii. 2).

Yes, the apostle virtually says to the Corinthians,—

You may be thoroughly assured that none of those refinements on the gospel system—none of those fresh and original exhibitions of it, whether in the new light of a higher philosophy or on the field of a wider and larger philanthropy, which have a certain attraction for you in certain moods of mind—possess the element of stability ; none of them have power to impart the security which the gospel itself, rightly apprehended, gives ; in none of them can you stand at all so safely, or so surely, or so uprightly, as in it. They may seem to have some advantages in the way of overcoming initial difficulties on the heavenly road, or in the way of leading that road subsequently along a loftier range of vision and attainment. The first and primary act of faith, in closing with Christ, may apparently be rendered simpler and easier by substituting, for the free and universal gift of Christ to sinners as their Saviour, some vague notion of the Creator's equal fatherly favour for all his creatures, even apart from their being converted by his Spirit and reconciled to himself by the blood of his Son. And there may be a doctrine or discipline of so-called perfection, connected with mystical conceptions of the spiritual life ; or there may be an assumption and affectation of a humanity less straitened than that of ordinary, old-fashioned godliness ; such as may leave far behind the tame and narrow routine of a humble and holy walk with God in the midst of an evil world. But after all, where but in the old gospel of the free grace of God in Christ is a poor tempest-tossed dove to find a resting-place for the sole of its foot? Where but in the ark is a weary spirit to find safe repose? It is in the gospel that we "stand." For it is the gospel alone that can furnish, what is the indispensable condition of our standing securely, the means of a thorough healing of the breach, a thorough settlement of the misunderstanding, which sin has caused between us and our God. In the gospel alone, in the gospel system of a free and full justification by grace, through faith in Christ as "the righteousness of God," "the Lord our righteousness,"—we have guilty man confronted face to face with his Judge, and made to see how in righteousness his guilt is cancelled, and he is himself restored to the place and privilege of a child. There alone we have, in the cross of Christ, the Ruler and the criminal, the Father and the prodigal, the Holy One and the sinner, righteously reconciled. This is our standing in the gospel. "Being justified by faith we have peace with God through our Lord Jesus Christ : by whom also we have access by faith into this grace wherein we stand" (Rom. v. 1, 2).

III.—"By which also ye are saved" (verse 2).

This gospel is indeed "the power of God unto salvation to every one that believeth." And it is so, because "therein is the righteousness of God revealed

from faith to faith ; as it is written, the just shall live
by faith" (Rom. i. 16,17). "Christ crucified" may be to
some a stumbling-block, for "he was crucified through
weakness" (2 Cor. xiii. 4). "But the weakness of
God is stronger than man ;" and "to them that are
called, Christ crucified is the power of God." All the
elements of salvation are provided for us and secured
to us in this gospel. In it we have free forgiveness,
complete acceptance in the sight of God, a sure
standing in his favour, present peace. In it we have
also renewal of nature, a new heart, a right spirit, a
new principle implanted in us of holy loyalty and
love to him who first loved us. And in it we have,
moreover, the gift of the Holy Ghost, and his indwelling in us, to shed abroad in our hearts the love
of God to us, to quicken our love to God, to cry in us
Abba Father, to "witness with our spirits that we are
the children of God, and if children then heirs, heirs
of God and joint heirs with Christ ;"—to be thus in
us "the earnest of our inheritance," giving us, more
and more, in our growing sense of God's fatherly love
to us, and our growing exercise of filial love to God,—
in our advancing likeness to him, and our increasing
capacity for knowing, trusting, and delighting in him,
—an ever brightening foresight, an ever deepening
foretaste, of the eternal blessedness of heaven. Such
salvation is there in "the gospel which I preached
unto you, which also ye have received, and wherein

ye stand." Surely, then, it is not a gospel to be lightly abandoned, or superseded, or changed.

IV. So the apostle, in substance, reasons, when he puts it, as it were, to the Corinthians to say if they mean to "keep in memory,"—or rather simply to keep, to retain and hold fast,—"what he preached unto them";—"if ye keep what I preached unto you" (verse 2). Is it not worth the keeping? Is it not still, as at the first, "a faithful saying, and worthy of all acceptation?" If it is a gospel which you once received ; if it is a gospel which is of such power to "strengthen, stablish, settle you," to give you a firm footing and sure standing in the favour and in the family of heaven ; and if it is a gospel which conveys and secures to you, in present possession and in future prospect, such a fulness of saving benefits ; is it to be supposed possible that you will hesitate about keeping it? It cannot, of course, minister to you either stability or salvation, unless you keep it; grasping it tenaciously and refusing to let it go. It is satisfying and saving only if you keep it.

If you keep it! Can that be matter of doubt? If so, it comes to this, that "ye have believed in vain" (verse 2). You make void and vain all the Lord's gracious dealings with you, and all your experience hitherto of his love and mercy. All that you have ever heard and seen of Christ is of none effect. You in effect nullify your whole past Christianity. Surely you are not prepared for such a result! An alternative like that you cannot face! And yet that is the inevitable consequence of your giving up and parting with the gospel which "I have preached unto you." You are at sea again ; unsettled and unquiet. Questions that concern your best interests for time and for eternity—questions which once seemed to be well adjusted—are again involved in all their old perplexing uncertainty. You have to begin the search for saving light and solid peace anew. And the probability is that, if you yield to the temptation, you may become like those who are "ever learning, and never able to come to the knowledge of the truth" (2 Tim. iii. 7). Keep therefore what you have received. Hold fast that which is good. When at any time you are in danger of being seduced from your steadfastness, let the still small voice of Christ sound in your ear, "Will ye also go away?" And let your reply be prompt, "Lord, to whom shall we go? Thou hast the words of eternal life" (John vi. 67, 68).

2

THE SUBSTANCE OF PAUL'S PREACHING

*For I delivered unto you first of all that which I also re-
ceived, how that Christ died for our sins according to the
scriptures; and that he was buried, and that he rose again
the third day according to the scriptures.*
— 1 Corinthians 15:3, 4

THE gospel which Paul preached was very simple.
He gives a very simple account of it. I. The articles
of the creed on which he insisted were few and plain
— " Christ died ; he was buried ; he rose again."
These three facts formed the staple of his preaching ;
they furnished to him his heads of discourse ; they
made up together his confession of faith. These were
the truths which he was accustomed to "deliver" at
Corinth. II. He delivered them "first of all." They
were among the first things of which he spoke. He
put them always in the van and forefront of all his
teaching. III. He delivered them as "that which he
also received." They constituted his message and his
mission ; both of which came to him directly from
the Lord.

I. The articles of this apostolic creed,—the heads of our apostle's customary discourse at Corinth,—are three, or rather two propositions. They are three, if we take them simply as matters of fact—Christ died ; he was buried ; he rose again. They are two, if we take them in connection with that appeal to the Old Testament Scriptures which gives them their real meaning and value, as embodying and unfolding the essential principles of the Divine government applicable to the salvation of man.

The first proposition, then, is "that Christ died for our sins according to the Scriptures."

It is not the mere historical fact of our Lord's death that is insisted on ; but, first, the meaning of that fact—" He died for our sins ;" and, secondly, the place which it holds in the economy of God as revealed from the beginning of the world—" He died for our sins, according to the Scriptures." In either view, the historical fact becomes a religious doctrine.

1. To say that Christ died, is to state a historical fact ; to say that Christ died for our sins, is to teach a religious doctrine. It was not, therefore, an ordinary death that he died. It was not the common case of a man giving up the ghost, breathing his last, and, as the phrase is, paying the debt of nature. His death and our sins are intimately connected : the guilt of our sins being the cause of his death ; the removal of

that guilt being the fruit and effect of it. To this death of Christ, thus viewed, I was always, says the apostle, directing your eye: "I determined not to know anything among you save Jesus Christ, and him crucified" (ii. 2). I held him forth before you, lifted up on the cross, dying for our sins.

Who is he who is seen dying there? Jesus Christ the righteous, the Lord from heaven, the Son of the Highest, himself the mighty God, who has become man for this very end, that he may be capable of dying. And who are they who inflict on this high and holy one the doom of this death? Not Herod and Pontius Pilate, the Gentiles and the people of Israel; but our sins; your sins and mine.

But if our sins slew him, is it not the worse for us? No. For he bore our sins, that he might relieve us of their burden. He died for our sins, that we might not die in our sins. He consented to their slaying him, that they might not slay us.

Christ died for our sins; by reason of them; on account of them. His death, therefore, was penal. It was the death which is the wages of sin. It was the death which we for our sins deserved to die. It was death by the sentence of law; the holy, un-changeable, righteous law of God. To die for our sins is to be subjected to their punishment. It is to be subjected to the curse, or condemnation of the law. It is to bear the wrath of the lawgiver and judge. It is to suffer what is necessarily implied in the utterance of that exceeding bitter cry, "My God, my God, why hast thou forsaken me!"

Shall we still choose to die for our sins?—to endure, and that for ever, what Christ endured when he died for our sins? Nay, rather let his death save us from thus dying. He died for our sins; for the cancelling of their guilt, for the annulling of their criminality. His death, being penal, is expiating and atoning. It is a real sacrifice of substitution. He takes the place of sinners. He dies for our sins instead of us. His dying for our sins is instead of our dying for them ourselves. No wonder, therefore, that he says so emphatically, "Whosoever liveth and believeth in me shall never die" (John xi. 26).

2. And all this, the apostle observes, is " according to the Scriptures." Paul identifies his own statement concerning Christ, that "he died for our sins," with all former revelations from the beginning. And he does so, not merely that he may confirm what he says himself by the authority of holy men of old who "spake as they were moved by the Holy Ghost;" nor that his teaching may add weight to theirs; nor even that their thorough agreement may prove the truth of both. He has a higher purpose to serve. He means to indicate the place which this great truth holds in that moral government of God, which it is the object alike of the Scriptures of the Old Testament, and of

the apostolic preaching in the New, to illustrate and unfold.

That "Christ died for our sins," is not a fact of local and temporary significance, like other great facts in the world's history which, however linked on with what goes before and comes after, may yet be, each in itself, isolated, separately estimated, disposed of, and set aside. Considered simply as a historical event, the death of Christ has a locality and a date. It took place in Palestine nearly nineteen centuries ago. It was that event which put an end to Judaism and originated Christianity. Christ died; and in consequence of that fact, an old religion passed away and a new religion began its course. But the doctrine —" Christ died for our sins "—lifts the fact of Christ's death out of the category of a mere historical event, having a locality and a date in past time. It becomes now the embodiment, or the enacting, of a principle in the Divine administration ;—a principle common to all times and places—common therefore to all the revelations of God to man. It was "according to the Scriptures " that Christ died for our sins, because it was according to the fixed, unalterable rule of that moral government of God to which the Scriptures throughout are intended to bear testimony.

For it is a necessary law or principle of the Divine administration, that he who would save sinners must save them by dying for their sins. Therefore, from the first it was announced, and continued always to be announced, as a discovery of divine revelation, that he who was to save sinners was to save them by dying for their sins. It was so in that earliest prophecy of mercy, when God said to the serpent, "I will put enmity between thee and the woman, and between thy seed and her seed ; it shall bruise thy head and thou shalt bruise his heel." The rite of animal sacrifice also, then instituted,—the slaying of a lamb, a goat, or a bullock, with confession of guilt over its head,—proclaimed the same universal, invariable, and indispensable law, that "without shedding of blood there is no remission." Sinners can be saved only by one dying for their sins. The whole Levitical institute, with its continual offering of slaughtered victims on behalf of the unclean—kept up the instinctive sense of that righteous rule of the Divine government which requires penal death for sin ; and kept up also the hope that ere long the rule would have its accomplishment in a worthy ransom being found thus to die. And with increasing clearness, as time rolled on, inspired prophets threw light on this hope ;—as when Isaiah said of him who was "to grow up before the Lord, as a tender plant, and as a root out of a dry ground ;"—"Surely he hath borne our griefs, and carried our sorrows ; yet we did esteem him stricken, smitten of God, and afflicted. But he was wounded for our transgressions, he was bruised for our iniquities : the chastisement of our peace was upon him ; and with his stripes we are healed. All we, like sheep, have gone astray; we have turned every one to his own way; and the Lord hath laid on him the iniquity of us all" (Is. liii. 4-6).

Thus Christ, on the one hand, "died for our sins." And thus, on the other hand, his dying for our sins was "according to the Scriptures."

And thus always we are to consider his death; not so much with reference to its mere occurrence, as an event in history, but rather in its bearing on that essential rule or principle in the holy administration of God which, as we trace it through all the Scriptures, the death of Christ is seen to assert and vindicate ; so that we·may be impressed with right views of the exceeding evil and demerit of sin ; the inevitable certainty of judgment ; the impossibility of escape otherwise than through the shedding of blood; the inflexible rectitude of that moral government by law which cannot even in mercy be relaxed, whose claims must be met if anarchy is not to reign ; the infinite love, above all, of the Father who, when no other adequate substitute can be found, does not spare his only begotten Son,—as well as the infinite love also of the Son who, knowing the inexorable condition that he can save sinners only by dying for their sins, is heard saying, "Lo! I come; I delight to do thy will, O my God" (Ps. xl. 7, 8).

The second proposition embraced in the apostle's preaching is the supplement or counterpart of the first. It is this—"He was buried, and he rose again according to the Scriptures." These two statements might be separated. And if, like the former, "Christ died for our sins," they were so put as to bring out their doctrinal value, or, in other words, their bearing on the plan of the Divine government in the salvation of sinners, it might be of importance to consider them separately. But they are not so put here. Elsewhere they are so put, as when it is said of Christ, that he was "delivered for our offences, and was raised again for our justification" (Rom. iv. 25); and when it is said of believers, that they are first "buried with him," and then "risen with him" (Col. ii. 20, and iii. 1). In this very chapter, as the argument goes on, the full significancy of the fact of the resurrection, as affecting both our present peace and our hope for the future, is illustrated at length. But in the brief summary of his preaching now before us, Paul mentions the burial and resurrection of Christ simply as matters of fact, establishing, when viewed in connection with his death, the completeness of the transaction which that event consummated and sealed. It is to prove the sufficiency and efficacy of Christ's death, as an atonement for sin, that his burial and resurrection are here brought in.

"Christ died for our sins." But he did not continue dead. He was not long under the power of death. "He was buried," indeed. And for a time it seemed as if he was to have no power to save; as if the cross were fatal to him, and therefore also fatal to those for whose sins he died; as if they had nothing for it but to re-echo the sad complaint of the mourning disciples, "We trusted that it had been he which should have redeemed Israel" (Luke xxiv. 21). But he rose again. Whatever his endurance of death implied,—including the body's occupancy of the dark and noisome grave, as well as the soul's separate sojourn in the unknown region where disembodied spirits dwell,—was temporary. It came to a speedy end.

It must be so, for so it had been foretold. "He rose again the third day according to the Scriptures." The Scriptures announced that he was to rise again. Thus the prophet Hosea speaks, with evident reference to the Messiah's resurrection, as being in fact the revival of God's people,—"Come, let us return unto the Lord; he hath smitten, and he will bind us up; after two days will he revive us; in the third day he will raise us up, and we shall live in his sight" (vi. 1). We may not perhaps interpret that text as fixing the third day for his resurrection, although some eminent divines have so understood it. But surely it intimates that his resurrection was to follow his death very closely. And then, still more explicitly, we find the Psalmist in Christ's person, hopefully "rejoicing;"

and giving this as the reason of his joy, "Thou wilt not leave my soul in hell, neither wilt thou suffer thine Holy One to see corruption" (Ps. xvi. 10).

Thus it was "according to the Scriptures" that Christ rose again the third day. And it was so because his resurrection after burial, like his death in order to burial, was no mere ordinary event in providence, but one that touches an essential principle of the Divine administration, which it is the object of all "the Scriptures" to unfold.

For if it is true, in virtue of a fixed rule or law in the holy, moral government of God, that whoever would save sinners must save them by dying for their sins, it is no less true that, if he is to save them, his dying for their sins must be followed up immediately by his rising again. He must be one of whom it can be said, "It was not possible that he should be holden of death" (Acts ii. 24). He must be one who can say of himself, "I am he that liveth and was dead, and behold I am alive for evermore; and have the keys of hell and of death,"—of the invisible world and of the entrance thereto (Rev. i. 18).

He is to die for our sins. They are to slay him. He is to suffer death on account of them, as a bleeding victim on the altar of atonement. Is that all? Then, a succession of such sufferers must be found, in quick relay, ransom after ransom, lamb after lamb, each dying for our sins, and continuing dead until now. But that cannot be all. The true saviour must be one who, dying for our sins, receives and takes again the life which he lays down. He must be one who can meet our doom. But he must also be one who cannot remain under it.

A divine person, the everlasting Son of the Father, his equal, his "fellow" (Zech. xiii. 7), taking our nature,—becoming capable of enduring the penalty of our sins, yet not capable of continuing to endure it,—such a Saviour alone can meet our case and, consistently with the eternal principle of righteousness in the government of God, effect our salvation.

Therefore, from the beginning, Christ is promised in the Scriptures as the seed of the woman, whose heel the serpent is to bruise, but who is himself to bruise the serpent's head. He is to bid defiance to death and to the grave, " O death, I will be thy plagues ; O grave, I will be thy destruction" (Hos. xiii. 14). He is not to die for our sins, as a merely mortal substitute or victim might be put to death for them. He is so thoroughly and conclusively to die for our sins, that once for all he is to "finish transgression and make an end of sin, and bring in an everlasting righteousness" (Dan. ix. 24). " As the righteous servant of the Father," he is " by the knowledge of himself to justify many, for he is to bear their iniquities." And he is to have done with bearing them. When " his soul shall have made an offering for sin," he is "to see his seed, he is to prolong his days, and the pleasure of the Lord is to prosper in his hand" (Is. liii. 10, 11).

"According to" such "Scriptures" as these, announcing the only Redeemer possible under the fixed rule, or law, or principle, of the righteous government of God, Christ died for our sins, was buried, and rose again the third day. And now it is our unspeakable privilege and joy to know that our Redeemer, though he was dead, liveth ; and that "he is able to save unto the uttermost all that come unto God by him, seeing he ever liveth to make intercession for them" (Heb. vii. 25).

These, then, are the facts on which Paul used to insist, in preaching the gospel to the Corinthians ; the death, burial, and resurrection of Christ; with a reference always to their doctrinal value and spiritual bearing, as connected with the teaching of the Scriptures from the beginning, and with that plan of the divine government which it is the business of the Scriptures to reveal.

II. But the apostle not only reminds the Corinthians of the topics he was accustomed to handle ;— he is anxious to remind them also of the place which they occupied in all his teaching among them ;— "These things I delivered unto you first of all ;" or, more exactly, "among the first things." The apostle attaches much importance to his having always given them this foremost place. At the very beginning of my preaching the gospel to you, I opened up to you these things. And all throughout, in all my ministry, however I might exhort you to "leave the first principles of the doctrine of Christ and go on to perfection," I never ceased to insist on them as the first and fundamental facts and doctrines of Christianity.

1. They were the first things of which I spoke to you ; these pregnant and significant facts ; giving an insight, such as nothing else can give, into the scope and meaning of the Old Testament Scriptures, and the fixed essential character of the government of God, of which these Scriptures are the exponent. I did not seek to introduce you gradually to the consideration of such topics, and to prepare the way by previous appeals likely to be more welcome. I plunged at once into the very heart of an obnoxious theme. I held up, in spite of its offence, the cross. I did not hesitate to commend to you, as your Saviour, one who died the death of a guilty slave. I did not hesitate to tell you the story of his resurrection. I knew that these truths would be most unpalatable to you : that the idea of one who died on the cross being your Saviour would hurt your pride ; that the idea of a resurrection from the grave would shock your reason. But I did not, on that account, keep back—no, not for a moment—these truths of God.

I did not try to win you by putting forward, as I
might have done, speculations or theories, that might
have better pleased your fancy. I wasted no time in
trying to disarm prejudice, and conciliate favour. I
spoke right on. I went straight up to the fortress.
I dispensed with all preliminaries, and summoned it
at once to the surrender, in the name of a crucified
and risen Saviour. You are my witnesses. My very
first words to you, without preface or preamble of
any sort, were these strange words for Grecian ears
polite ;—that an obscure native of Galilee, bred in
the house of a common carpenter, condemned as a
malefactor to a servile death, had by that very death
become the Saviour of men from their sins ;—and
that after being unquestionably dead and buried, he
returned again to life within three short days. You
know how I spoke to you, from the very beginning,
of these events, and referred you, for proof and explanation of them, to the old records of a nation that you
were accustomed to despise.

2. Nor is this all. You are my witnesses also to
something more. You know how, all throughout my
ministry among you, however much I might be bent
on carrying you on to the highest attainments in the
knowledge of Christ, and in the life of God, I still
always kept these truths prominently in the fore-
ground. I did not, indeed, wish you to be for ever
working at the foundation. I exhorted you to go on

from what was merely rudimental and elementary in the Christian experience, to what might interest and engage the loftiest movements and aspirations of your souls. But you must remember that I never ceased from reminding you of these first principles of the gospel, which from the beginning I made the staple of my teaching among you. I never ceased from setting before you, as the first and foremost topic in all my appeals to you, Christ; Christ crucified; Christ raised from the dead. "I delivered unto you" always, "first of all, how that Christ died for our sins according to the Scriptures; and that he was buried, and that he rose again the third day according to the Scriptures."

III. And how, the apostle virtually asks, referring to the "necessity laid upon him" to preach this gospel—how could I do otherwise? They were the very things—these things which "I delivered first of all"—that made up the essence, the sum and substance, of my message. It was my mission to deliver them. And I had no mission to deliver anything else. "I delivered unto you first of all that which I also received." I did not deliver it as a discovery of my own. I did not deliver it as a lesson I had learned from any master on earth. I delivered it as what I had received, not of man, or by man's teaching, but by the revelation of Jesus Christ. No wonder, therefore, that I delivered it "first of all;" that I made it from the beginning my first theme; and made it my first theme always to the last. It was what I had received. The Lord Jesus gave it me to deliver; it was he who gave it; and it was all he gave. I spoke as his commissioner, his deputy, his ambassador, when I was for ever telling you how "he died for our sins according to the Scriptures, and was buried, and rose again according to the Scriptures." I stood before you "as though God did beseech you by me," when I "prayed you, in Christ's stead, to be reconciled to God." And I always urged as the great argument and reason for your being reconciled, that first truth of the everlasting gospel; its first and last; its Alpha and Omega; "God hath made him to be sin for us, who knew no sin; that we might be made the righteousness of God in him" (2 Cor. v. 20, 21).

3

THE EVIDENCE AND AUTHORITY
OF PAUL'S PREACHING

And that he was seen of Cephas, then of the twelve: After that he was seen of above five hundred brethren at once; of whom the greater part remain unto this present, but some are fallen asleep. After that he was seen of James; then of all the apostles. And last of all he was seen of me also, as of one born out of due time. For I am the least of the apostles, that am not meet to be called an apostle, because I persecuted the church of God. But by the grace of God I am what I am: and his grace which was bestowed upon me was not in vain; but I laboured more abundantly than they all: yet not I, but the grace of God which was with me. Therefore, whether it were I or they, so we preach, and so ye believed.
— 1 Corinthians 15:5-11

WHAT Paul preached, or "delivered," to the Corinthians concerning the death, the burial, and the resurrection of Christ, he was accustomed to preach, or "deliver," confidently and boldly. And he was well entitled to do so. He was in a position to take his stand upon these facts as incontrovertibly true. They were the truths which constituted the groundwork or staple of all his teaching. And as matters of fact, they were thoroughly established by most competent evidence. The last of them in particular, the Lord's resurrection, the crown and consummation of the whole, rested on proof that could not be called in question. The apostles, and he himself as one of them, had actually seen the risen Saviour; and their testimony,—not to speak of several hundred additional eye-witnesses, most of them still alive,—was of itself amply sufficient (verses 3-10). It was so all the more on account of their entire agreement, not only in their testimony to the fact, but in the doctrinal use which they made of it. In their testimony and their preaching, they were all at one (verse 11).

Thus Paul asserts first, the authority, and secondly the harmony, of the apostolic teaching on the subject of Christ's resurrection.

I. Having described the gospel which he was accustomed to preach at Corinth, Paul indicates the character in which he preached it. He preached it as an apostle, as one of those who had seen the risen Lord. For it was their having actually seen the Lord after his resurrection that qualified the apostles for being eye-witnesses of that event; and therefore qualified them also for declaring that doctrine of the atonement which, as we have seen, depends on that event being proved to be a reality. Hence, in "delivering that which he received," concerning the death, the burial, and the resurrection of Christ, it was Paul's practice, not only to appeal to the testimony of the original apostles, but also to associate himself with them, as competent to bear the same testimony that they bore. He was consequently authorised to preach the same gospel that they preached, in the same character in which they preached it,—that of a " witness of the resurrection."

For the original warrant and authority of all apostolic preaching is to be found in the fact of which the apostles were eye-witnesses, that the Lord was seen after his resurrection. It was part of my preaching therefore, so Paul reminds the Corinthians, that Christ, after he was buried and rose again, was seen alive by " Cephas," and by the college of " the twelve"—still so called, though at the time, alas! shorn of its perfect number by the sin and doom of Judas (verse 5). It is not that the evidence of the fact of Christ's resurrection depends exclusively on the testimony of the apostles. " Once" at least "he was seen of above five hundred brethren ;"—of whom, though "some are fallen asleep, the greater part" still survive, and may be appealed to in corroboration of what the apostles testify (verse 6). That, however, was not the Lord's usual way of appearing during the forty days he was on earth before his ascension. He did not go in and out before the multitude, and among his disciples, as was his practice in the days of his public ministry. God shewed him openly, " not to all the people, but unto witnesses chosen before of God, even to us, who did eat and drink with him after he rose from the dead" (Acts x. 41). It was the apostles that were to be witnesses of his resurrection,—"he was seen of James ; then of all the apostles" (verse 7),—for it was as witnesses of his resurrection that they were to preach the gospel. Therefore, it was a necessary qualification for the apostolic office, that they who were to hold it must be men who could say, We have actually seen the risen Lord.

Paul accordingly claims for himself here, as elsewhere (ix. 1), this very qualification, and on the ground of it asserts his right to be recognized as an apostle, equally with Peter and James and the rest ; —"And last of all he was seen of me also, as of one born out of due time" (verse 8).

With fear and trembling indeed does Paul take his place among the apostles. He keenly feels his unworthiness. "His sin is ever before him," though "he did it ignorantly, in unbelief," the sin of his opposition to Christ and his cause. "I am the least of the apostles, that am not meet to be called an apostle, because I persecuted the church of God" (verse 9). But with confidence he claims his place. He would not dishonour or disown the grace of God to which he was indebted for it ;—a grace so sovereign, rich, and free, as to choose a persecutor to be an apostle;—and so abundant also, as to crown that persecutor's apostolic labours with fruit beyond what any of his fellow-labourers could count ;—"But by the grace of God I am what I am : and his grace which was bestowed upon me was not in vain ; but I laboured more abundantly than they all : yet not I, but the grace of God which was with me" (verse 10).

Grace, he cries ; it is all of grace ! It is by grace that I am saved myself, " counting it a faithful saying, and worthy of all acceptation, that Jesus Christ came into the world to save sinners, of whom I am chief" (1 Tim. i. 15). It is by grace that I am called to be an apostle ; of equal standing with all the apostles, though born, as to my apostleship, like a posthumous child ; permitted to see the risen Lord as well as they ; fitted, as they were fitted, for bearing witness to the resurrection. It is by grace that I am enabled even to surpass them all in labour, and allowed to see that I labour not in vain. By the grace of God I am what I am. It is not I who labour, but the grace of God which is with me. And if these my labours, so abundant and so successful, are the seal and confirmation of my calling as an apostle ; if in that view I seem to boast of them, though in them all I feel myself to be a debtor to grace alone; it is not that I may exalt myself above Cephas, or James, or the others who saw the Lord, but only that I may make good my title to be one of them, to be a partner with them in preaching common gospel, and a helper with them in establishing the common faith.

II. For in what we testify and in what we teach, we are all at one. This is the last consideration which Paul urges in behalf of the old doctrine, which some were for improving upon by their innovations. It has, he argues, this recommendation, that in declaring it, and in bearing witness to the great fact on which it rests, the apostles of the Lord are united and unanimous. "Therefore, whether it were I or they, so we preach, and so ye believed" (verse 11).

Thus, in closing his preliminary appeal, the apostle asserts the harmony and consent of the apostolic teaching; and at the same time again reminds the Corinthians of the glad acceptance which it once met with at their hands. You remember what I used to deliver to you as my message, which I had received from above. You remember how I spoke to you of the death, and burial, and resurrection of Christ. You remember how I referred you to the testimony of Peter and the other apostles, who had seen the Lord alive after his passion. I refer you to the same testimony still; corroborated, if you will, by a more numerous company, to whom, on one occasion, the Lord appeared. But I speak to you of what the apostles, as eye-witnesses of the resurrection, have to deliver to you concerning Christ. I am myself one of them, not less competent as an eye-witness, not less honoured as a labourer, than any of them. Nay, I have to acknowledge more grace than they all; for

who among them was so vile as I was when I persecuted the church? And who among them has been exposed, as I have been, to toil, and blessed, as I have
been, in seeing the fruit of my toil? But be that as
it may, in this we are all at one. We all speak the
same thing. We have all the same message to deliver,
the same gospel to preach. And it is a gospel which,
once at least, seemed to meet your case, and win your
approbation. "So we preach, and so ye believed."

Shall I not say,—so ye believe still? Alas! if I
am obliged, if you oblige me, to speak in the past
tense of your believing acceptance of what we, the
other apostles and myself, all of us, they and I, not
only used to preach once, but continue to preach now!
Is it then really a past event—"So ye believed?"
We have not changed our preaching. Can it be that
you have changed your belief? We, whether it be
Cephas, or James, or the other apostles, or myself, not
less an apostle than any of them—we continue to be
all agreed in what we have to tell of Christ, and of
the way of salvation in Christ. What we preached
at the beginning, we all with one accord constantly
preach still. As we preached then, "so we preach"
now. And "so" also "you" once at least "believed."
Must I stop short there? May I not venture to add,
—so you believe still?

It is, in one view of it, a keen and somewhat caustic
stroke of humour—a sort of covert yet kindly irony ;—

" So we preach, and so ye believed." That old gospel of ours was good enough for you, as well as for us, once. It is good enough for us still. But you, it seems, have outgrown it. You must have something less offensive to philosophic reason and fine taste, or something more recondite, transcendental, spiritual, and sublime. Be it so. By all means perfect the Christian system, and polish it to your heart's content. Meanwhile we, for our part, old fashioned as we are, will be content to preach as you used to believe. We will persevere in proclaiming the same gospel which formerly you received.

But in another view it is a deeply affecting appeal. It is fitted to bring before your eyes, O ye Corinthians, the venerable company of devoted men who first de-, clared to you and to all the churches "the unsearchable riches of Christ" (Ephes. iii. 8). It is fitted to set you upon asking what, in comparison with them, are those broachers of novelties, to whose subtle teaching you have been tempted to listen? What are all their various and conflicting speculations, springing out of abstract theories about mind and matter, or built upon one-sided and partial views of human nature and human life, when compared with " the simplicity that is in Christ" (2 Cor. xi. 3), as the apostolic fathers of Christianity have been wont to set him forth, "delivered for our offences, and rising again for our justification" (Rom. iv. 25) ?

May we not imagine a prompt reply to this pathetic appeal,—all the more pathetic for the touch of irony there may be in it? Paul shall not have occasion to use the past tense any more. What he and the other apostles preach, we will still believe. We are not to be "carried about with divers and strange doctrines." We call to mind how "good a thing it is that the heart be established with grace" (Heb. xiii. 9). We will not have new wine put into our old bottles. Having tasted the old wine, we will not desire the new; for the old is better. We are prepared to give heed to the exhortation,—"Remember them which have the rule over you, who have spoken unto you the word of God: whose faith follow, considering the end of their conversation. Jesus Christ the same yesterday, and to-day, and for ever" (Heb. xiii. 7, 8).

PART ONE

INFERENCES FROM THE DENIAL OF THE RESURRECTION OF THE DEAD (1 CORINTHIANS 15:12-34)

THE apostle having, in his introductory appeal, prepared the way for a favourable reception, or at least a fair hearing, of the argument which he has to maintain, proceeds to open it up at large. He presents it, as I apprehend, in two distinct aspects or points of view. In the first part of his reasoning (verses 12-34), he brings out the doctrinal import or value of the resurrection of the dead generally, and the resurrection of Christ in particular; shewing what is implied in the denial of his resurrection, and what in the admission and belief of it. In the second part, again, of his reasoning (34-58), he deals with a question or objection that might be raised, and is led on to consider, in connection with it, the nature and functions of the resurrection body, as contrasted with the body that is laid aside at death.

It is the first part of the argument which bears most directly on the object which the apostle seems to have in view. That object is not to prove or illustrate the doctrine of the resurrection of the dead, but rather to defend one of the fundamental truths of Christianity which the rejection of the doctrine of the resurrection tends, in the apostle's judgment, to undermine and overthrow. In fact, it is not the resurrection but justification that is the main theme of the argument, at least in the first part ; and the former subject is handled chiefly, if not exclusively, in subordination to the latter. What Paul is really concerned about, is the believer's hope of pardon and eternal life in Christ ; and it is because it so deeply affects that blessed hope that he regards with such intense alarm any speculation or theory that sets aside, or explains away, the literal bodily resurrection of the dead. This must be kept in mind throughout, if we would rightly understand what the apostle says with reference to the state and prospects, on the hypothesis of there being no resurrection of the dead, both of living believers and of saints who have fallen asleep in Jesus.

4

FIRST INFERENCE FROM THE DENIAL: CHRIST IS NOT RISEN, AND WE ARE YET IN OUR SINS

Now, if Christ be preached that he rose from the dead, how say some among you that there is no resurrection of the dead? But if there be no resurrection of the dead, then is Christ not risen: And if Christ be not risen, then is our preaching vain, and your faith is also vain. Yea, and we are found false witnesses of God; because we have testified of God that he raised up Christ: whom he raised not up, if so be that the dead rise not. For if the dead rise not, then is not Christ raised: And if Christ be not raised, your faith is vain; ye are yet in your sins.   —1 Corinthians 15:12-17

THE fact of the resurrection of Christ and the belief of a general resurrection of the dead are intimately and inseparably connected. So the apostle Paul here as well as elsewhere teaches. He asserts or assumes that connection; and, indeed, the whole of his reasoning in this chapter proceeds upon it. The resurrection of Christ, and the general resurrection of the dead, are so related to one another that they stand or fall together. If Christ is risen, then the dead rise; if the dead rise not, then is Christ not raised. It is in this last form that the apostle presents the case at the beginning of his argument.

He expresses surprise that any who had been made acquainted with the fact of Christ's resurrection, and with the evidence of that fact, should have embraced a doctrine which denies that there is or can be such a thing as a literal resurrection of the body ;—" Now, if Christ be preached that he rose from the dead, how say some among you that there is no resurrection of the dead" (verse 12) ? And still more, he expresses his surprise that they should do so apparently without perceiving that they must, in consistency, be driven to deny the resurrection of Christ ;—" But if there be no resurrection of the dead, then is Christ not risen" (verse 13). This, he says, is not only a fair and legitimate inference from that theory or opinion of " some among you," but a necessary part of it.

You think that the only possible resurrection is a spiritual one,—a resurrection which in spiritual men is " past already" (2 Tim. ii. 18). That anything whatever of the dead body which you consign to the rottenness of the tomb is hereafter to live again ; that in its dust, mingled and lost in the kindred dust of earth, the germ is to be found of a corporeal frame identically the same with the " mortal coil shuffled off" at death,—only beautiful and glorious beyond all comparison ; such a faith as that is, in your judgment, not only a fond imagination, but offensive, as savouring of a gross materialism. Your idea of the future life is of a more purely spiritual character. The notion of taking up again, in any sense or with any change, the very flesh which you lay aside when you quit this earthly scene, is to you intolerable. You say that there is, that there can be, no such thing as a bodily resurrection of the dead.

But have you considered how impossible it is, according to your views, to maintain the truth of the resurrection of Christ? And have you considered what the effect on your Christian life and experience must be, if his resurrection is denied? It is not merely that a historical testimony is set aside. The whole gospel which we preach, and which you once at least believed, is made void ;—" If Christ be not risen, then is our preaching vain, and your faith is also vain " (verse 14).

You pay us a poor compliment by that dogma of yours about there being no resurrection—involving, as it does, the conclusion that there was no resurrection on that third day on which, as it is at all events reported among us, Joseph of Arimathea's new tomb was found empty,—and after which, he who was laid in it shewed himself alive in the body by many infallible signs. You make us out to be not only poor preachers, but false witnesses ; poor preachers, because, if you are right, we merely amuse and beguile our hearers with an idle dream of corporeal felicity as a substitute for spiritual perfection ; and false witnesses, for we profess to attest, as a fact, on personal knowledge, what on your principles must be a fable ;—" Yea, and we are found false witnesses of God ; because we have testified of God that he raised up Christ : whom he raised not up, if so be that the dead rise not" (verse 15). That, however, is comparatively a small matter. What is far more important, is the bearing of your dogma on your own spiritual state. I repeat, therefore, what I said before, that since it sets aside the resurrection of our Lord, it cuts up by the roots the entire gospel method of man's recovery, and so renders that very spiritual resurrection to the faith of which you cling, thoroughly and hopelessly unattainable ;—" For if the dead rise not, then is not Christ raised : and if Christ be not raised, your faith is vain ; ye are yet in your sins" (verse 16, 17).

But how is this ? How should the denial of the resurrection of Christ lead to so fatal a result ? How does it follow, that if Christ be not raised, my faith is vain, and I am yet in my sins ?

The answer to this question is all important in its bearing on the real nature of the death of Christ, and the value, in a spiritual point of view, of his resurrection. Paul, indeed, apparently does not apprehend the necessity of an answer ; he does not anticipate the putting of any such question at all. He seems to have thought that his brief logic—his rapid summary of inevitable consequences—would commend itself at once as self-evident. And so it does, to one rightly impressed by the teaching of the Scriptures on the subject of Christ's death, as doubtless many of those were to whom Paul was writing. It may have been his purpose rather to alarm such persons by an abrupt appeal, than to convince them by long argument. In this, the divine wisdom with which he was endowed is apparent. To reason the matter fully out with such ingenious and speculative minds as he had to deal with, was the very way to set their subtle intellects on edge, to throw them into a combative and controversial mood, and to pique their powers of argumentative, not to say sophistical, debate. A winged and pointed word of warning to their consciences, compelling them, as earnest men,—as sinners hoping for salvation by grace alone,—to pause and think, was far better. And such a word in season was that pregnant syllogism ;—" For if the dead rise not, then is not Christ raised : and if Christ be not raised, your faith is vain ; ye are yet in your sins."

Ye are yet in your sins, because Christ is yet in your sins ; and your faith, committing you to Christ, and uniting you to Christ, makes you sharers with him in whatever is his condition,—in whatever is his fate. You cannot be better off than he is. The utmost your faith can do for you is to make you one with him, to bring you into fellowship with him, to identify your interests with his, to secure that as he is so you shall be. If, therefore, he is yet in your sins, then of necessity you also must be yet in your sins yourselves.

He was " in your sins " when he died. They were about him ; they were upon him ; they were his. He owned, he felt them, to be his. "Innumerable evils have compassed me about ; mine iniquities have taken hold upon me, so that I am not able to look up ; they are more than the hairs of mine head ; therefore my heart faileth me" (Ps. xl. 12). So your iniquities took hold of him as if they were his own. He made them his own. Making common cause with you, and putting himself in your place, he was in the midst of them,—he was under them. I repeat it solemnly; Jesus Christ our Lord was " in your sins " when he died.

He was " in your sins " when he was buried. They were still around him and upon him as he lay in the dark tomb. He had not got rid of them ; for he was still, in the soul's separation from the body and the body's occupancy of the grave, suffering their penalty ; he was still bearing their doom.

And if he is not risen, he is even yet " in your sins ;" your sins are around him and upon him even now. All your faith in him as able to save you from your sins is vain. " Ye are yet in your sins "—alas!

how hopelessly,—if he who should have saved you from them is yet in them himself.

If this is the real force of the apostle's argument or appeal, and one can scarcely see how otherwise it has any meaning, it suggests very solemn thoughts as to Christ's communion with us,—and ours, through faith, with him,—in his death, his burial, and his resurrection.

I. As to his death, it gives a character of stern and living reality to the statement, that "Christ died for our sins." He died for our sins, in the sense of dying in them ; literally and fully in that sense. He bore our sins;—"his own self bare our sins, in his own body, on the tree" (1 Pet. ii. 24).

How he bore them ; what his bearing of them implied ; what unparalleled sufferings, what "unknown agony ;" no heart of man can conceive. But we may partly understand in what character he bore our sins, and what relation he sustained to us in the bearing of them, if we consider what is here so impressively taught as to these sins of ours being really his, and his being really in them. They did actually so cleave to him at his death, as that, but for his rising from the dead, they must have been cleaving to him still.

The supposition, indeed, is one which, in this view, can scarcely be entertained without a shudder, as if it were on the verge of blasphemy ;—the supposition, I mean, of Christ not having risen, considered thus in the light of the position which he occupied and the character which he bore when he died. Had it been possible for him to be "holden of death," he must have continued to occupy the position and to bear the character of the guilty criminals whom he represented when he died. Their sins, then laid on him, must have been upon him still. His purpose of saving them from their sins must have failed. He has himself become inextricably involved in their sins, if the supposition in question is correct; and consequently involved also in the irremediable and irretrievable ruin which, in that case, their sins must be held to have entailed on them.

Does not this prove conclusively the strictly penal and piacular or expiatory nature of the sufferings and death of Christ? He made our sins his own; he made them so thoroughly, so personally his own, when he died for them, that if he had continued in the state of death, he must have continued in these sins of ours still. They must have adhered to him to this day. Their whole guilt, and the entire debt or obligation of their punishment, he made his own, and took upon himself. It was, in very deed, a vicarious death that he died. He identified himself with us as sinners, as criminals condemned to die, already dead in our sins. He substituted himself for us, when he died, bearing the condemnation in our stead. This is

what is meant by his being the propitiation for our
sins. Thus " Christ, our passover, is sacrificed for us."
All vague, indefinite views of his great sacrifice, as if
it were a mere pageant or spectacle,—exhibiting, in
the crucified God-man, God's holy love and the surrender of man's will to that love,—and intended to
operate by an influence similar to what a pure and
high ideal of excellency exercises over a sensitive
mind ; all such views of Christ's sacrifice of atonement are set aside by this one consideration,—the
tremendous consequence which, as to himself as well
as us, his death must have involved if he had not
risen from the dead. That consequence must have
been nothing less than his continuing in the sins for
which he died ; in their guilt ; in their condemnation.
Can his death, then, be anything else than a real and
actual judicial transaction, in which the blame or
criminality of our sins is laid upon him, and he
undergoes the sentence which we have incurred ?
" He made his soul an offering for sin." " The Lord
laid on him the iniquity of us all."

It is this view, and this view alone, of the death
of Christ that shews us either the real moral nature,
malignity, and ill desert of sin, or the real moral
nature of that God with whom we have to do. There
are many things in the system which God has established, and in the government which he exercises by
the ordinary universal laws of matter and mind, that

shew his opposition to sin. It is impossible to look intelligently at the order in which events follow one another, and the relations of cause and effect that control so regularly the course of affairs, without perceiving that the Ruler of all is one who hates evil and loves good. Sin and suffering are, in the long-run, inseparably joined. As certainly as, by the law of gravitation in the physical world, a body loosened from yonder heaven-reaching spire must reach the ground,—so surely, by the law of holiness and love in the spiritual world, a soul loosened from heaven's high standard must sink into the depths of hell's foul wrath and woe. All that is true ; but it is not the whole truth. The divine administration, in its dealing with moral evil, is not the mere development of a self-acting and self-enforcing law ;—such as in the lapse of ages must, by its own force or influence, work out of the system whatever is opposed to it, and bring all intelligences and all hearts into harmony with itself. The moral law, of which sin is the transgression, is not such a law as that to which a man, in some sense, runs counter when he thrusts his hand into the fire ; nor is the penalty with which the transgression of the former law is visited, of the same sort with the pain by which that other law may be said to avenge its own violation. The divine law is the image and exponent of the divine nature. But it is more. It is the assertion and vindication of the divine authority. There is a personal Lawgiver; a personal Judge; and he reckons personally with the breakers of his law, as personal offenders against himself and his government. They are criminals. As criminals he judges them, and punishes them. Guilt and condemnation are terrible realities. They are seen to be so, when Christ is set forth crucified before our eyes; treated as one guilty; condemned and punished in our stead. His penal death on the cross proclaims the fatal demerit of sin and the inexorable doom of judgment.

II. The burial of Christ, or his condition as to his body while his soul or spirit is in Paradise,—viewed in the light of the apostle's argument or appeal,—is very significant. It is an evidence of the completeness of the transaction which was accomplished on the cross when the Lord said "It is finished." His burial shews how fully he underwent, to the very letter, the curse, or sentence of condemnation, pronounced against those whose sins he bore, and in whose sins he died.

There hangs, indeed, a cloud of mystery over the interval between the death and the resurrection of our Lord. It is, so far as the living race of men are concerned, a dark eclipse. It is as if there was then a solemn pause in the march of time. In heaven, and in hell, there is an awful suspense. Alas! it is on earth only that this last of the Jewish Sabbaths passes away, just as usual;—with little heed of that sepulchre which, if men had only known what it meant, might well have stopped every pulse of busy life, and hushed the whole world in breathless and expectant silence.

The separation of the soul from the body at death is a part of the doom of sin. It is, along with the ills of life, one principle badge of man's subjection to vanity on account of sin. While that separation continues, it cannot be said that there is complete deliverance from the penal fruit, or wages, or punishment, of sin.

To the pious dead, indeed, this part of the doom of sin is so mitigated and stripped of its terror, that the thought of it need not occasion anxiety or uneasiness. Their souls are in the blessed region assigned to holy disembodied spirits. And their bodies "being still united to Christ, rest in their graves till the resurrection." "Precious in the sight of the Lord is the death of his saints." Their very dust is dear to him.

In the case of Christ himself, this must have been, and in fact was, pre-eminently true. His human soul is immediately after death in Paradise ; in the bosom of his Father and his God. He has commended his spirit into his Father's hands. The cup is drained to the dregs ; the bitterness of the curse is borne ; the agony is over; the expiation is complete. "It is finished!"

His body also is cared for. His Father sees to it that it shall be reverentially and honourably handled. The time may not admit of its being anointed with sweet spices by the weeping women. But Joseph of Arimathea is moved by the Spirit, in concert with Nicodemus, no longer "coming to Jesus by night," to render to the precious remains all highest offices of respect. A new tomb, "wherein never man lay," is found; and under the guardianship, not of Roman soldiers, but of heavenly angels, the corporeal frame of Jesus awaits its reunion to his soul.

Thus to Christ personally, in that intermediate state, there is really no more endurance of shame or pain.

Still there is that mutilation of the perfect manhood,—that separation of soul and body,—which sin has entailed on the fallen race of man. So long as he lies under that portion of the penalty or curse of sin, our Lord's deliverance from what is implied in his being "made sin," and "made a curse," for us, cannot be regarded as fully and finally accomplished. The man Christ Jesus, as to his whole manhood, body as well as soul, has not yet got rid of our sins. In their penal effect or issue, they are still with him, and upon him. In a vitally important sense, he is still "in them;"—so long as his body lies empty and lifeless in the dark and narrow cell in which loving friends have laid him.

For the whole doom of our guilt, as well as our guilt itself, he must make his own. The full penalty of our sins,—the entire legal consequence and judicial punishment of that "iniquity of us all" which "the Lord laid upon him,"—he must, as our substitute, bear. Wrath, condemnation, the sword of vengeance, he must bear on the cross. The severance also of soul and body, in fulfilment of the sentence "dust to dust," he must bear in the tomb.

Thus the consigning of the Lord's body to the earth and its temporary lodgment there, is the last instance and proof of his surrender of himself—his entire self—as the atoning victim, into the hands of his Father, the righteous Lawgiver and Judge of all. And therefore,—because he thus makes our sins so thoroughly his own, in all their guilt, and in the full measure of their righteously deserved doom, he is qualified to be our Saviour from sin and all its consequences. He is "the Lamb of God that taketh away the sin of the world;"—taking it away by taking upon himself its deepest ill-desert and utmost doom.

III. He is declared or proved to be so by his resurrection from the dead. Up to the moment of his resurrection, he is bearing our sins. Whether it be in the one part, or in the other, of that nature of ours which he assumed for this very end, he is still bearing our sins.

In his soul he bore our sins, when his Father hid his face from him ; when his Father's sword pierced him ; when the exceeding bitter cry was wrung from him, " My God, my God, why hast thou forsaken me." In his flesh he bore them, when the nails lacerated his feet, and the spear opened his side ; when death's thirst parched his lips, and his body, scarce cold, was hurried to the rich man's tomb.   All the time he was in that tomb our sins, in their penal consequences, were cleaving to him.   He was in them.   They had done their worst to his soul ; that unutterable and unknown anguish was over.   But they had not let go his body.   His body was still underlying and undergoing the curse.   He was not rid of these sins of ours which he made his own.   And if he is not risen, he is not rid of them even now.

Ah ! then, how can he ever rid us of them, if he is not rid of them himself ?   We may believe in him ever so sincerely, we may trust and love him ever so well, we may be ever so willing to give ourselves to him, and be one with him, and make common cause with him, as he makes common cause with us.   But it is a common cause of despair and ruin, if in respect of his complete manhood, or in respect of any part of his complete manhood, our sins are on him, in any sense or to any effect, and he is in them still !   Well may Paul say, " If Christ be not raised, your faith is vain ; ye are yet in your sins."

But on the other hand, if Christ is risen, how complete, how surely and gloriously complete, is our deliverance ! He is rid of our sins now. And if we are in him, we are rid of them too, in the very same sense, and to the very same extent, that he is. He was in them once ; in their guilt, in their curse ; so thoroughly in them that there was no escape for him, either from a criminal's death, or from a criminal's grave. But he is not in them now. Nor are we, if we are in him. " There is now no condemnation to them who are in Christ " (Rom. viii. 1). Our faith in him is not now vain : for, as " he was delivered for our offences," so " he was raised again for our justification " (Rom. iv. 25).

5

SECOND INFERENCE FROM THE DENIAL: THE PIOUS DEAD ARE LOST, AND WE ARE MISERABLE

Then they also which are fallen asleep in Christ are perished. If in this life only we have hope in Christ, we are of all men most miserable.   —1 Corinthians 15:18, 19

THIS is the climax and close of the apostle's argument concerning the resurrection, in its negative form. He reasons with the deniers of the possibility of a resurrection, after the manner of what is technically called in logic *reductio ad absurdum;* pointing out the conclusion in which their doctrine must, by a few short and necessary steps, inevitably land them.

This is a perfectly legitimate and warrantable mode of reasoning, if, in using it, I avoid the too common unfairness of imputing to my adversary the actual holding of dogmas, or principles, which may seem to me to follow from the proposition he is maintaining, but which he himself does not see or admit to be implied in it. To candid minds, it is a mode of reasoning fitted to be very convincing. Shew me that my views, if reasoned out, or acted out, lead to consequences from which I recoil as much as you do; and I cannot but be moved to reconsider the grounds on which I have adopted them.

In the present instance, it is a most fair, and what is more, a most affectionate appeal.

Have you thought seriously of the bearing of your new belief on your Saviour's work, and on your own faith and hope? Study it, and look at it, in that light. Surely you must perceive that at all events, and in the first place, it involves a denial of the resurrection of Christ. However you may try to explain the fact of the Lord's empty sepulchre,—and these strange words reported to have been uttered by him " Handle me, and see, for a spirit hath not flesh and bones, as ye see me have,"—it must have been a spirit after all that spoke. It might be Christ as he disappeared when, having cried with a loud voice " Father, into thy hands I commend my spirit," he gave up the ghost. It could not be Christ with anything about him of that material frame which thereafter hung for a little longer, empty, on the cross, and was then hastily buried in Joseph's tomb. Your doctrine, that there is no resurrection of the dead, with the ground on which you defend it,—the essential vileness of matter and its incompatibility with a perfect state of being,—makes that impossible. Plainly, if there be no resurrection of the dead, Christ is not risen. Are you prepared to face such a result of your philosophy?

Then you must be prepared to face also what immediately follows from it. I do not speak of your
virtually giving the lie to our testimony as apostles ;
a testimony which can be corroborated, if need be, by
five hundred other witnesses. That might be comparatively a small matter. But you cut up by the
roots the gospel which we preach, and your own faith
founded upon it. For of what use is your faith, uniting
you to Christ, and giving you an interest in Christ,
as dying for your sins, if the death which they entailed
on him has not been wholly reversed, undone, destroyed ? If in any respect, and to any effect, with
reference to any part of his person, these sins of yours,
for which, and in which, he died, have proved per-
manently fatal to him, how can he redeem you from
them ? " If Christ be not raised, your faith is vain ;
ye are yet in your sins."

And if it be so with you, what of those who are
dead and gone ? You still live, and may try some other
way of getting quit of your sins, if that which has
hitherto satisfied you fails you now. You may try
some new doctrine or discipline of perfection, based
on that very spiritualizing of the resurrection which
upsets your old faith in the atonement. But alas for
your departed brethren ! They have perilled their all
on what now, it seems, turns out to be an error ;—
" Then they also which are fallen asleep in Christ are
perished." Our case, in fact—the case of all of us,

living and dead—is sufficiently deplorable ;—" If in
this life only we have hope in Christ, we are of all
men most miserable."

I. "Then they also which are fallen asleep in
Christ are perished." This does not mean that upon
the supposition made they have ceased to exist. The
question of the continued existence of men after death
is not raised in the argument. It is a mistake to say
that in reasoning on the subject of the resurrection of
the body, the apostle loses sight of the distinction
between that particular doctrine and the general
doctrine of man's immortality. It is a mistake also
to think that in this verse he is teaching the depend-
ence of either doctrine on the admission of the fact
of Christ's resurrection. His statement is not put
thus : Then they also which are fallen asleep in
Christ shall never rise again ; their bodies shall never
be raised. That would be a true statement. It is an
inference or deduction of which Paul may afterwards
make use. But it is not his point here. Neither is
his statement put thus : Then they also which are
fallen asleep in Christ, have undergone total and final
annihilation. That idea is not once suggested in the
whole of this chapter. The glorious resurrection of
the bodies of his believing people may be connected
with the resurrection of Christ ; so that if his resurrection, as a matter of fact, is denied, their resurrec-

tion, as a matter of doctrine, must be denied also. But it does not follow that their spiritual immortality, or continued existence out of the body, is on that account denied. It does not follow that they must have perished, in the sense of ceasing to exist.

The fact is, what the apostle has in his view as to those who are fallen asleep in Christ, is not their perishing, in the sense of ceasing to exist, either in the body or out of the body ; but their perishing in the sense of not being saved,—in the sense of being lost. It is a far more solemn and awful conclusion that he asks you to face concerning the pious dead than either of these two :—either first, that they are not to live again in the body, or secondly, that they are not to survive and live after death at all.

The first of these conclusions, as flowing from the denial of the fact of Christ's resurrection, a spiritualist, jealous of physical impurity, and enamoured of an ideal immaterial perfection, might rather hail and welcome than repudiate. Such a consequence deduced from his belief would not alarm or shock him. The second of these conclusions, again, he would deny to be logical or legitimate. I do not see, he might urge, how the fact, if it be a fact ;—and you say it must be a fact, upon my view of the resurrection being present and spiritual, not future and corporeal ;—I do not see, how the fact of there having been no corporeal resurrection in the case of Christ, any more than I expect that there will be a corporeal resurrection in the case of his followers, implies that they cease to exist after death, any more than it implies that he ceased to exist after death. He would have had an immortal life, even if his body had not been raised. So they may have an immortal life also in him, even although you shut me up into the admission that his body has not been raised.

Such might have been a fair rejoinder or reply, if the apostle's argument in this eighteenth verse were to be understood as having reference to the mere continuance of life, embodied or disembodied, in the other world. Do you mean to argue thus : If Christ be not raised, then they also who have fallen asleep in Christ have perished—in this sense, that nothing of these corporeal frames of theirs which we bury is afterwards to reappear and be revived ? I accept that result. Or do you mean to argue thus : That upon that supposition they perish, in the sense of not surviving at all, but being altogether annihilated ? I do not see how that follows. The spiritual part of me may live on for ever, though all that is material about my person perish,—and perish irrecoverably.

What the apostle really reasons about is not immortality, whether spiritual or corporeal, but salvation. The conclusion to which he shuts up those with whom he is arguing, is not that they who have fallen asleep in Christ have perished, in the sense of

not living again in the body ; nor that they have
perished, in the sense of not continuing to live at all ;
but that they have perished in the sense of their being
lost as guilty and unsaved sinners ; irremediably lost ;
hopelessly consigned to everlasting perdition.

The statement or argument, in short, concerning
believers who have died, is immediately connected
with the statement or argument concerning believers
who are living. " If Christ be not risen," ye who still
live, although you believe in Christ, " are yet in your
sins." " If Christ be not raised," your departed
brethren, although they fell asleep in Christ, must
have died in their sins, and must even now be in them,
reaping their fruit, in condemnation and utter ruin—
and that for ever. If Christ be not raised, you now
believe in vain ; you believe in one who cannot save
you from your sins, seeing that he is not himself saved
from them. And your friends who have fallen asleep
in Christ have believed in vain. They fell asleep
believing in one who could not save them. They are
lost, therefore, finally ; they have perished.

Are you prepared for that consequence, inevitably
flowing from this speculation of yours about the
resurrection ? ˙Are you prepared, not only to make
void your own faith, which hitherto has sustained you
in the hope of your salvation from your sins, but to
make void also the faith of venerated fathers, beloved
brothers and sisters, whose peace, as they fell asleep

in Jesus, depended altogether on the assurance of
justification through his resurrection from the dead?
Was it a lie that these holy men and women grasped
in their right hand, when they walked so fearlessly
through the valley of the shadow of death? And are
their eyes now opened in that other world to the sad
and awful truth, that for all their faith in Christ they
are yet in their sins; that they have believed in one
who died, indeed, for their sins, but is not to this
hour himself extricated from them? Is the melan-
choly complaint of disappointment and despair theirs,
as well as yours—"We trusted that it had been he
who should have redeemed us?"

Surely this is a startling appeal, well fitted to
make the boldest innovator pause.

II. For in truth, adds the apostle, the innovation
involves us all, the dead and the living, who have
believed in Christ, in one common ruin;—"If in
this life only we have hope in Christ, we are of all
men most miserable" (verse 19).

Is there exaggeration in this utterance?—the
exaggeration of rhetoric or of feeling? Is it an over-
strained emotion, partly of enthusiasm—partly, also,
of vexation and annoyance—that here breaks out?

So it might seem, if the point at issue were either
the resurrection of the body, or the immortality of the
soul; if the question were merely, Are we to live

again in the body? or even, Are we to continue to live after death at all?

For, first, as to the first of these questions,—Why should believers in Christ be of all men most miserable, even though it should turn out that they are not to live again in the body? Surely there is enough in that immortal blessedness into which they enter when they depart to be with Christ,—"absent from the body and present with the Lord,"—to compensate, and far more than compensate, for all the toil, hardship, self-denial, and persecution which, for a few short years, their faith in Christ may entail upon them here. They may be more in trouble than other men; they may be more plagued than other men; there may be "bands in their death" (Psalm lxxiii. 4) from which other men are exempt. But if, when all on earth is over, the Lord Jesus receives their spirits, even though their bodies are to be wholly left behind for ever,—if that is their hope, —they cannot well be said to be "of all men most miserable."

Nay, take even the other supposition. Let the case put be that of our not continuing to live at all. Let that be the conclusion to which the denial of Christ's resurrection shuts us up. Let it be granted that we have no evidence or assurance of even the spiritual part of us surviving our bodily dissolution. Still, believers in Christ need not be condoled with,—they

are scarcely entitled to condole with one another,—
as being " of all men most miserable." They have, at
least, as good prospects and presumptions with reference to the world to come, as that great Roman orator
and philosopher had, who, in the evening of life, amid
the wreck and ruin of earth's holiest ties, would not
let go his grasp of immortality. " If it prove to be a
dream, I can be none the worse for it ; meanwhile, by
means of it, I have fellowship with the excellent who
are gone." And, what is more, more than the wisest
and best heathen ever had, they enjoy, in their experience or imagination of peace with God and reconciliation to him, what may well make their present life not
wretched but most enviable ;—even though it should
be a life of incessant trial, and a life that is to termi-
nate conclusively at death.

What, then, is the precise ground of the apostle's
passionate ejaculation, " If in this life only we have
hope in Christ, we are of all men most miserable ? "

It is in entire accordance with his previous argument. It proceeds upon the inference or deduction
that, if Christ be not raised, the very peace and reconciliation which make this life at its worst not only
tolerable but even desirable to believers in Jesus, are
themselves a delusion. In this life we have hope in
Christ. And there may be pleasure in such hope in
Christ while it lasts. But it is a hope which, if there
be, as there assuredly is, a hereafter, will be found to

be utterly hollow and untrue. For it is a hope based upon the faith of our being saved from our sins. But we are not saved from our sins "if Christ be not raised." On the contrary, we "are yet in our sins." Whatever hope we have in Christ, as regards our being saved from our sins, rests on what, it seems, is an error and a fable. It cannot last beyond this present life. At death, if we survive death, even although we fall asleep in Christ, we shall too surely discover—as "they which have fallen asleep in Christ" before us have already discovered—that our faith is vain and our hope delusive ; that since Christ is not raised, we are yet in our sins ; and alas! must continue in our sins for ever.

Is not this truly a miserable case ? If it is really ours, are we not deeply to be pitied ? Are we not " of all men most miserable ?"

The "hope in Christ," then, of which Paul speaks, is not the hope of the resurrection ;—nor even the hope of immortality ;—but the hope which has for its object the pardon, the favour, the approbation, the love of the Most High. It is the hope which cheers the broken heart of the man whose sin has found him out, when first, amid the anguish of his godly shame and sorrow, his eye fixes itself on Jesus lifted up on the cross, a sacrifice for sin. It is a hope which, if it be well founded, it is rapture to him to cherish, for present peace and pure joy in God, apart from all thought of what is to befall him in the future.

Yes! If it be well founded. But if you fling a cold doubt across that great fact on which it is built; if he to whom the Holy Ghost has been moving me to look as dying for my sins may, after all, not have risen again; if my sins are still upon him, keeping his body in the tomb; if, through his bearing my guilt, the precious substance of that holy human frame which the Holy Ghost prepared for him in the Virgin's womb is lost inextricably and irrecoverably, in the common dust of this doomed earth—the ground cursed for man's sin;—if thus the great Redeemer himself has failed to procure, even in his own case, a reversal of the sentence, dust to dust;—if the very "ransom God has found to deliver from going down to the pit" is itself marred, and the person of Emmanuel is no more complete, as it was when it was formed within the womb of his mother Mary;—if the grave has triumphed and the expiation has broken down;—in a word, if Christ is not raised, and they who have believed on him for the remission of their sins are in their sins still, and die in their sins, and perish in their sins;—Oh! what better is my hope to me than the hope of the hypocrite, whose "soul, whatever he has gained, God taketh away!" (Job xxvii. 8).

"If in this life only we have hope in Christ!" Any hope we can have in Christ respecting the for-

giveness of our sins must, on the supposition now
made, be a hope which we can have only in this life.
We may cling to it, and lean on it, for a little longer,
while we live.   We may desperately grasp it as the
only solace of our anxious souls.   We may try
earnestly to persuade ourselves that there is for us an
atonement—that there is for us a pardon in Christ.
But the atonement ; what is it ? — the pardon ;
where is it ?—if our sins, for which Christ died,
are upon him still, subjecting him still to the power
of death ?

The bubble must one day burst.   The fond per-
suasion, the flattering hope, must be cut off.   At death,
if not before, we must be awakened to the discovery
that, believing in Christ for the saving of our souls
from sin, we have believed in vain.   We are yet in
our sins after all.   We perish, as they who have fallen
asleep in Jesus have perished, hopelessly and for ever.
If this be so, "are we not indeed of all men most
miserable ? "

The apostle is not here formally comparing himself and his fellow-believers with the rest of mankind.
When he calls himself elsewhere the "chief of sinners,"
he is not measuring himself by others.   It is of himself
alone, and of his own aggravated guilt, that he is there
thinking.   So it is here.   It is himself and his fellow-
believers alone, and not any others, that he has in his
mind, when, using the strong language of seeming

comparison, he cries — "If in this life only we have hope in Christ, we are of all men most miserable!"

Yes. We are so! We who have had our eyes opened to see the exceeding sinfulness of sin, and the infinite preciousness of salvation from sin! If our hope is dashed; if it is found to be a hope which, however we may cling to it for a while, must fail us at the last; we cannot fall back again upon the fat, contented slumber of easy unconcern and worldly security. Our natural peace has been broken. Our consciences have been pricked. Our hearts have been stirred. We have been made to know ourselves, and to know our God. We have been forced to feel what every sin of ours deserves, and how terrible a thing it is to "fall into the hands of the living God" (Heb. x. 31).

We had got a hope, a trembling hope, of the forgiveness of sin and the favour of God being ours. It was a hope based and built on a satisfying atonement having been offered on our behalf by the Eternal Son, through the Eternal Spirit, to the Eternal Father;— offered on our behalf, and accepted too. Our conviction of its having been an adequate satisfaction—our faith in its having been accepted—rested on this belief, that whatever our sins, when he died for them, brought on Christ, had been undone.

But you tell us, no. The ruin of his body was irreparable. Our sins slew his body, and it lies slain to this hour.

Then where is our hope? Where is the hope we so fondly cherished that our sins were fully atoned for ; their guilt expiated, their condemnation thoroughly taken away? They still keep Christ under the power of death—the death he died for us. They must keep us in the doom which we, wicked as we are, brought on him, the Righteous One. It is, on that supposition, a doom from which he is not himself completely delivered. How then can he deliver us? They must keep us, these sins of ours, in that doom of guilt and ruin evermore.

Is not that enough to make us miserable, "most miserable?" What matters this present life, with its gleam and faint spark of hope, kindled by the death of Christ, if that is to be the end of it? Touch our hope, as you do touch our hope, of the full, free, everlasting forgiveness of our sins, through Christ dying for our sins and rising again, and what refuge have we? We cannot in any other way find rest or peace. We cannot lay any flattering unction to our souls, as if we might, somehow, otherwise be saved. We cannot do without the atonement.

And must it not be misery unspeakable to conclude that, after all, he whom we have admired, believed, trusted, loved, cannot save us?—that in spite of his dying for our sins, we are yet in our sins?—that, like others who have gone before us, when we fall asleep in him, we perish?

But it is not so. Christ is risen from the dead. He who was dead is alive for evermore. Therefore, we live now ;—we who believe in him. And they live too ;—they who have fallen asleep in him. Death could not hold him : no ; not any part of him. Sin could not destroy him : no ; not any part of him. He goes down to the pit. But see ! He comes forth, leaving no part of him behind. Therefore, guilt is expiated. Therefore, the ransom is sufficient. Therefore, the redemption is complete. Therefore we, as well as our predecessors in the life of faith, have a hope which neither death nor sin can touch.

They have not perished. Though absent from the body, they live now. In the body they are to live hereafter. No part of them has fallen, or is to fall, a victim, either to death or to sin.

We, also, believing, are not in our sins. No wrath for sin is upon us now. No death for sin awaits us at last. Ours now is a life in Christ, free from the doom of guilt. When we fall asleep in Christ, we do not perish.

In the risen Saviour, then, let us rejoice to hope. In the risen Saviour, let us rejoice to have fellowship in our hope with all them that have already fallen asleep in Christ. They have fallen asleep, as we hope to fall asleep, not to perish, but to have everlasting life.

6

FIRST INFERENCE FROM THE ADMISSION OF THE RESURRECTION: CHRIST IS RISEN AND IS BECOME THE FIRSTFRUITS OF THEM THAT SLEEP

But now is Christ risen from the dead, and become the first-fruits of them that slept. For since by man came death, by man came also the resurrection of the dead. For as in Adam all die, even so in Christ shall all be made alive. But every man in his own order: Christ the firstfruits; afterwards they that are Christ's at his coming.
                                                —1 Corinthians 15:20-23

From the dreary supposition on which he has been reasoning, in order to expose the miserable consequences which it involves, the apostle gladly turns to the glorious fact and its glorious issue : "But now is Christ risen from the dead, and become the first-fruits of them that slept."

Enough ! one seems to hear him saying to himself —enough, and more than enough of this base hypothesis. I will not argue upon it—I will not look at it—any longer. You see to what your notion about there being no resurrection leads you. It forces you to deny the resurrection of Christ. And if you deny that, you are landed, for yourselves and for those who have gone before you, in the cheerless and hopeless gloom of absolute despair.

But let us admit the fact that Christ is risen. Confess that, when you began to entertain that new opinion about the only possible resurrection being a spiritual one, you did not perceive its bearing on the resurrection of Christ. Confess that you cannot face the conclusion which forces itself upon you, now that you do perceive that. No. You cannot spare from your creed the fact or doctrine of your Saviour's resurrection. He is risen. And if he is risen, the resurrection of the body must be possible. There is, there must be, a resurrection of the dead. For "Christ is risen from the dead, and become the first-fruits of them that slept." His resurrection implies and ensures theirs.

How it does so, we are now to inquire. What is the nature of the connection between Christ's resurrection and that of them that sleep in him?

It is not said, either here or anywhere else in Scripture, that the resurrection of the dead generally is a consequence of the resurrection of Christ; that apart from him there would have been no resurrection at all. There is no reason to believe that the general resurrection of the dead is any part of the remedial and mediatorial economy, or is in any sense the result of the interposition of a Redeemer. If man had not sinned, it is probable that the successive generations of the human family, as one after another they completed their probation here,—"walking with God" (Gen. v. 22),—would have been translated in the body, as Enoch and Elijah were, to some other region in the universe, where they might be kept in rest and glory until the entire race was gathered in. But sin entered, and death by sin. If there had been no provision of salvation, it is equally probable that the separation of the soul from the body which death entails would not have been for ever. When " death had passed upon all men, because all had sinned," they would all have been raised up—to stand again before God in the body, and receive in the body the sentence of the second death, the due reward of their deeds done in the body ; " Depart from me, ye cursed, into everlasting fire, prepared for the Devil and his angels "(Matt. xxv. 41). It cannot, therefore, be the general resurrection of mankind universally that the apostle here connects with the resurrection of Christ. If Christ had not come at all, if he had neither died nor risen from the dead, there would have been a general resurrection of mankind universally notwithstanding. It is the resurrection of the just alone that is meant. And even as regards the resurrection of the just, it is not the mere fact that they are to rise again that is connected with the fact of Christ having risen. His resurrection is not really the procuring cause or condition of their resurrection. It is simply the cause and condition of their resurrection being not a resurrection of damnation, but a resurrection of life, blessedness, and glory.

"Now is Christ risen from the dead, and become the first-fruits of them that slept" (verse 20). They, therefore, who are fallen asleep in Christ are not perished. They have not gone down to the pit of utter and endless ruin. Their union to Christ, their interest in Christ, secures for them a participation in his resurrection. And consequently, in addition to whatever present benefit it may confer, it secures to them ultimately a resurrection of the same kind as his.

Is that a hope for yourselves, and for your brethren who have gone before you, to be lightly thrown away? Is not the inference to be drawn from an admission of Christ's resurrection better than that which a denial of it must force upon you? Who among you now would take offence at what some scout as the materialistic idea of a literal bodily resurrection? Will the most sensitive spiritualist still persist in saying that there is no resurrection of the dead, when it is such a resurrection that is pointed at?

For the question is now seen to turn on this simple but most serious and weighty alternative ;— either Christ is not raised, and they which are fallen asleep in Christ are perished ;—or Christ is raised, and is become the first-fruits of them that slept. And accordingly, the principle upon which the apostle proceeds is the same when he reasons on the assumption of Christ's resurrection being admitted, as when he argues on the hypothesis of its being denied. That principle is the substantial oneness of Christ and his believing people. Their faith unites them to Christ, and identifies them with him. It commits them to share his fortune. It involves them in his destiny, whatever that destiny may be.

If Christ be not risen, then, since he died for your sins, and in your sins,—continuing dead, he continues in your sins still ; they are upon him still ; he has not got rid of them. Nor have you ; you are yet in your sins. You die in your sins ; and in spite of all your faith in Christ,—nay in that case on account of your faith in Christ,—you perish in your sins. But if Christ is risen, your sins—for which and in which he died —are upon him no more. Nor are they now any more upon you. Their guilt, their condemnation, cleaves no more to him. And therefore "there is now no condemnation to you who are in him." You are not now in your sins ; you do not die in your sins ; you fall asleep in Jesus. You are for a time to be as he was, when his body rested in Joseph's tomb. That is not a dismal prospect. And, ere long, you are to be as he is, now that he has risen from the dead. Your union to Christ, which would be your destruction if Christ were not risen, now that he is risen, is your life and glory.

Thus the oneness of believers with Christ is the explanation of the connection between his resurrection and theirs. It is because Christ and they are one by faith, that his resurrection involves theirs, and their resurrection is of the same kind as his. They are themselves in him; and their resurrection consequently is also in him. His resurrection is theirs.

Thus believers are by grace in Christ, as "the first fruits of them that sleep,"—in the same sense in which they are all naturally in Adam, in whom they sinned, and with whom they fell. The two economies —the original and remedial; the original economy of nature, or "of law working death," and the remedial economy of grace, with its "resurrection of life;" have several features in common for those who have experience of both. Representation, union, and subordination,—are the three principles or characteristics which the two economies have in common.

I. In both economies there is representation, one man representing his fellows;—"For since by man came death, by man came also the resurrection of the dead" (verse 21). It is by or through a representative man that death reaches us. It is by or through a representative man that the resurrection of life awaits us. Christ, in his resurrection, represents us precisely as Adam, when he incurred death, represented us. Man, a man, the first Adam, representing us, sins and dies. Man, a man, the man Christ Jesus, the second Adam, representing us, takes away sin and rises from the dead. The connection between us and the man by whom comes death, as well as the connection between us and the man by whom comes the resurrection of the dead, is a connection of representation. In both cases alike we are dealt with on the principle of representation. A representative man is constituted, by whom there comes to us whom he represents either weal or woe.

This is an act of mere sovereignty on the part of God. It is an arrangement, or dispensation, of which no account can be given, excepting only that such is the divine appointment, such is the divine will.

II. Secondly, in both economies there is union ;—"For as in Adam all die, even so in Christ shall all be made alive" (verse 22). Those who are here spoken of—believers who are said to fall asleep in Christ—are all "in Adam," and therefore they all die. They are all "in Christ," and therefore they shall all be made alive. They are all "in Adam," not only as being represented by Adam, but also as being one with him ; partakers of his nature ; inheritors of the loss and damage which his nature sustained when he sinned and fell. They are all likewise "in Christ," not only as being represented by him, but also as becoming one with him ; partakers of his nature ; associated with him in his relation to the Father ; in his righteousness, life, and glory. They all "in Adam," or as one with Adam, die ; they all " in Christ," or as one with Christ, shall be made alive.

The representation, in short, is through union. We are represented by another, because we are naturally, or we are to become by grace, one with him who represents us. This is not necessarily the principle of representation. It is not always so. Whether the representative is chosen by us, or chosen for us, it may be a purely arbitrary arrangement, a simple exercise of discretion. Beyond its being settled and understood that by what he does, as our representative, we stand or fall, there may be no real or known connection subsisting between him and us. When God, however, deals with us on the principle of representation, he deals with us as really one with him who represents us. There is, no doubt, in such a procedure, an act of absolute sovereignty on the part of God. He wills that one should represent us. But he wills also that the representation should rest on the substantive ground of union. That there may be representation, he secures or effects union. We are in the man Adam, by whom came death. We are in the man Christ Jesus, by whom comes the resurrection of the dead. It is as being in Adam by nature, that we all die the death which comes by him. It is as being in Christ by grace, that we shall all be made alive with the life, the resurrection of the dead, which comes by him.

It is a real union, in either case, though differently ordained and constituted. It is by necessity of nature in the one case ; it is by election of grace in the other. It is hereditary in the one case ; it is personal in the other. It is involuntary and without consent on our part in the one case ; it is with our own full and free concurrence and choice in the other. We are in Adam, in the man by whom came death, as his natural seed—inheriting, by descent from him, his standing, character, and fortune, as the first representative man ; and as to that, we cannot help ourselves. We are in him whether we will or not. We are not thus in Christ, in the man by whom comes the resurrection of the dead. We are not in him by any general or universal law of nature. We are in him, if we are in him at all, by a special act of grace towards us, and a special work of grace in us. We are in him, not by our natural birth, but by our new spiritual birth ; not by any baptism of water, which may be without intelligence on our part, and without consent, but by the baptism of the Holy Ghost, making us the Lord's "willing people in the day of his power" (Ps. cx. 3).

If it be thus that we are in Christ—intelligently, willingly, by grace, through faith ; if it be thus that we are in that second representative man, by whom comes the resurrection of the dead ; is it not even more clear and more demonstrably certain that we must share his destiny, than it could ever be that we must participate in the fault and fate of the first man, by whom came death? We do not believe in vain when we believe in him by whom comes the resurrection of the dead. It is not in vain, or for nothing, that we are " found in him " (Phil. iii. 9). We so believe in him, and are so found in him, that he and we are henceforth inseparably one ; and whatever he is, we are to be. Therefore, as in Adam we all die, even so, nay, rather much more, in Christ we, believing, shall all be made alive. His resurrection from the dead,—his glorious life, as risen from the dead,— is ours, inasmuch as we, believing, are one with him.

III. It is ours, let it be noticed in the third place, in due time, in due " order." As there is representation in both of the economies that are here contrasted, and as in both of them the representation is through union, so in both of them there is also subordination. Especially there is subordination in the economy of life ;—" But every man in his own order ; Christ the first-fruits ; afterward they that are Christ's at his coming " (verse 23).

That the principle of representation may be kept clear and entire, there is a distinction of order or rank between the representative man Christ Jesus, and those whom he represents. It is most fitting that it should be so. The sheaf of the first-fruits at the passover, severed from the ripening crop of which it was the pledge and earnest, had its place apart.* It was, itself alone, waved before the Lord, and accepted for the people. Then, in due course and order, came the general harvest. The sheaf of the first-fruits of the harvest now is " Christ our passover, sacrificed for us " (1 Cor. v. 7). For " Christ is risen, and become the first-fruits of them that slept." He is himself alone the first-fruits. That is his position, his rank and order. Most gladly and gratefully do we concede it to him. And most cheerfully do we consent to wait, that the due distinction may be observed between the sheaf of the first-fruits waved before the Lord, and the rich harvest-home which it inaugurates, sanctifies, and blesses. Yes ! " Every man in his own order : Christ the first-fruits ; afterward they that are Christ's at his coming !"

" At his coming." For he who presents himself as the first-fruits, is himself to present us as the harvest. He is to come again for that end. He is to come when the harvest is complete ; ripe and ready to be gathered. Then the relation in which

---

* And the Lord spake unto Moses, saying, Speak unto the children of Israel, and say unto them, When ye be come into the land which I give unto you, and shall reap the harvest thereof, then ye shall bring a sheaf of the first-fruits of your harvest unto the priest : And he shall wave the sheaf before the Lord, to be accepted for you : on the morrow after the Sabbath the priest shall wave it.— Lev. xxiii. 9-11.

he stands to his people, and they to him, will be gloriously developed and acted out. Now he is risen for them. Then they rise in him. They rise because he has risen. They rise as he has risen. They rise to be as he is, and where he is, now that he is risen. They rise, as "his body, the fulness of him that filleth all in all" (Ephes. i. 23). For his resurrection is not complete until they rise in him. It is his body that is still lying in the tomb wherever his buried saints are laid. It is his body that lies bleaching on the plain, or sinks plunged in the deep, wherever the bones of his unburied saints are scattered, or given to the sea to keep. And even that body of his is, in an important sense, not to see corruption. His natural body literally saw no corruption, being actually raised and restored to life before corruption had time to begin its horrid work. That was when he became the first-fruits. And is not that the sure pledge that his mystical body too is, in a high sense, to share the same incorruptibility?

These saints of his, when they fall asleep in him, have, as to their material frames, a cold, dank, dreary abode. The grave is no cheerful house. Their bed is in the darkness. "They say to corruption: Thou art my father; to the worm: Thou art my mother and my sister." The reptile, or the raven, feeds foully on their remains. Surely they see corruption. Their bodies all rot away. Not one of them has in itself

any element of life—any principle of vitality—that
can defy corruption. True. But yet in every one of
them,—even in what of every one of them earth or
sea has got,—there is that which neither earth nor sea
can hopelessly corrupt. And at his coming, when
earth and sea give up their dead, the Lord takes his
risen saints to be for ever with him. Their resurrection is the complement or completion of his own.
He presents himself and them before the throne of
his Father's glory. And then, with reference to his
mystical body, the church—as now, with reference to
the body of his own human nature—he joyfully and
triumphantly owns that faithfulness of the Father in
which he trusted when he said, "Thou wilt not suffer
thine Holy One to see corruption" (Ps. xvi. 10).

Thus, these three principles ; — representation,
union, subordination ;—are the cement and seal of
that connection between Christ and us, on which the
connection between Christ's resurrection and ours
depends. While we live, believing on him—when
we die, falling asleep in him—we are represented by
Christ ; we are united to Christ ; we are subordinate
under Christ. Christ for them ; they in Christ ;
Christ before them ;—such is the "threefold cord"
which "cannot be quickly broken," binding Christ
and his people together. Is it not in every view of
it a blessed connection? Is not this a better and
brighter prospect than any that they could have, if

there were no resurrection of the dead, and if consequently Christ were not risen ?

The resurrection, thus regarded, is not a mere
mode of the future life.   The question about the
resurrection is not a question affecting merely the
manner of our existence after death.   If it were, we
could afford, perhaps, to make a present of it to the
schools of the philosophers.

It might be a question of that nature.   It might
be a question about some spiritual or physical theory
of another life ; such as this—How are men generally
—or,—How are believers in Christ,—to be fashioned
and constituted in the world to come ?   Are they to
be mere and pure spirits ?   Or are they to be clothed
with some sort of filmy and shadowy corporeity, such
as may continue to cleave to them when, leaving their
grosser clay for us to bury, they pass from our sight
at death ?   Or are they, at some date or crisis beyond
that, to receive back again out of their graves material
frames, bearing as real a relation of identity to the
bodies now lying there, as the wheat rising out of
the ground bears to the seed from which it springs ?

Questions like these might be left for debate to
subtle speculators and inquirers.   They are questions
which do not, to any great extent, touch the hope of
future happiness which the righteous man has.   He
would probably feel that his happiness might be quite

compatible with any one of these suppositions. He
would be disposed to decline too minute an inquiry
into the subject, as savouring of that "doting about
questions and strifes of words," which Paul condemns.
I am content, he might say, to receive, as the pardoned
thief on the cross received, the Saviour's full and comprehensive assurance, "To-day shalt thou be with me
in Paradise." I ask for no explanation of the different
or successive modes of happy being which that wide
promise may contain.

But it is not as bearing upon any such questions
as these, that the apostle here treats of the resurrection of Christ. He views it in its connection with a
far more vital question—What hope have they who
are in Christ of being saved now, and saved for ever?
They are represented by him ; they are one with him ;
they are in an order of close association and sequence
under him, and as it were, behind him. What he is,
that they are. As he is, so are they. To them, his
resurrection is not a mere historical event, in any
question about which they may consent to be neutral
or in doubt. It is their all in all. Their life in time
and for eternity is bound up in it. Because he liveth,
proved by his resurrection from the dead to be no
more "in their sins," and "declared to be the Son of
God with power," (Rom. i. 4)—therefore they live,
justified in and with him, now ;—therefore they are
to live, glorified in and with him, hereafter.

Well, therefore, may we sing with joy, Christ our Lord is risen! He is risen, and is become "the author of eternal salvation to all of us who obey him." He is risen, and is become the first-fruits of them that have fallen asleep in him. They and we are safe in him now. We are not now in our sins. They are not perished. At his coming, the glorious harvest of which he is the first-fruits will be reaped. "The dead in Christ shall rise first : then we which are alive and remain shall be caught up together with them in the clouds, to meet the Lord in the air : and so shall we," all of us, "be ever with the Lord" (1 Thess. iv. 16, 17).

7

SECOND INFERENCE FROM THE ADMISSION OF THE RESURRECTION: THE END—THE DELIVERING UP OF THE KINGDOM TO THE FATHER

Then cometh the end, when he shall have delivered up the kingdom to God, even the Father; when he shall have put down all rule and all authority and power. For he must reign, till he hath put all enemies under his feet. The last enemy that shall be destroyed is death. For he hath put all things under his feet. But when he saith, all things are put under him, it is manifest that he is expected, which did put all things under him. And when all things shall be subdued unto him, then shall the Son also himself be subject unto him that put all things under him, that God may be all in all. —1 Corinthians 15:24-28

In these verses an important question is virtually raised. It is the question between a simultaneous resurrection of all the Lord's believing people collectively, at the close of this dispensation, and successive resurrections of them individually and one by one, during its currency and continuance. If the Lord and his believing people are so intimately one that his resurrection involves theirs and their resurrection must be of the same nature with his,—how comes it that they are not raised, as he was, before they see corruption? Why do their bodies lie in their graves so much longer than his? Why does not every believer separately, as he falls asleep in Jesus, resume, as Jesus did, his corporeal frame, on the third day after it has been consigned to the tomb?

To such inquiries, the answer is partly given in the twenty-third verse—"But every man in his own order : Christ the first-fruits ; afterward they that are Christ's at his coming." There must be order and due subordination. The consecrated first-fruits must take precedence of the harvest of which it is the pledge. It is fitting that, in some marked way, Christ should be seen to occupy a position apart. He receives his natural body, raised from the dead, ere he leaves the world and goes to the Father. He is to receive his mystical body, raised from the dead, "at his coming."

But the principal answer is to be found in the view which the apostle gives of the great transactions that are to signalize the Lord's coming.

"Then cometh the end ;" the catastrophe of the world's drama ; the winding up of its history ; the close and consummation of the economy of probation. It is to be a crisis or era ; an occasion on which an august ceremonial is to be presented before the eyes of all intelligences. And in immediate connection with what is then to be done, the resurrection of the Lord's people has its fitting place.

That this may be clearly seen, let us try to realise what is briefly sketched as a sort of programme of the august ceremonial, or procedure, which is then to be observed. It is a procedure in which Christ is conspicuously the prominent party.

I. There is a remarkable and significant transaction between the Son and the Everlasting Father :—" Then cometh the end, when he shall have delivered up the kingdom to God, even the Father" (verse 24). What is this transaction? What is the kingdom? What is meant by its being delivered up?

Plainly, the kingdom here means, not the realms or territories over which kingly authority is exercised, but the kingly authority itself. It is not certain dominions that Christ delivers up, but the right of dominion. And the right of dominion, or kingly authority, then to be delivered up, is evidently that which Christ wields, as having "all things put under his feet" (verse 27). It is that by which "he puts down all rule, and all authority, and power" (verse 24). It is his mediatorial sovereignty ; his prerogative of supremacy and empire, as Messiah the Prince.

But how does he deliver that up "to God, even the Father?" Does he so deliver it up that it passes from him, and he ceases to reign? Is it an entire surrender of authority,—a resignation of the kingly office,—an abdication of the royal throne?

It cannot well be that, most believers will be ready to reply. Is it not repeatedly intimated in

Scripture, that Messiah is to reign for ever?—that "of the increase of his government and peace there shall be no end?" (Is. ix. 7)—that "his throne is to endure as the days of heaven?" (Ps. lxxxix. 29). Nor can such intimations be easily explained as meaning no more than this;—that whereas the authority of other kings, who die and give place to successors, passes from hand to hand, Christ's authority, vested in himself personally, is not thus transferable, but is to last out the whole time of the dynasty or dispensation to which it belongs. "To him that overcometh will I grant to sit with me in my throne, even as I also overcame, and am set down with my Father in his throne" (Rev. iii. 21;) —"We shall reign with him" (2 Tim. ii. 12);— promises like these surely point to the future and endless life. And, indeed, even apart from the express declarations of Scripture, there is something against which the spiritual instinct revolts, in the idea of that relation of loving loyalty in which his believing subjects stand to him as their King ceasing and being dissolved; at the very time, too, when, by their actual bodily participation with him in his resurrection, their union to him is to be most illustriously manifested and sealed. It cannot surely be such an abdication that is here meant.

But if not, what is it? What is it that Christ's "delivering up the kingdom" implies?

It is admitted that he reigns as Mediator by a delegated authority. His mediatorial sovereignty is distinct from that which he shares, as the Son, with the Father and the Holy Ghost, in the essential unity of the Godhead, from everlasting. His mediatorial sovereignty is not from everlasting. It has a beginning in time. It does not, on that account, follow that it is to have an end in time. Though not from everlasting, it may be to everlasting. And the constitution of Christ's person, in respect of which he is Mediator, and as Mediator, king ; his being God as well as man, and therefore, in his person and in his offices, unchangeable ; together with the fellowship with himself into which he admits his people ;—all this would seem to intimate that his reign, as a reign over them at least, is to be for ever. But except in so far as it is a reign over them, this delegated mediatorial sovereignty of Christ may have an end.

Let it be observed, that as Mediator, he may be said, in an important sense, to abdicate his original and eternal sovereignty, at the first beginning of his mediatorship. In that respect, he does not eagerly retain or grasp his equality with God. "Made of a woman, made under the law," he becomes, instead of a sovereign or king, a servant and subject. And in that new character, he consents to receive, as the reward of his obedience unto death, a new kingdom. He is invested with a new and distinct right of sovereignty. He reigns by a new title; under a new and special commission from him whom, as his servant and subject, as well as his son, he was wont to adore; —"I thank thee, O Father, Lord of heaven and earth" (Matt. xi. 25).

That commission, in the first instance, confers on him a right to reign over the people "given to him by the Father." In virtue of it, he "rides prosperously in his majesty;" with "grace poured into his lips," and "his sword girt on his thigh." His sharp arrows of conviction "pierce the hearts of those who have been the King's enemies." His quick and powerful word, carried home by his quickening and all-powerful Spirit, "subdues the people under him." "His people are willing in the day of his power." They "kiss the Son." They own him as their Saviour, and become obedient to him as their King. His reign over them as Mediator—as having in that character redeemed them, bought them, subdued them, won them—is established as a reign that is to know no interruption and no end. His throne is "for ever and ever" (Ps. xlv.)

But at present, and as things now are, the commission which Christ has, as Mediator, to reign thus over the people given to him by the Father, would be frustrated and made void, if it did not embrace also a far wider right—a right and power to reign over all this world, and all "the rulers of the darkness of this world" (Ephes. vi. 12). He cannot, as mediatorial Lord and redeeming King, "bring many sons unto glory," unless his lordship as mediator, his kingly prerogative as Redeemer, extends over the entire territory through which, as "the captain of their salvation," he has to lead them, and comprehends all the powers, of whatever kind, by which their progress may be either hindered or advanced.

But now, let all the sons whom he thus leads be brought safely to glory. Let the redemption of the people given to him by the Father be complete. Let even the last badge and token of their "subjection to vanity on account of sin,"—the mouldering of their mortal bodies in the tomb,—come to an end.

It is plain that, in these altered circumstances, the reason for the present widely-extended sweep of his mediatorial sovereignty ceases. Having all his people with himself,—having his body, mystical as well as personal, whole and entire ;—there being no longer, any where, any evil power or principle outstanding that can touch them, and therefore no longer any possibility of assault or injury from without ;—Christ, their King, need not now, in the character in which he is their King, claim or retain any kingship outside of them. His sovereignty over them, the sovereignty which he has bought so dearly,—buying them to be his subjects with his own precious blood,—he will not, and cannot, relinquish. They themselves could ill brook the idea of his relinquishing it. But it would seem that for the exercise of that sovereignty, in his capacity of their redeeming King, over others besides them, on their behalf, there is really no occasion now, and no room. It may be fitly merged, therefore, in the general sovereignty which the Godhead has over all things.

Behold, then, Christ the Son "delivering up the kingdom to God, even the Father!"

Contemplate him as coming forth from the Father. A province in the great universal empire of God has apostatized. Its inhabitants have thrown off their allegiance, and are in open rebellion. A usurping prince, with his legions, has got possession of the soil, and has won the hearts of those who occupy it. Suddenly, though after long warning, the Son, the heir of the rightful monarch, makes his appearance. He comes on a strange errand. He comes to expiate the crime of their rebellion on behalf of all who will adhere to him, by bearing for them, and as their substitute, its deserved and inevitable doom. He comes as his Father's delegate and viceroy, invested with full power and absolute authority over the whole province, and all within it. The universal power and authority thus conveyed to him he is commissioned to use, on the one hand, for attaching all who are to be his adherents to himself, and on the other hand, for the overthrow of every hostile force. The war is long; the struggle is severe; but at last it is over. The Captain of Salvation has gathered around him the entire number of the people that are to be saved. He has been wielding his delegated sovereignty for their salvation; and he has wielded it effectually. He needs to wield it no more. In their name, as well as in his own, he surrenders it. As representing them, —himself one with them and having them one with himself,—being still their Head, and Lord, and redeeming King,—he delivers up the kingly power which in that character he has been exercising over a province, once rebellious, but now subdued.

Thus, in their name, and as their king, he resigns the universal "government" which, in their name and as their king, he has had "laid upon his shoulders." In resigning it, as well as in receiving it, he acts as the representative of his people. Continuing still to be their king, representing them and acting for them in that character and capacity, he abdicates his more extensive power and prerogative, as "head over all things to the church." That universal power and prerogative he was entitled to claim, so long as the strife was hot. But now that the strife is over, he claims it no longer. Thus, and in these circumstances, "he delivers up the kingdom to God, even the Father."

II. This view of the transaction in question between Christ and the Father is confirmed by a consideration of the victorious position which he is represented as occupying when it takes place ;—"He shall have put down all rule, and all authority, and power" (verse 24).

He has completed the work for which he received the kingdom ; he has executed triumphantly the commission with which he was charged.

The Father has " given him power over all flesh, that he may give eternal life to as many as he has given him" (John xvii. 2). He is "set far above all principality, and power, and might, and dominion," and made "head over all things to the church, which is his body, the fulness of him that filleth all in all" (Ephes. i. 21-24). Such is his inauguration into his kingdom of universal authority and power. But he receives this authority and power, as "the man Christ Jesus," for a special purpose. That purpose is the subjugation of all authority and power on the earth, whether human or satanic, that is hostile to the Father's government and the Father's glory. He commands in an enemy's country. Armed with full kingly sovereignty, he wages war in a territory which has submitted to a usurper. Rallying round him, as the strife goes on, age after age, from among the very rebels with whom the war is waged, successive bands of faithful followers, whom he buys for himself with his blood and wins to himself by his Spirit,—leading them, shielding them, saving them,—he makes head

against his enemies and theirs; against the enemies
of the Father's throne,—the throne of "his Father
and their Father, his God and their God."

For years and long centuries, it seems a doubtful
contest. Evil influences, evil principles, evil powers,
evil men, evil spirits, are apparently as strong and
dominant as at the first. Ignorance, misery, crime,
lust, oppression, tyranny, bloodshed—the dark troop
of obscene harpies that track the malign steps of the
reign of this world's god—brood as ominously as ever
over the nations and families of mankind. The
Church, the Lord's struggling host, scarcely keeps her
precarious and ambiguous ground. The enemies of
God and of godliness are still confident and bold.

One might almost conclude that the best thing
the King and Captain of the Lord's host can do, is to
carry his loyal subjects hence, from this doomed
globe, to some better and brighter sphere, and leave
the field here for the Adversary to work his will in.

Yes! I may be sometimes tempted to exclaim,—
let it just come to this! Let the fortress be surrendered. Let the debateable land be evacuated.
Let the besieged garrison, the beleaguered army,
march off, one after another, under their leader :—
not conquered indeed, but not caring to prolong the
weary and interminable strife.

What though this earth be abandoned to the
Devil and his angels, to the prince of this world and

his slaves?—Away among those orbs of quenchless light that set the starry firmament in a blaze, may not some purer and more beauteous planet be found, where Christ may gather round him, as one by one they fall, the little ones whom the Father giveth him, when they have fought the good fight, and finished their course, and kept the faith, and won the crown of righteousness?

So let it be. Let them depart to be with Christ. And when they have all departed, when the last of them is gone, let this earth, which has been the scene of their trial and training for a better world, be left forsaken of "the Lord and his Christ," a worthless prey to the adversaries who have so long been saying, "Let us break their bands asunder, and cast their cords from us" (Ps. ii.)

But what! Leave this earth at last in the hands of enemies; this earth which holds the dust of his redeemed! Abandon and give over to hostile powers the place of his people's graves!—the graves in which those bodies lie that, belonging to the children who are one with himself, must as certainly be raised as his own was raised! Nay, if it were for nothing else than the raising of these bodies, this earth which is their burial-place must be rescued from the usurper, and recovered, before all is done, victoriously and gloriously for its rightful owner.

And it is most fitting that the raising of these

bodies should be the crowning trophy of the glorious victory. " He must reign, till he put all enemies under his feet " (verse 25). His last act of universal sovereignty is to be the rescuing of the bodies of his saints from the power of corruption. " The last enemy that shall be destroyed is death" (verse 26). It is fitting, I repeat, that it should be so.

He returns to this earth, once the scene of his agony, now to be the scene of his triumph. Then he was crucified in weakness ; it was "the hour and the power of darkness ;" he seemed to fall before his enemies ; it was for them to raise the shout of exultation. Now he has put them all under his feet ; he has overthrown every power, and overturned every government, that exalted itself against him. All who have been working evil on the earth, counterworking his good, are now impotent, and at his disposal. Their machinations and menaces alike are at an end. The earth is rid of them. And instead, Lo ! Christ is come in the clouds. He is come to consummate his success ; to follow it up with judgment ; to "avenge his slaughtered saints ;" to take vengeance on the oppressors. He is come, bringing with him the mighty multitude of saved souls that have been with him in paradise.

What time more suitable than that, what occasion more opportune, for the resurrection of those bodies which, when they departed to be with him, they left behind them here? All other enemies are under his feet; all the other enemies that were wont to tempt and try,—to vex and harass them. They are safe and free, completely and for ever, even if they are to dwell now again on earth, from all the adversaries of whatever sort, spiritual or carnal, that used to torment them when they dwelt on earth before. But they are not yet wholly free from death.

True; even before they fell asleep in Jesus, they were, to a large extent, most mercifully set free from death's power. They had ceased to be, "through fear of death, all their lifetime subject to bondage" (Heb. ii. 15). And when they came actually to die, there was no sting in their death, no curse, no sense of condemnation, no fear of wrath. Still death got hold of them in part, and has kept hold of them ever since.

But now Christ comes, and they come with him. And all their other enemies whom they had to meet when they were here before being under the feet of Christ their Lord, this last enemy, too, is to be destroyed. Whatever grasp he has had of them, even in the corporeal part of their nature, the grim king of terrors must let go. They rise. While "the wicked rise to the resurrection of damnation, and are cast out" (Matt. xxv. 41), they "rise to the resurrection of life," and remain. They are then sharers in the full blessedness of the resurrection of their Lord. And thenceforth there is no more, on all the earth's surface, a grave; there is no more, in all the earth's history, a death!

What a scene here bursts and breaks on the enraptured view of faith! What a crisis! Christ, the man Christ Jesus, standing again on this earth, in the body; all his redeemed with him in the body; not a breath, not a whisper, of opposition or rebellion anywhere to be heard, throughout all its continents and kingdoms; not a tomb anywhere; not a dying groan; not a trace of sin's, or of sorrow's, ravages; not the faintest vestige of the footsteps of the Archfiend who first brought sin and sorrow to its shores! Yes! The Lord's work is done! The end for which he got the kingdom is fully and for ever attained. Well may he then utter once more the exclamation of deep satisfaction—"It is finished"—and so "deliver up the kingdom to God, even the Father."

Shall we dare to penetrate a little farther into futurity, and look beyond that scene? What do we see? A renovated earth, with renovated heavens, wherein dwelleth righteousness. And who possess and own it? Saints changed or risen; with one like unto the Son of Man going in and out among them; not for a thousand years, ending with another fearful apostasy and fall; but for endless ages. Christ and his redeemed occupy that earth for ever. In some sense, and to some extent, they are wielding kingly power in it, and exercising kingly power over it ; he above them, and they under him. But it is only in the sense in which originally man was commanded to subdue the earth ; and with no claim, and indeed no ambition, as to any sovereignty beyond that. The dominion which, as the redeeming man, and for redeemed men, Christ had over all, is no more needed. His special and temporary mediatorial government, as Messiah the Prince, is merged in the everlasting and universal government of the Godhead. As the Eternal Son, he has that government still upon his shoulders. But as Christ, his people's Lord and King, as the man Christ Jesus, sharing with them the occupancy of Paradise restored, he is in the position in which the first Adam, if he had not fallen, might have been ultimately, with his children, in the Paradise that was lost. He continues to reign over the seed given to him and purchased by him. He is ever presenting them as the subjects whom he has brought back from rebellion to be, in him, now loyal subjects under the ordinary moral administration of God. As his, in that new earth which he has won for them, they own allegiance to the sovereign authority by which all the universe is governed. On earth, as elsewhere, " God is all in all " (verse 28).

Then the ideal of the eighth Psalm, as interpreted in the Epistle to the Hebrews (ii. 6-8), is fully realized. The last Adam occupies the place which the first Adam should have secured. And the wondering company of the redeemed, finding themselves, in their redeeming Lord and King, lords and kings upon this renovated earth,—yet owning still, nay, owning more than ever, in and with him, subjection to the universal supremacy of God,—take up, as applicable to him for them, and to them in him, the triumphant song of thanksgiving and praise—"What is man, that thou art mindful of him? and the son of man that thou visitest him? For thou hast made him a little lower than the angels, and hast crowned him with glory and honour. Thou madest him to have dominion over the works of thy hands; thou hast put all things under his feet; all sheep and oxen, yea, and the beasts of the field; the fowl of the air, and the fish of the sea, and whatsoever passeth through the paths of the seas. O Lord, our Lord, how excellent is thy name in all the earth!"

8

BAPTISM FOR THE DEAD AND OTHER PERILS —WHAT GOOD IS IT IF THE DEAD RISE NOT?

Else what shall they do which are baptized for the dead, if the dead rise not all? Why are they then baptized for the dead? And why stand we in jeopardy every hour? I protest by your rejoicing which I have in Christ Jesus our Lord, I die daily. If after the manner of men I have fought with beasts at Ephesus, what advantageth it me, if the dead rise not? Let us eat and drink; for tomorrow we die.
—1 Corinthians 15:29-32

THIS passage, which is on all hands confessed to be one of extremely difficult interpretation, may be considered, first, in itself and in its details ; and secondly, in its general meaning and connection, as a part of the apostle's argument.

Without entering particularly into all difficulties of detail connected with this passage considered in itself, it may be proper briefly to notice the most considerable of them in their order.

The first and chief difficulty is in the twenty-ninth verse : "Else what shall they do which are baptized for the dead, if the dead rise not at all ? why are they then baptized for the dead?" What is meant by being baptized for the dead?

The idea naturally suggested by the original phrase is that of a vicarious baptism; the baptism of one person in the place, or room, or stead of another. And in accordance with this idea, it has been supposed that there is a reference here to a practice which at one time partially prevailed in the church. The practice was this. If a convert to Christianity happened to die unbaptized, a Christian brother might volunteer to be his substitute and representative, and so might have the baptismal rite administered to him, on behalf of his deceased friend. This was held to make up for the loss which the dead man might sustain in consequence of his not having been himself baptized, while yet alive. It was held to be equivalent to his having been in his own person made partaker of the initiatory sacrament of the church. It was a posthumous baptism by proxy.

Some interpreters of high name have been inclined to understand Paul as alluding to that practice; and they have admired his allusion to it as an instance of the tenderness with which he dealt with a usage, to say the least of it, of dangerous tendency; while they have commended the skill with which he turned it to argumentative or oratorical account in pleading with those among whom it may have had some supporters. They represent him as reasoning thus : " Out

of your own mouth I argue with you. There are
some of you who have received baptism as personating
the dead, and, to use a familiar phrase, standing in
their shoes. For what good end did you do so, even
on your own theory of what such a procedure might
mean and might effect, if the dead rise not at all?"

There are grave and obvious objections to this
view. It shocks one's sense of propriety. It seems
unlike the apostle's usual manliness and genuine
truthfulness that he should deal thus with so fond
and frivolous, not to say so gross and fatal a superstition ; employing it merely to point a rhetorical
appeal, without one word of warning or denunciation
against it. Besides, there is not a trace of the usage
in question till many years after apostolic times, and
then only within a very narrow section of the church,
suspected with good reason, upon other grounds, of
unsoundness in the faith. And it is far more
probable that in a subsequent age of declining spirituality and increasing corruption the practice originated
among a few heretics, misinterpreting perhaps the
apostle's language, than either that it existed at all
in Paul's day, or that if it did, he could treat it so
lightly. The text, misconstrued, may have suggested
the usage ;—not the usage the text.

Of the other meanings that have been put upon
the phrase, none are entirely satisfactory and unob-
jectionable. That which, perhaps, most commends

itself,—at least to the fancy and the heart,—is the one which, retaining still the general idea of substitution, gives it a different turn ; making it not a vicarious representation of the persons of the dead, but, as it were, a vicarious occupancy of the position which till death they filled.

The vacancies left in the ranks of the Christian army, when saints and martyrs fall asleep in Jesus, are supplied by fresh recruits, eager to be baptized as they were, and pledged by baptism to fall as they fell at the post of duty and danger. It is a touching sight which the Lord's baptized host presents to view, especially in troublous times. Column after column advancing to the breach, as on a forlorn hope, in the storming of Satan's citadel of worldly pomp and power, is mowed down by the ruthless fire of persecution. But ever as one line disappears a new band of volunteers starts up, candidates for the seal of baptism, even though in their case, as in the case of their predecessors in the deadly strife, the seal of baptism is to be the earnest of the bloody crown of martyrdom.

It is surely somewhere in the line of this thought that the key to the perplexing phrase, " baptized for the dead," is to be found. It implies that somehow baptism forms a link of connection between the baptized living and the baptized dead—committing the living to the fortune or fate, whatever it may be, that has already overtaken the dead. Your baptism constitutes you the substitutes and successors on earth of the holy men and women who have gone before you. It binds you to do their work in life ; and to share their destiny in death.

But what destiny is that, if the dead rise not at all ? What means, in that case, your being baptized for the dead ?

The second difficulty, less formidable than the first, is in the affecting question and emphatic protest : " And why stand we in jeopardy every hour ? I protest by your rejoicing which I have in Christ Jesus our Lord, I die daily" (verses 30, 31).

The apostle points to the dangers which always and everywhere beset believers, as " baptized for the dead ; " and most pathetically describes his own condition as being one not merely of continual exposure to death, but of the continual endurance of death. It is singularly strong language that he uses. It is one of the instances in which personal feeling seems to rise within him with a certain uncontrollable and even indignant vehemence. He cannot contain himself. " I protest," he cries. And mark the ground of his protestation. " By your rejoicing which I have in Christ Jesus our Lord." " Your rejoicing which I have." The phrase is a strange one. It means substantially this :—The joy which I have in you ; the joy which I have in your joy, in Christ

Jesus our Lord. Your rejoicing in our common Lord is my joy. But I protest to you that it is a joy that is on my part very dearly bought. It is bought at the cost of an experience almost literally equivalent to a daily death. " I die daily."

And is it you who are " my joy and crown ;" you whose rejoicing is my joy in Christ Jesus our Lord ; you, to share whose joy in our common Saviour I am content to die daily ;—is it you who would yourselves cast away, and would have me to cast away, that hope of the resurrection which alone can make our joy, yours and mine, reasonable—which alone therefore can make my daily death endurable ? Where, if the dead rise not, is that "rejoicing of yours which I have," —which is my joy,—"in Christ Jesus our Lord ?" Why should I, for so vain a dream of fancied mutual blessedness, be doomed to " die daily ?"

There is yet a third difficulty. The apostle refers to a particular personal experience as illustrative of this " dying daily ;"—" If after the manner of men I have fought with beasts at Ephesus, what advantageth it me, if the dead rise not ?" (verse 32).

"I die daily ;"—and that not in a figure merely. Here, at Ephesus, where I am now writing this epistle, I have just escaped from a conflict which, humanly speaking, is tantamount to one of the cruellest deaths with which you, as frequenters of the ordinary public spectacles in Grecian cities, must once have been familiar;—the death inflicted by the fangs of wild and infuriated animals on the victims exposed upon the stage to their relentless rage;—"fighting with beasts."

To what exposure of himself the apostle here alludes, is not clear. It may be the same as that which he elsewhere indicates when he speaks of the trouble which came to him in Asia—how he was "pressed, out of measure, above strength,"—as if in a literal fight with wild beasts,—"insomuch that he despaired even of life" (2 Cor. i. 8). We know that once, during his three years' residence in Ephesus, he was in danger of being torn in pieces or stoned by a tumultuary assembly, roused against him by the fanaticism of the worshippers of Diana, who had been stimulated by the self-interest of the craftsmen, and inflamed by the rancour of the Jews (Acts xix.) He may have had similar hairbreadth escapes more than once. The Corinthians would understand well enough to what peril he referred. And they could feel, as in our ignorance of minute details we cannot feel, the full force of this most affecting appeal; "If after the manner of men I have fought with beasts at Ephesus, what advantageth it me, if the dead rise not?"

I. There are many among us, they seem to hear their once-loved pastor exclaiming, who, in being baptized, have nothing but death before us. We had everything to lose, as regards this present life, and

absolutely nothing to gain, when we were baptized.
So far as this world is concerned, our baptism
was virtually our death. We embraced the gospel,
knowing that those who had gone before us had
lost all, even their very lives, in the cause. I myself
held the clothes of Stephen when, amid a shower of
stones, seeing the heavenly glory, he "fell asleep."
I was baptized for the dead when, but a few days
after, I was by baptism enlisted to occupy his vacant
post. My baptism came in place of his death. What
if the vision of a risen Saviour was a delusion to the
martyr Stephen, as it must have been if the dead rise
not? Then the appearance of a risen Saviour to me,
as I was on the way to Damascus, was a delusion
also. But it was on the faith of that appearance that
I was baptized, as I may say, in Stephen's room.
Well may I ask, "What shall they do which are
baptized for the dead?"

II. And why do I, and those similarly situated
with me, hold on in a course implying uninterrupted
liability to destruction? Our having been baptized
for the dead is bad enough ; — our having rashly
served ourselves heirs to such men as Stephen, and
committed ourselves to a like fate with theirs.
Why should we not own our error now? Why not
acknowledge that it was under a mistake that we
thus identified ourselves with the martyrs, and cast
in our lot with them ; that we were misled when we

consented to be baptized for the dead? "Why stand we in jeopardy every hour?"

III. For my part, I can assure you, it is so with me. You know how I rejoice over you, and in you, and with you. You have not forgotten how you and I rejoiced together in Christ Jesus our Lord. It was, and is, a great joy—a great mutual joy—to be rejoicing in and with one another, in Christ Jesus our Lord. But "I protest to you" that, if it costs you little sacrifice, it costs me much. "I die daily." I enter daily into the death of Christ. It is only through my entering daily into the bitterness of his death that I enter, for myself and you—for myself with you—into the joy of his resurrection. Will you rob me of that joy, yours and mine—my joy in you, my joy with you—by persuading me that there is no resurrection?

IV. And if that consideration does not move you, what do you say to my actual, outward estate here at Ephesus, where I am now writing to you? Speaking to you as men are wont to speak to one another of their trials, I tell you frankly that it has seemed to me as if it were rather with wild beasts than with human beings that I have had to contend. If I have not literally been cast as a prey on the red and slippery stage to savage monsters; or forced to wrestle naked and unarmed with fierce lions for the amusement of a blood-thirsty populace; have I not really had to bear the brunt of an encounter quite as painful and as perilous, in braving the hostile passions of exasperated men?

And to what purpose is all this? Why should we pledge ourselves in baptism to a partnership with the fallen martyrs? Why should we continue in that partnership, incurring danger every hour? Why should we, for a visionary and ideal joy, however brotherly that joy may appear, and however divine, go through a daily experience of dying? And why should we face the enmity and wrath of a world that rages furiously, like a wild beast, against all that condemn its principles and practices? Why thus, in baptism, take the place of dead saints?—why continue, in spite of hourly jeopardy, to occupy their place?—why seek to retain and cultivate the joyous fellowship of believers at the expense of dying daily?—why provoke the resentment of wild beasts at Ephesus?—if, after all, there is no resurrection of the dead! Why not rather act on the Epicurean and worldly maxim—" Let us eat and drink, for to-morrow we die?"

9

HOW IS THIS QUESTION RAISED IN CONNECTION WITH THE ARGUMENT ABOUT THE RESURRECTION? (1 CORINTHIANS 15:29-32)

" LET us eat and drink, for to-morrow we die ;"—that is the conclusion to which the apostle sees that the argument of his antagonist is tending. It is a conclusion sufficiently startling and serious. It implies that all future hazards, as regards the life to come, are to be braved, and that present satisfaction alone, in the life that now is, must be sought. And this is alleged to be the necessary consequence of the denial of the resurrection.

A question naturally occurs ; more so now than in the time of the apostle ;—How does the doctrine which denies a bodily resurrection,—even though it involves a denial of Christ's own corporeity after his death, and of ours hereafter in him,—make void all our hope ? How does this dreary maxim of infidelity —" Let us eat and drink, for to-morrow we die "— present itself as the inevitable conclusion resulting from a denial of the bodily resurrection? May there not be a doctrine of immortality independent of that article of faith? If the pious dead continue to live ; if "the souls of believers are at their death made perfect in holiness, and do immediately pass into glory ;" is not that enough for them, and for us, even though their mortal frames, and ours, when we follow them, should never be resuscitated or quickened again?

Surely I may consent to be "baptized for the dead ;" to cast in my lot with them, and share their death, if they survive at all in blessedness. My doing so may imply that I stand in jeopardy ever hour. It may imply that for the "fellowship of joy" which I have with living Christians "I die daily," being "crucified with Christ." In meeting the enemies of my peace, the "principalities and powers" with which I have to "wrestle in the heavenly places," I may have to submit to what is tantamount to "fighting with wild beasts at Ephesus." The dead, into partnership with whom, as one of their substitutes and successors, I am baptized, have had all that to endure; and I, as baptized for the dead, may lay my account with having to endure it too. That undoubtedly, is a hard case, if they have utterly perished ; for I cannot hope to come better off at the last than they. But the question is about the material part of their complex being exclusively. It is, at the worst, only what is physical that is to be irretrievably lost. What is spiritual and immaterial is indestructible and immortal. And if, when they die, they "depart to be with Jesus"—to be "absent from the body and present with the Lord"—then, even although that absence from the body should be perpetuated and prolonged for ever, it was worth while for them to live as they lived—it was worth while for them to die as they died. And it is worth while for me, it is gain to me and no loss, to live and to die as they lived and died—or, in other words, to be "baptized for the dead."

So I am apt to feel and to reason;—being familiar with the notion of the soul living on in blessedness, while the body lies mouldering in the grave, and of that life of the soul continuing, even though the body should never quit the grave in which it lies.

And so perhaps some of those Corinthian speculators with whom Paul had to deal might argue. You do us injustice when you assume that because we cannot see our way intelligently to admit the theory of a future literal and bodily resurrection, we therefore, either virtually or formally, deny the fact of a future spiritual life. We hold, as you do, that whosoever liveth and believeth in Jesus shall never die. We are persuaded that our believing friends, who have gone before us through the dark valley, are living now, and are enjoying a happiness which

But Not Salvation (15:29-32) • 135

makes up to them a thousandfold for all that they had to sacrifice and to suffer here below. Instead of them, thus dead, we count it all joy to be baptized ; though this baptism of ours for the dead may cost us sacrifices and sufferings as grievous as theirs. It is enough if we are to share their felicity, as they have it imparted to their spirits now. What matters it though neither their bodies nor ours are ever to see the light of life again ?

Evidently this is not the apostle's view. He considers the whole future state of himself and his fellow-believers to be at stake. With Paul it is a question of life or death ;—and it is so in the strictest and most formidable sense of that alternative.

And yet Paul must have been well read in those arguments of philosophy—Grecian and Oriental—that grappled with the question of immortality. He must have had the idea of the soul's separate existence in his view. He himself, more than once in his writings, asserts that doctrine most articulately. He could not, like the Sadducees, confound or identify the denial of the resurrection with the denial of immortality. He must have been prepared to admit that there might be a spiritual immortality without a bodily or physical resurrection ;—that men might live on, in Christ, and with Christ, as to their souls, though their bodies were to perish altogether. What he could not admit was the possibility of there being life, either of the soul or of the body,—real life—saved life—life for the redeemed, either out of the body or in the body,—apart from the resurrection of Christ.

For it is here, if one may be allowed the expression, that the shoe pinches. It is here that the real stress and pressure of the argument lies.

Take away the doctrine of the resurrection, and you take away, as a matter of fact, the resurrection of Christ. Take away that, and you take away the ground or foundation on which any believer in Christ can have life now, or can look for life after death, either out of the body or in the body.

In vain you tell me of an immortality of the soul. In vain you bid me apprehend the surviving of the whole spiritual part of me, after death has dealt with my mortal frame. I care not for such a survivorship, unless it carries with it safety, life, and glory. But how can it, if there is no resurrection? For if there is no resurrection, Christ is not risen. And if Christ is not risen, if there is no resurrection, why mock me with the delusion of a life separate from the body, when, even if such a life were sure to me, it must be a living death?—such a living death as, in some terrible sense, the death of the man Christ Jesus himself must have been, if, dying for our sins, he had not been raised again for our justification! In his case, and therefore in ours, the motto is—No resurrection, no life.

For it comes to that. If there be no resurrection there is no life ; none of that life for which alone, as a believer in the Lord Jesus Christ, I care ; no life in and with my risen Saviour, my living Lord and Head.

The resurrection of my body at the last day is not that life, although it is the consummation and completion of it. The life itself I have now. And I shall continue to have it after death, while my body lies in the grave. Death is no break, no interruption in that life. The resuming of my body is but an incident in that life. It is a life whose continuity stretches, in one unbroken and unending line, from the moment of my believing, and being found in Christ, onward throughout eternal ages. It is the same life—a resurrection life throughout. It is life depending on a resurrection ; it is life flowing from a resurrection ; it is life realized in a resurrection. My life is my oneness with Christ in his resurrection. He is to me the resurrection and the life. He is my resurrection and my life.*

Grant me this resurrection life, to begin now and here, while I am in the body ; to survive when I am absent from the body ; to be perfected for ever when I am in the body again. Grant me this life ; a life intimately and inseparably, from the first throughout, bound up with the belief of the resurrection. Then I am ready for any forlorn hope. I will fill the

---

* See Supplementary Discourse on John 11:25.

bloody footsteps of any of the fallen brave. I will
accept a baptism for any martyrdom. All the live-
long day and night, for all the days and nights of my
earthly pilgrimage, I will stand in jeopardy. The
most humbling daily death will I die. The wildest
beasts of Ephesus will I face. And all this I will do,
not in gloom, as if all the present were misery, to be
compensated by some future reward ; but in gladness,
for I have the compensation now. I have it in that
resurrection life on which I have already entered. I
have it ;—I protest, by the joy of my fellowship
with all the saints in our common risen Saviour,
that I have it. By our mutual rejoicing with one
another in Jesus Christ our Lord, I protest that I
have the compensation now.

There are several important practical lessons involved in this representation. I mention two of them.

The first is, that the resurrection for which Paul
pleads, is the resurrection which virtually includes in
it the whole life of the believer, in this world, in the
intermediate state, and throughout eternity. The
apostle is not merely arguing about an event that is
to happen at the last day. If that were all, the
matter might seem of minor consequence. The resuming of our bodies may be the signal and the occasion for a large accession of glory and blessedness.
Still, if it were viewed as an isolated incident in our
history, and if otherwise, apart from it, our spiritual

life in God's favour and likeness were secure to us,
the necessity for making so much of it as Paul does
might not be very apparent. But the whole drift of
the apostle's reasoning is to shew that, apart from the
resurrection, we can have no spiritual life at all,
either here or hereafter. Whatever spiritual life we
have, now or hereafter, we must accept as resurrection
life ;—for it is the resurrection life of Christ that we
accept.

He died for our sins, and in our sins ; and it is
only in his resurrection that he appears as delivered
from our sins ;—himself saved from our sins, and so
saving us from them. In his resurrection he stands
forth complete ; thoroughly and for ever, as to his
whole person, rid of all the guilt and condemnation
of our sins which he made his own ; thoroughly and
for ever, as to his whole person, accepted and justified ; alive, therefore, for evermore. That is his
resurrection life.

And into that life—into fellowship and participation with him in that life—we enter, when the
Spirit, working faith in us, unites us to him. Our
resurrection life then begins ; we "are risen with
Christ" (Coloss. ii. 12, and iii. 1). And it goes on
unfolding and developing itself before our death, and
after our death, until at last, in the most exact and
full sense, as to our whole person, body as well as
soul, the resurrection life of Christ becomes ours. Thus

it is a resurrection life throughout. It is a life wrapt up in a justifying resurrection from a penal and expiatory death.

Hence, to deny that resurrection is to cut up by the roots this life. It is to fling us back on such life as we may have apart from Christ and the resurrection ;—independently of Christ and the resurrection.

And what life is that? It may be a life with a hereafter ;—a hereafter for the immortal soul ;—a hereafter even for the revivified body. But it is a life to which sin, guilt, condemnation, corruption, wrath, all hopelessly cleave. It is, I repeat, no better than a living death. There is nothing in it to make amends for a martyr's bloody baptism of death. There is nothing in it fitted to make amends even for the self-denial and self-sacrifice which ordinary christian fellowship and service demand. If we have nothing better than that to gain through Christ, we may certainly as well take things easily ; making the most of the world as we find it ; and acting on the pleasing, seductive maxim—"Let us eat and drink, for to-morrow we die."

The second lesson to be learned is this ; that what reconciles believers to present trial, is not the distant and prospective vision of a future reward, but the present sense of a resurrection life.

It is a poor thing to conceive of the apostle as arguing thus : I would consider it worth while to submit to hardships, privations, persecutions, even to death itself, were I sure of living hereafter, and being recompensed and requited hereafter. A generous and noble spirit might reply : There are some things worth the suffering for, and worth the dying for, even if there were no life or resurrection of any sort in the future world after death. Truth is one of these, and righteousness, and charity. I would be baptized for the dead ; I would stand in jeopardy ; I would mortify myself and crucify myself daily ; I would fight with wild beasts, any day and every day ;—as a confessor in the cause of truth, or of righteousness, or of charity ;—without ever asking if I am to survive death, and to be paid my wages after death for my work and warfare now. I am paid already. I have the wages in my own bosom, conscious of right, and triumphant over wrong. And when you make your christian bemoan himself, as if he could not be faithful and honourable in his master's service here unless he were sure of getting the resurrection of his body as his hire hereafter, you degrade him below the level of many a heathen, who darkly struggled on in the cause of the true and the good,—hopeless, or all but hopeless, of any life at all beyond the grave.

But this is not really a fair statement of the case. What the apostle urges is, that if you take away the resurrection, you not merely take away the future reward—you take away the present value and virtue

—of the struggle. There is no sense or meaning now in any service I may render or in any sacrifice I may make. The whole is a delusion and a dream.

But give me, on the other hand, in sure possession now, this resurrection to life,—Christ's resurrection to life for me and my resurrection to life in him. Then, not in the remote distance before me, but in my present actual realization of it, I have a joy in the midst of all my tribulations,—the joy of my "life, that is hid with Christ in God;"—a joy for which I may well consent to die daily, to be in jeopardy every hour, and to fight with all manner of wild beasts, in any sort of Ephesus.

10

CONCLUSION OF THE FIRST PART: DANGER OF ANTINOMIAN LICENSE

Be not deceived: evil communications corrupt good manners. Awake to righteousness, and sin not; for some have not the knowledge of God: I speak this to your shame.
—1 Corinthians 15:33, 34

THERE is undoubtedly a difficulty in understanding why Paul should be so very earnest in insisting on the resurrection of the body :—as if he thought that without that element, the belief of immortality might not only fail to exercise a good influence, but might even exercise an evil influence, over one who so embraces it. It is a difficulty that is not unnatural when we look at the question from a modern point of view. We are apt to regard it as a question between parties, both of whom equally hold the doctrine of a future state of reward and retribution, and who differ merely in their conceptions of the nature of that state. If the question is thus narrowed, it may not be easy to make it very palpable how the one opinion is less favourable to holiness, or tends more to licentiousness, than the other. The indestructibility of the soul being maintained as a tenet of natural, as well as of revealed, religion, — why make so much of a material resurrection of the body? Whether in or out of the body, man is an heir of immortality.

Even in that view, however, the question is one of more importance than at first sight appears. It is one thing to think of my future life hereafter, as the final escape and emancipation of my soul, my better part, from that gross physical frame whose companionship clogs and debases it here. It is quite another thing to look forward to my soul's resuming that very frame, and having it for a companion through eternity. In the former case, I am apt to feel that it matters comparatively little how I use this body of mine, what liberties I take with it, what indulgences I allow it. It is not properly myself, nor any vital part of myself, but rather an extraneous encumbrance. The pure ethereal spirit in me is to shake it off. And being rid of its temporary associate's lower tendencies and agitations for ever, it is itself to soar aloft, on the wings of its own higher aspirations, in the regions of cloudless mental serenity and repose.

You tell me, no doubt, that I may still have to answer, in my soul or spirit, for deeds done in the body. And I can see how my spiritual essence may retain for a time, as it departs, some flavour of the sordid cask in which it has for a time been lodged.

But the idea still haunts me, that when I " shuffle off this mortal coil," I part with what has been the real occasion of my sufferings and sins, and pass into a purely spiritual mode of being, in which ultimately I must emerge out of all the degradation of earth into heaven's own pure and perfect light.

Thus the unseen future after death stretches itself out before me, when the immortality of the soul, and that alone, is my hope. It wears a dreamy, ideal, unsubstantial character ; apt to become more and more dim, intangible, impersonal. I am almost fain to lose myself, like the old visionaries of the East, in the great thought of all finite intelligences being at last absorbed into the one Infinite Mind.

Some such tendency as this has always been found associated with the mere belief of the soul's natural immortality, apart from that of a bodily resurrection. It was a tendency most marked and decided in the case of those heresiarchs who were already, in the apostle's time, marring the simple gospel by the intro-duction of Oriental subtleties.

The favourite dogma of these " gnostics," or know-ing ones,—that matter is in itself essentially and incurably corrupt and the cause of all corruption,—compelled them to deny the possibility of a literal bodily resurrection. Nothing but a spiritual resurrec-tion could find a place in their creed ; and they held that, in the case of believers, or at least in the case of the initiated, that spiritual resurrection was "past already." The soul, renovated by faith, is raised to newness of life. In its new life, it is hindered and held down by the body, until death sets it free. Then, either instantly or after a period of probation or purgation, the slough of the flesh is thoroughly cast off. And ever after, for ever, all is well.

From this speculative theory of theirs, two practical conclusions flowed. It led them to throw the blame of whatever evil still adhered to them, not on the risen soul, but on the material body, which would not let the soul live purely and freely according to its renovated nature. And, worse than that, it led them to argue that the amount of evil, more or less, which might still adhere to them, was really very much a matter of indifference, since, being all centred in the body, it would be all got rid of when the body was cast aside.

Thus by brief stages their error led to sin. The speculative argument for license was but too congenial. They might wallow in the filth and mire of moral pollution ; it would affect only that mortal part of them which was already hopelessly corrupt and doomed at any rate. The leprosy, however loathsome, would ere long be buried in the tomb,— with that mortal frame which alone it touched. Their spiritual nature would then be pure and free.

Even in these early apostolic times, this vicious

logic of debauchery was beginning to infest the
church. The apostle refers to it elsewhere : "Shun
profane and vain babblings : for they will increase
unto more ungodliness. And their word will eat as
doth a canker: of whom is Hymenæus and Philetus ;
who concerning the truth have erred, saying that the
resurrection is past already ; and overthrow the faith
of some " (2 Tim. ii. 16-18). It was, indeed, a canker,
a gangrene, eating into the very heart of whatever
society it touched, and turning it into a foul Epicurean sty. Ere long, it made sad havoc in some of
the once fairest portions of the church ; such havoc
as at a later period was wrought among the fanatics
whose violent crimes and licentious excesses, justified
in much the same way, were the shame and scandal
of the Reformation.

No wonder that Paul was filled with intensest
alarm, if there was any symptom of a plague like
this breaking out at Corinth. And, in truth, there
was but too much cause. The shameless laxity of
morals which made the city famous, or infamous,
throughout all the civilized world of antiquity, might
well awaken anxious concern for the purity of the
church being kept unblemished there. The unwise
and unfaithful tolerance of incest in a member of
the church, with the grounds of expediency, false
tenderness, and false security, on which that tolerance seemed to be vindicated or excused, made the

danger more palpable (chapter v.) And now an opinion is openly broached, as an article of religious belief, of which the plain meaning is,—and of which the obvious effect must be,—to license, as all but harmless, whatever one calling himself a saint may choose to do in the body.

Well might the apostle, in these circumstances, utter the solemn warning: " Be not deceived : evil communications corrupt good manners " (verse 33).

Thus introduced, the brief, proverbial saying— " evil communications corrupt good manners "—must be understood somewhat differently from what the common mode of quoting it would make it. The " evil communications " here indicated are not practical but theoretical. It is not the keeping of evil company, in the ordinary sense of that phrase, that is meant ; but our becoming familiar with unsound doctrine on a vital point of christianity. That is the import of the maxim here.

Are you tempted to listen to the speculations of these deniers of the resurrection ? Are you beginning to take part and find pleasure in their discussions ? You little know what risk you are running.

Their views have a certain plausibility ; a show of more than ordinary spirituality. Their conceptions of the future state are a refinement on the commonplace teaching of vulgar christianity, with its local heaven, its material hell, and its actual, bodily resurrection of the dead. There is something in their lofty ideal of the unseen and eternal,—dim and shadowy perhaps,—but yet fitted to captivate the imagination. It is so calm and pure ;—the region, the domain, of mind alone ;—of mind expanding with its own high thoughts ; and with no bodily senses, no bodily organs, to let in the disturbing forces of any material world any more. You listen : you are fascinated. Surely, to say the least of them, such " communications " as these must be harmless. To be familiar, to be conversant with them in their highest sublimity, may elevate the soul ; and cannot surely debase it. Why not suffer yourself to be interested and charmed ?

" Be not deceived." Consider the practical bearings of that line of thought which you are beginning to like so well. Consider to what these " communications "—these communings you are so fond of— really tend. They are " evil " in themselves, and therefore mischievous. They have an irresistible tendency to " corrupt good manners."

You may fancy that you can indulge in them with impunity. Your convictions are so strong, your principles so fixed, on all the great fundamental tenets of christian faith and practice, that on this confessedly obscure topic, the precise nature of the future state, you may allow yourselves a little latitude. Even if these deep thinkers push their views a little too far,—

and in their recoil from other men's gross materialism, overdo, as it were, their own spiritualism,—is it not, at all events, an error on the safe side? One would almost rather err somewhat with these high intellects, these enthusiastic souls, than tamely trudge on, with the uninquiring crowd, in the dull level track of an immaculate, stereotyped, orthodox creed about a literal resurrection from the dead.

So you may be apt to feel. But beware. This super-refined spirituality which so fascinates and intoxicates you, has in it the germ of the most unblushing sensuality. It carries in its bosom a principle which, when fairly followed out, makes self-denial and self-sacrifice mere folly, and the freest, foulest self-indulgence innocent and good. Beware, lest the spell of a sort of opium-inspired dream be upon you. "Awake to righteousness, and sin not" (verse 34).

Awake! as from the deepening lethargy of weariness and wine. Shake off the drowsiness apt to steal over you, as you yield yourselves up to some fond vision, carrying your rapt soul away into the realms of bright spirit-land and fairy-land. Awake, so as to take a right view of things as they really are. From the visionary ideal, awake to the actual reality. Let there be a righteous awakening; an awakening according to righteousness. You have been dreaming of some transcendental state of heavenly perfection, to be reached by the soul's absolute rejection of the body ; the ethereal particle which thinks and feels becoming perfectly pure, as it quits for ever its tenement of clay. I call for a righteous awakening ; such an awakening as may bring you back to a right apprehension of the realities of your position, in the view of the righteous Lawgiver, and his righteous government and law. Thus only can you be preserved from deadly sin ;—"Awake to righteousness and sin not."

Alas ! that so peremptory a call should be needed. And yet so it is. "For there are among you some who have not the knowledge of God" (verse 34). They may affect to know much, far more than others, of mind, soul, spirit, human and divine. Theories of all sorts, concerning the Infinite Mind, and the way in which finite minds are to converse and commune with the Infinite, may be familiar to them as household words. And they may be at home in speculating upon the human spirit's ascension, or absorption, into the divine. But of God personally they are ignorant; —of God, in that character of holy, righteous, judicial sovereignty, in which, as lawgiver and judge, he stands forth before the eyes of all who are "awakened to righteousness," by the Spirit "convincing them of sin, of righteousness, and of judgment."

And surely this ignorance, in your case, is inexcusable. After all that you have heard of Christ and

of his cross—of Christ as a ransom and of his cross
as a redemption—that any of you should still prefer
the heathen dream of a spiritual immortality to the
Gospel assurance of your whole selves, body as well
as soul, being redeemed and saved ;—this implies an
amount of ignorance, as to what God, the Righteous
One, is,—and as to how he deals with you in
righteousness,—that is as little creditable as it is safe.
" I speak this to your shame " (verse 34).

Such, generally, is the import of this earnest
practical appeal of the apostle's, as to the danger of
familiar communing with false doctrine, and the
teachers of false doctrine, on the subject of the resurrection. Error in opinion leads to sin in conduct.
That is the real import of the proverbial saying.
And it is realized very seriously when it is this new
idea of the resurrection that is in vogue. It must
be so if the apostle's previous reasoning holds.

The substance of that reasoning is, that the denial
of the general doctrine of the resurrection, implying
as it does a denial of the fact of Christ's resurrection,
cuts up by the very roots the hope of those who have
believed in him ; and that, too, with reference to, not
exclusively or specially to the future state after death,
but with reference to the life that now is as well as
that which is to come. The argument is based on
the union between them and Christ, in virtue of

which they are dead in him, because he died for
them. It was a penal death that he died for them;
it is a penal death that they die in him. And if, as
these speculators tell us, there is and can be no such
thing as a resurrection; if, in consequence, we must
explain away, on some ideal theory, the opened tomb,
the absent body, the eating of broiled fish at the Sea
of Galilee, the "handle me and see, for a spirit hath
not flesh and bones as ye see me have:"—if, in short,
Christ is not risen bodily; then all proof is wanting
of his emancipation, and his people's emancipation in
him, from the penalty of sin. All proof is wanting
of his righteous justification for them, and their
righteous justification in him.

It is this making void of the whole doctrine of
redemption that the apostle dreads, as the issue to
which these rash speculations about the resurrection
of the body tend; and it is from this source that he
anticipates a tide of licentious error as about to flow
in upon the church.

You lose,—such in substance is his appeal,—you
lose your apprehension of a new life, to which, as to
your whole manhood, body as well as soul, you are
already raised, in Christ your risen Lord. To apprehend that life as a life begun now; as a life moreover
to be perfected, not by the soul's quitting the body,
but by the body's rising again; to recognise yourselves, your entire persons, as already raised together

with Christ, in your being justified,—and as destined ultimately to be raised together with Christ, in your being glorified ;—this is an animating faith and hope ; —a faith and hope coming home, with a living sense of intense personality, to your bosoms. It may well nerve you for great works and great trials. It may reconcile you to the crucifying of all worldly and fleshly lusts.

But where are you if there be no resurrection, and if, in consequence, Christ be not risen ? All idea of such personal dealing with you on the part of God ;— his judicially absolving and accepting you, as on the supposition of his having raised Christ from the dead, he must be held to have judicially absolved and accepted him ;—all idea of his thus raising you to a justified life in the risen Christ must be abandoned. You can but fall back on the vague hope that some-how this Christ may have made provision, not for expiating your guilt and reconciling you personally to God now, but for drawing out of you some spiritual element that may survive the destruction of your body, and may ultimately, through that destruction of the body, unite itself, in some transcendental spiritual fashion, to him who is a spirit, and who alone is good. From such a hope the inference is not far to seek, that with the body, and in the body, you may do what you please.

To make this difficult subject, if possible, some-what plainer, let me ask attention once more to two practical views of the bearing of this doctrine—the doctrine of the resurrection—on personal holiness.

I. How does it affect our present state and standing, as believers, in the sight of God?

The apostle's doctrine clearly is, that if there is no resurrection there is no justification. We must abandon the notion of any judicial procedure on the part of God, either with Christ for us or with us in Christ. It is not in any such way that we can hope to be saved. If that was the divine plan—with reverence be it said —it has, if there is no resurrection, proved a failure. A ransom, no doubt, has been found; a voluntary substitute has presented himself—unexceptionable—infinitely worthy. The Father, as the righteous judge, has laid on him our iniquities, and inflicted on him our doom. He has died for our sins. But he is dead still. Death has got, and still keeps, hold over him. His soul, indeed, may be free. But as to his entire manhood, which for us men and for our salvation he assumed, he is not delivered. He is not really saved from death. His human nature which, that he might die, he took, is still the victim of death. It suffers mutilation. What survives the cross and the grave is not the entire manhood, but some ethereal, spiritual essence extracted out of the manhood.

And what is the necessary conclusion? Even

the Son of the Highest could not take our nature,
that he might stand in our place, without coming
under that law of death which attaches to our nature
by reason of sin ; and so coming under it, that he
cannot be delivered except at the expense of the
bodily part of that nature being, even in his case, left
to lie and rot hopelessly in the tomb! Even he, the
Holy One and the Just, cannot save or sanctify the
body. He may succeed in extricating from it the
soul. He may begin and carry on now a dealing
with the spiritual part of us which, when the fleshly
part of us is cast away, may result in our spiritual
perfection. But he cannot, as our substitute, reinstate
us as we now are, bodily, in the position of favour
with God which for our sin we have lost. He cannot present us now, as we are, in the body, before his
Father, that we may be justified. For he is not himself justified, in the body, for us, if he is not raised
from the dead.

If this be a gospel at all, it is certainly a very different gospel from that which we have been accustomed
to believe. It sets altogether aside the whole doctrine
of atonement by sacrifice, in any fair sense of these
terms. The fundamental idea of guilt expiated, and
the guilty justified, through union with him who,
being made sin, died,—and being the righteousness
of God, rose again,—can have no place in such a
system. Hence appeals like these become irrelevant

and unmeaning; "Ye are not your own, ye are bought with a price; therefore glorify God in your body and in your spirit, which are God's." "Christ hath redeemed you from the curse of the law, being made a curse for you." "He died for your sins, and rose again for your justification." "Reckon ye yourselves to be dead indeed unto sin, but alive unto God, through Jesus Christ our Lord."

But are not these the very appeals which stir the believer's heart, like a trumpet-call to arms, and summon him to "glory and virtue?" Are not these the considerations which the Holy Ghost brings home to him as motives to holy watching and heavenly devotedness?—that he is to regard himself as, in his whole manhood, redeemed; that he has passed through an ordeal of judgment; that he has seen the sentence of death recorded against him executed upon the person of the Son of God in his stead; that believing and accepting this substitution, he has been crucified, and is crucified, with Christ; that nevertheless he lives, being quickened together with Christ; that "the life he now lives in the flesh, he lives by the faith of the Son of God, who loved him and gave himself for him;" and that "the love of Christ constrains him to live, not unto himself, but unto him who died for him, and who rose again."

These are the views of the resurrection, in its bearing on our present state and standing before

God, which sentimental spiritualists would have us to cast aside. And what do they give us in their place ? What is their scheme of christianity ?

At the best, it is little more than an improvement on the methods which thoughtful men have been always trying, for extricating their better part, or, as they say, the divine part that is in them, from the polluting contact of what is fleshly, or of what is earthly. Jesus is now somehow our leader, pattern, guide, in this process of emancipation ; which, going on more or less in this world, will at last be perfected, or put in the way of being perfected, after death, in the world to come. This is all, or nearly all, they have to say.

Alas ! it will but ill meet the case of a really awakened man, whose conscience testifies to him that his guilt is a reality, and whose heart longs for real peace with his God, as the only way to purity and love.

Hold fast, then, your faith in the resurrection, and especially in the resurrection of Christ, both as a matter of fact and as a matter of doctrine. You believe it as a matter of fact. That is well. But believe it also, with an intelligent eye to its doctrinal significancy. This was what these Corinthians lost sight of. And losing sight of that,—the bearing of the resurrection as a matter of doctrine,—they were the more easily persuaded to let it go as a matter

of fact. But be ye fully persuaded, not only that it
is a fact, and a great fact, but that it has a meaning,
and a great meaning. Recognise in it a double
justification; Christ's justification for you, and your
justification in Christ; a double justification, but
yet one and the same. Behold the Father, as the
righteous judge, justifying him; pronouncing him
to be no longer laden with the guilt of your sins
which had been laid upon him; well pleased in him
for his righteousness' sake; acquitting and accepting
him; "declaring him to be the Son of God, with
power, by his resurrection from the dead." And
believe—you have full warrant for believing, whatever your guilt, whatever your unbelief hitherto—
believe in God the righteous Father as acting towards
you now precisely as he acted towards Christ then;
treating you now precisely as he treated him then;
justifying you now as surely and as fully as he then
justified him; loving you henceforth for ever, even as
he loveth him. Believe this and live. Live, as thus
believing. This is gospel peace and gospel holiness.

II. How does this doctrine of the resurrection
affect, not our present standing merely in the sight of
God, but our hope as regards the life to come? And
in this view what is its bearing on personal holiness?

Here let it be again emphatically said, it is this
doctrine of the resurrection which alone gives any-

thing like tangible reality to the future state, considered as a state of reward and retribution.

If, when I die, I am to go out of this body, the body which connects me with the scene of my personal history in this present life,—and if I am to be out of it for ever after,—I can never quite rid myself of the idea that I am to leave that personal history itself behind me, and that its chequered recollections and experiences are to trouble me no more.

Yes! And the idea is apt to be but too welcome. Willingly, I often feel, most willingly and right gladly, would I have the whole warp and woof of the web that has been woven for me, or woven by me, upon earth, cut for ever clean out of the great loom of time. Willingly would I consent to the entire record of my passage from the cradle to the grave being blotted out for ever, by one sweep of the pen of oblivion over it. Sunny spots there have been, bright days; but no day so bright as to be without its clouds; no spot so sunny as to want its shadow. And what weariness have I felt amid them all! How vain and hollow have been my joys! How manifold my bitter griefs! And everywhere what sin and self-reproach! Yes! It were well to have it all, from first to last, cancelled; and for all its busy stir and strife, its laughter, its tears, to have nothing but a blank, which neither I nor any other spirit could ever read again.

Would I have any exception made? Are there some few dear friends to whom I would not like to say farewell for ever? Still, how in that other world would I choose to meet them? Passages of love come rushing on my memory as I am leaving them, interchanges of kindly confidence and fondness. Shall we talk over these when we are together again? There is for a moment rapture in the thought. But, ah! here too what sin and self-reproach! I cannot, without many a keen pang of regret, nay, of remorse, recall our past endearments and familiarities. Better, after all, that when we are re-united in a holier and happier region, we should begin our loving intercourse anew. We shall have fresh materials there in abundance for the exchange of thoughts and feelings then freshly purified. And our converse will be all the closer if no memories of a former fellowship, less pure and holy, are suffered to intrude.

Yes! I am still willing to be for ever absent from the body. It has wrought me sin and sorrow enough. Let me have no more of these bodily infirmities and changes. Let my soul live before thee, oh God!

Such, I am persuaded, must often have been the frame of mind in which even believers in Christ have been inclined to look forward to a future state.

Now, if it is thus that I contemplate my hereafter, may I not be falling into the very error which Paul condemns? I do not, it is true, avowedly adopt

a creed which formally denies a future reckoning.
But I fill and soothe my mind with vague notions of
a dreamy sort of immortality of bliss for the soul.
The thought of my having to give an account for the
deeds done in the body recedes gradually into the
background. And my anticipations of the life that is
to come, growing more and more transcendental and
ideal, grow less and less influential over the actual
bodily doings of the life that now is. Insensibly I
find myself, in my secret heart, beginning almost to
reason like those speculators of old, and feel as if,
with reference to this or that small instance of sloth
or of self-indulgence, it cannot really matter much
how I act. It is but an affair of the body after all.
It is a transient and accidental infirmity of my bodily
constitution. The essence of my soul's life in Christ
is untouched. My spiritual walk with God in Christ
is safe.

Let me beware of the first approach of this most
subtle and insidious temptation. And that I may
beware of it, let me hold fast my faith in the doctrine
of the resurrection. I may well indeed rejoice in the
thought that at death I am to be absent from the
body ; not, however, because absence from the body
is in itself to be desired ; but because to be " absent
from the body" is to be "present with the Lord." I
"depart to be with Christ, which is far better." But
never let me forget that the real eternity before me

is not what begins at death, but what begins at the resurrection. Then I live again in the body; in the very body, as to all essential properties, and as to all practical issues, in which I live now.

I am to be alive again in this body. And I am to live in it for ever. If so, dare I dream of separating this body, or anything done in this body, or anything that touches this body, from myself? Can I now imagine, for a moment, any portion or passage of my present bodily history left behind, cancelled, and obliterated?

Fain would I often break, even in this life, the thread of continuity between the past and the future. Fain would I cherish the hope that it may be broken, when I pass into the life to come. But no; it cannot be. The fact of the resurrection—Christ's and mine —gives the lie to the delusion. I am to live, not a ghost, a spectre, a spirit. I am to live then, as I live now, in the body.

Oh! that I were so living now, and always, in this my body, as I shall wish I had lived, when I come to live in it again! Let me never, at any time, in any circumstances, lose sight of this solemn thought, that the deed which I am now doing in the body,—the thought I am thinking now, the word I am speaking now, the work I am working at now, in the body— must follow me. I may perhaps lay it down at death; but I must take it up again at the resurrection. This deed of mine must follow me into that future and eternal life.

For what purpose? To shame me before the Judge? to sting me? to vex me with a sense of my deep ingratitude to him who died for me,—my heedless selfishness and shameful guilt in wounding him afresh? What terror is there in the prospect!

And yet, if I am in Christ, and fall asleep in Christ, it need not be all terror; it need not be terror at all.

When the broken thread of my bodily life is united again at the resurrection, its earthly history will doubtless come up again. It will come up more clearly far than I can trace it now. It will all come up. And many, too many, things will there be in it that, when discovered anew, may well startle and appal me. They passed almost unnoticed at the time; I got over them easily; I soon forgot them. But I see them now; I feel them now. The risen Saviour, as the Judge, is shewing them to me, as one of his risen saints.

Yes! he is shewing them to me;—not, however, that he may visit me for them; not that he may upbraid me with them;—but that he may give me a new insight into the riches of that love which, even in spite of them, has saved me. What he shews me, in that day, of these deeds done in the body, may be one more lesson of humiliation and godly sorrow. But along with them, he shews me anew, and more vividly than ever before, the blood which cleanseth from them all, the righteousness which covers them all, the charter of free forgiveness which cancels all their guilt. I " obtain mercy of the Lord in that day" (2 Tim. i. 18). With what new rapture, therefore, of admiring and adoring gratitude, perceiving now at last how much I am forgiven—and, therefore, loving much—shall I join in the song, "Worthy is the Lamb that was slain, for he was slain for us!"

Nor will this be all the experience of that hour when my bodily life begins again, and my earthly history comes up. It will not be all a bringing forth of evil. There are lines in that history, if it be the history of the lowly and loving walk of faith, which I may be glad to resume again ; interrupted studies to which I may apply myself again ; inquiries, begun only to be broken off, which I may prosecute again ; habits of activity in God's service which I may exercise again ; researches into his works and ways which I may carry on again ; friendships and brotherhoods which I may cultivate again.

It may be largely the same life as now ; but, oh ! how different! Now I study, as one examining, with bleared eyes, pebbles on the shore ; then I range, with open vision, over the boundless ocean of truth. Now I darkly grope and guess ; then I ask, and know, even as I am known. Now I flag and grow weary ; then with untired wing I fly on errands of love from the Father evermore. Now his works and his ways are shrouded in gloom, he walks in the sea, his path is in the mighty waters ;—then all is unveiled ; in his light I then at last see light. And then my fellowship of love with kindred spirits is unbroken. There is no more sorrow, or sighing, or separation. And, oh ! consummation of joy, there is no more sin !

Thus to take up again, in the body, our present earthly history, may well be felt to be blessedness indeed. The anticipation of it may animate us to holy watchfulness and diligence, and lead us ever to be asking the stirring questions :—Is the life I am leading now a life that I would wish to resume hereafter ?—Is the work I am doing now a work that I would wish to follow me hereafter ?

For there are works which will follow us to our joy. When the Judge, remembering what we have forgotten—noticing instances of good service of which we were at the time ashamed—righteousnesses which we felt to be filthy rags—points to some of his little ones whom we have pitied and helped ;—how will our hearts burn within us as we hear him say, " Inasmuch as ye did it to the least of these my brethren, ye did it unto me ! "

PART TWO

THE NATURE OF THE FUTURE BODY
(1 CORINTHIANS 15:35-58)

THIS is a subject—the nature of the future body—which, as I apprehend his argument in this chapter, the apostle is led to discuss, in so far as he does discuss it, incidentally. It comes up under the form of an objection put and answered ; a difficulty raised and solved. In dealing with it, Paul is led to open up large and interesting views respecting the corporeal frame of the risen saints, and the future world to which it is to be adapted. An insight is given to us, incomplete of course, but yet most suggestive, into what is to be the condition, and what the capacities, of man, when he reaches " the adoption, to wit-the redemption of his body," for which " he waits now," amid the groans of creation and his own groans (Rom. viii. 19-23). Still, the great object of the apostle's line of thought,—the bearing of the denial or admission of the resurrection on the justification and spiritual life of the believer, both here and hereafter,—is not overlooked. And in the end, the second part closes with a practical appeal altogether parallel to that which closes the first ; only positive rather than negative. For the warning in the thirty-third and thirty-fourth verses—" Be not deceived : evil communications corrupt good manners ; awake to righteousness and sin not : for some have not the knowledge of God ; I speak this to your shame,"—has its counterpart, as will be seen, in the exhortation at the fifty-eighth verse—" Therefore, my beloved brethren, be ye steadfast, unmovable, always abounding in the work of the Lord, forasmuch as ye know that your labour is not in vain in the Lord."

11

OBJECTOR'S QUESTION: HOW ARE THE DEAD RAISED? FIRST ANSWER: ANALOGY OF SEED-CORN

But some man will say, How are the dead raised up? and with what body do they come? Thou fool, that which thou sowest is not quickened, except it die: and that which thou sowest, thou sowest not that body that shall be, but bare grain, it may chance of wheat, or of some other grain: but God giveth it a body as it hath pleased him, and to every seed his own body. —1 Corinthians 15:35-38

THE reasoning of Paul now takes the form of an answer to a supposed or anticipated objection ; and for the right understanding of the reasoning, it is most important that we form a correct notion of the objection. This is all the more necessary, because modern ideas on the subject to which it relates are apt somewhat to mislead us. It will be proper, therefore, at the outset of our analysis or exposition of this second branch of the apostle's argument, to ascertain as exactly as possible the precise import and bearing of the question to which it is intended to be a reply ; " How are the dead raised up ? and with what body do they come ? " (ver. 35.)

There is no occasion, as it seems to me, for divid-

ing, as some are for doing, this question into two ;—
as if it were first asked, How can there possibly be a
resurrection of the dead at all ? and then, secondly,
If so, where are their bodies to come from ? and of
what sort are they to be ? The cavil is really one.

It is not quite the same as the Sadducean cavil to
which the Lord gave this reply, "Ye do err, not knowing
the Scriptures, nor the power of God " (Matt. xxii. 29).
There the Lord charges the Sadducees, who denied
the resurrection, with limiting the power of God.
Apparently, this caviller with whom Paul deals might
and would admit the power of God to raise the dead.
If it was the mere restoring of life to a dead man
that was in question,—the bringing of him back to
this present world, to live in the body here as he did
before he died,—there could be little difficulty in
admitting the possibility of that. The Sadducees
themselves could scarcely venture to question it. In
the face of such miraculous facts as Elisha's restoring
the Shunammite's child to life (2 Kings iv.), and our
Lord's raising Lazarus and the son of the widow of
Nain (Luke vii., John xi.) ;—not to speak of apostolic
acts of the same kind ;—it is not easy to see how any
one admitting as true the historical events of christianity, and its divine origin as proved by them, could
raise any doubt as to the possibility of a resurrection,
considered simply as a resuscitation of the body, or
the return of the deceased person in the body to a

life like this present life, with its ordinary animal functions, and its material offices and works.

Nor, I am persuaded, would such a reasoner have been much staggered by any additional difficulty which the body's decay and rottenness in the tomb might be supposed to present. He is not thinking of that at all. Very possibly, if it were a resurrection like that of Lazarus that he had to deal with, he might be little, if at all, troubled by any such suggestion as that of Martha ; " Lord by this time he stinketh ; for he hath been dead four days." The objector is supposed to be thinking of quite another question. It is not, How may the dead be raised up ?—as for instance, to such life as they have in this present world ; and, With what bodies may they come ?—as for instance, to such a world as this present world repeated over again. The power of God, he might say, to effect such a resurrection, I by no means deny or doubt. That the persons who have been named, not to speak of many others, were restored to this present life in the body after they were dead, I gladly admit. Nor do I raise any scruple as to the possibility of a resurrection like theirs taking place, even in the case of those whose bodies have not only been consigned to the grave, but left for years and ages to moulder there. That is not really my difficulty at all.

My real difficulty is this, Can the dead be so

raised up as to be fitted for the life to come ? What bodies, what sort of bodies, are they to have ? Are they to have the identical bodies which they have now ? Will such bodies be suitable for the spiritual and eternal world ? Will they do for heaven ?

We are apt to look at this whole argument from a modern point of view. And at this stage especially we are apt to have in our eye the miserable drivellings of modern infidelity, compared with which the inquiries of these old speculators,—"fools," as the apostle justly called them,—were yet at all events respectable. It was not with them a question of particles and atoms. They did not make a work about scattered bones ; burnt ashes ; carcasses eaten piecemeal by worms, or swallowed whole by ravenous beasts and monsters of the deep ; dead human flesh, decomposed into the elements of the food by which living human flesh is sustained and fed. Objections of that sort, based upon the supposed difficulty of extricating, from the mass of this earth's ever-changing matter, the identical bodily frame that once belonged to each one of its human inhabitants, are comparatively of recent date. It is not improbable that if the doctrine propounded for their belief had been that of a return of the saints, in the body, to the world as it now is, or some such world,—these "fools" would have raised no such foolish questions as those by means of which wise men, so called, have since

their time sought to perplex the minds and shake
the faith of simple Christians, in reference to the
great scriptural truth of a literal and bodily resurrection of the dead.

In point of fact, their hesitancy about admitting
that truth arose out of a much graver and more
serious consideration. They could not understand
how, even if the bodies of dead saints were raised,
they could be so raised as to be at home in that
future economy, that other heavenly world, for which
the present earthly world and economy is preparatory.
And hence the question, "How are the dead raised
up? and with what body do they come?"

Even in this view of it the apostle regards the
question as a foolish one. "Thou fool," he exclaims;
for art thou not in this matter a fool? Is not the
difficulty one which shews either great ignorance, or
great want of thought? A very simple analogy may
suffice to remove it. Look at what happens in your
own hands every day. "That which thou sowest is
not quickened, except it die" (ver. 36). You sow it
with a view to its being quickened, and living. But
you sow it, in the full knowledge that it can be
quickened, and can live, only by its undergoing a
process of death, being subject to decay and dissolution. And the process which it undergoes is such
as to change its whole nature and character; so that

what springs up is something altogether new :—"thou sowest not that body which shall be." What you sow, is "bare grain ;" it is the mere seed "of wheat, or of some other kind of corn." What comes up has a very different structure and organization from that which the "bare grain" you sow possesses. What sort of body it is that is to come up, depends on the sovereign will of the great Husbandman. "God giveth it a body as it hath pleased him." But whatever change there may be, identity is not in any wise lost. For there is to "every seed his own body" (ver. 37, 38).

Some* would read the first clause of the thirty-sixth verse thus :—"That which thou sowest is not quickened except it be dead ;" dead, that is, at the time of sowing it ; dead when it is sown. Thou sowest not the living plant, but the dead seed. And as it is the dead seed that, when sown, is quickened into a new living plant, so it is the dead corpse that, when buried, is quickened into a new living body.

It is doubtful if the words will naturally admit of that meaning ; nor does it seem to be the meaning required by the necessity of the analogy ; which, indeed, rather appears to be against it, if we consider the real nature of the objection to be met.

The question is, What sort of bodies are the saints

* See Dr. John Brown's "Resurrection of Life," pp. 181, 182. Edition 1852.

hereafter to receive? Are their bodies, when they are raised, to be of the same sort that they were when earth claimed them as its own? Will bodies of such a sort be fit for heaven?

Nay, you forget the process through which these bodies pass while lying in the bosom of mother earth. Death does for them there, what is done in the ground for the seed-corn which you drop in it. Death causes them to be as the seed-corn is when it lies in the soil,—rotting, and as it seems, almost melting away. The sort of dissolution which the seed-corn undergoes in the ground, the body undergoes in the grave. And the issue may be similar. The body that rises from the grave may be quickened as the seed-corn is quickened; quickened,—not to be such as it was when, like the seed-corn, it died and decayed; but quickened,—to bloom in a new and fresh life, fitted for the upper skies.

It is not, then, in respect of its being dead when sown, that the seed is compared to the body, viewed as dead when it is buried. Rather it is the process which the seed undergoes when sown, that is represented as similar to the gradual dissolution of the body in the grave. The seed decays and is dissolved; it is lost and disappears in the soil into which it falls. That is the indispensable condition of its being quickened. So also the body returns to its kindred dust, and becomes dust itself. This is the condition of its being

quickened too. In either case, the original frame,
—of the seed in the one case, of the body in the other,
—is broken up, and its former organization is utterly
destroyed. It is a new life altogether that it receives.
If, then, the body is to live anew, it must first die ;
it must undergo decomposition ; and, as in the case
of the seed "which thou sowest," lose for ever the
fashion which it had before. When it reappears, it
reappears refashioned, recast, remoulded. What is
sown, what is subjected to the process of dissolution,
is "bare grain." What afterwards lives again, is
something quite different. It is not the same sort of
body in its fashion and structure that it was before.
It has such a structure, or physical bodily organization, as it may please God to give it. For it is all
the Lord's doing. It is the Lord who raises anew to
life the "bare seed" that is sown and dies. It is the
Lord who, according to his pleasure, endows it with
whatever fashion he may think fit to give to it. It
may be a body in some respects wholly unlike the
body which is sown and dies. But what of that ?
Is it not enough to know that in this resurrection
metamorphosis there is still substantial identity ?
For " God giveth to every seed his own body ? "

It is dangerous to push an analogy of this sort
too far. But it seems fitted legitimately to suggest
three important practical conclusions.

I. Death, dissolution, decay, decomposition,—whatever may be the body subjected to that process, —is not only no obstacle in the way of that body living again, but affords a presumption that if it is to live again at all, it may be to live in a superior condition ; it may be to live as possessed of a new nature, a new organization ; adapted to the new sphere into which it is to be introduced.

The general law or principle to which Paul appeals as applicable now, in this present state of things, to all material substances,—or at least to all that have the character of living organized bodies,—would seem to be this ;—that death may be to them a step in advance. It may be the preliminary to their having any real life. What is sown is not quickened except it die. Not only is its death no presumption against its living again ; it may be the condition, and, as matters stand, the indispensable condition of its living a higher life than it lives now.

In its present state the body does not, in the fair and full sense of the term, really live. That warm-breathing frame of yours, with all its well-knit sinewy strength, its fine proportions, its beauteous form and colour,—what life has it ? Such life as the grass has, or the flower of the field. The wind passeth over it and it is gone. The last of it is its coming to be like a seed, a grain,—a pickle, as we say, of corn. And even that is destined to corruption. Can any life spring out of this death?—any living frame out of this dissolving carcass?

Why not? In the case of the seed, or the "bare grain," cast into the ground to die, the resurrection is to a new life;—to a life altogether new and fresh. The seed is quickened through decay into a new life. The old takes end in dissolution or death. The new emerges out of the soil in which the old has died. So in the case of this mortal body of mine, the life which it is to receive through its dissolution in the grave may be new and fresh; as new and fresh as was the life which man's body had, before the condition of mortality attached to it at all. Nay, it may be a better life even than that. Its death makes it capable of a new life. Its existence under the law of death comes to a complete end. If it is to exist again, it may be under a new law of life. Death is not the destruction, but the quickening of it. "That which thou sowest is not quickened, except it die."

II. The body which we are to receive in the resurrection may differ from that which we now have, very much as what springs out of the ground, and presents itself to view in ripe autumn, in the shape of a luxuriant stalk of corn, differs from the "bare seed" dropped into the ploughed earth in spring.

The body that now is, and the body that is to be, are not to be exactly the same. In structure and organization they may differ widely. It is expressly said—"That which thou sowest, thou sowest not that body that shall be." It is then a different body that is to come forth when the grave is opened at the last; a body different from that which mourning friends laid there. What the difference is will afterwards, as the argument advances, partly appear. In the meantime, the fact is clearly enough asserted. And the assertion of it may meet both of the two difficulties which we sometimes have in apprehending the reality of the resurrection of the dead. First, how can the scattered particles of my material frame be gathered and compacted together again, so as to be once more organized into symmetrical strength and beauty? And, secondly, if that were possible, what sort of body would I thus have with which to enter heaven?

As to the first difficulty, I now perceive that there is no occasion for "considering too curiously" what becomes of the dust or ashes that remain when the body is buried or burned. Nor need I perplex myself with nice and subtle inquiries as to how the matter of my body is to be separated from the matter of other bodies, of which it may have become the food. To all such silly questions, the old and sufficient answer is, that the substantial identity or sameness of my body, even in this life, does not depend on its consisting, or being composed of, identically the same matter. It has been computed, that once in seven years the whole matter of my body is changed, so

that at this moment, my body has not in it one particle, one atom, of the matter that it was made up of
seven years ago. And yet to all intents and purposes
it is the same body. An additional, and even perhaps
a more satisfactory reply, is furnished by the analogy
of the seed, or "bare grain." It is sown "bare grain."
It reappears in the full-grown stalk of corn. Identity
of particles, sameness of matter, is there out of the
question. All is changed; all is new.

And the analogy meets also, and still more
directly and satisfactorily, the other difficulty. If my
present material frame, I ask, were reconstructed and
reorganized, would it be a fitting tabernacle for my
immortal spirit, in its unchanging and eternal home?
What better solution of such a perplexing doubt than
this—"God giveth it a body as it hath pleased him!"
Leave it to him. "Jehovah Jireh," the Lord will
provide. It is the "bare grain thou sowest" that
will be quickened; but it will not be "bare grain"
when it is quickened. There will be a body corresponding to that which is sown. It will be such as
God sees fit that it should be. Is not that enough?

III. Still there is real identity;—"To every seed
his own body." I cannot doubt that this is added of
set purpose, to meet a painful misgiving that might
be felt, in consequence of the analogy which has
been used, and the appeal which has been made to
the divine sovereignty.

If my present body is to have no more likeness
or relation to my resurrection body, than the "bare
grain" has to the stalk of wheat that comes up when
it is dead ;—if, in fact, my resurrection body may be
any body that God is pleased to give ;—how am I to
recognize myself, how am I to be recognized by others,
as the same person then, bodily as well as mentally,
that I am now ? If all corporeity is to be new,
according to the free discretion of God, what will
there be to connect me with the past, and with those
who, in the past, were my companions in the body ?
Nay, but it is not so. "Every seed is to have his own
body." It is to be such a body as God may be
pleased to give, but still it is to be "his own body."
It is to be a body which the individual himself, and
all who knew him, may and must recognize as his
own. It may be changed from what it was when the
tomb received it,—weak, wasted, worn. It may wear
the bloom of summer life, instead of the cold wintry
deadness of the "bare grain." It will not, however,
be so changed but that the instinct of conscience will
feel it to be the body in which the deeds of this life
were done. It will not be so changed but that the
eye of affection will perceive it to be the very form,
on whose clay-cold lips, years or ages ago, it im-
printed the last long kiss of fondness.

Yes! I am to rise again in my body ; different,
but yet the same ; with such difference as it may

seem good to God to make ; with such sameness as shall identify me personally, in body and in soul, to myself and to all my friends. When I die and become pure spirit, I know that I shall resume my bodily frame again ;—changed, much changed, in its structure and organization ;—yet so thoroughly one with the bodily frame which I lay aside now, that I must answer in that body for the deeds done in this. When I see thee die, O my brother, I know that I shall embrace thee in the body again ;—altered, greatly altered for the better ;—but with the same kind smile that now lingers on thy wan countenance ; —and the same hand that now presses mine in a parting grasp ;—and the same heart that beats in unison with mine, until, alas ! it beats no more !

12

SECOND ANSWER: VARIETIES OF TERRESTRIAL AND CELESTIAL BODIES

All flesh is not the same flesh: but there is one kind of flesh of men, another flesh of beasts, another of fishes, and another of birds. There are also celestial bodies, and bodies terrestrial: but the glory of the celestial is one, and the glory of the terrestrial is another. There is one glory of the sun, and another glory of the moon, and another glory of the stars: for one star differeth from another star in glory. So also is the resurrection of the dead.

—1 Corinthians 15:39-42

WITH reference to the question—"How are the dead raised up? and with what body do they come?"—the apostle may be supposed to ask—Is it not answered now? Is not the analogy of the "bare grain" coming up with a new body enough to answer it?

If not, then there is another analogy, or another argument, founded on plain facts, that should at least silence you. Consider the variety that there is, as regards their physical framework or constitution, among the various material bodies within the reach of your cognizance. First, bodies on earth differ from one another as to the kind of flesh they possess (verse 39). Secondly, Heavenly bodies differ from earthly bodies (verse 40). Thirdly, Heavenly bodies differ among themselves (verse 41).

First, here on earth, and within the range of our earthly knowledge and experience, we find instances of great variety in the structure and organization of bodies. "All flesh is not the same flesh : but there is one kind of flesh of men, another flesh of beasts, another of fishes, and another of birds" (verse 39).

What folly to imagine that there can be any real difficulty in the case! Do you not perceive that even on this earth there is a great variety of bodies, and that, too, although they all consist of flesh? There are animal bodies, all composed of flesh, yet differing widely from one another. Men, beasts, fishes, birds —all have bodies. God gives them bodies as it has pleased him. All of them, moreover, have bodies that are fleshly. But the flesh is not the same in all ; nay, it is not the same in any two. They all differ from one another, as regards the flesh of which they are made.

Now, if God can form here, on the earth, so many different sorts of body ; all of flesh, but of flesh all but endlessly diversified; how should it be thought a thing incredible that he may provide for his risen saints bodies suited to their new condition? Even assuming that the substance of which these bodies are to be formed is the same as what animal bodies on earth are composed of,—that it is flesh,—still we have presumptive proof from analogy, that it may be flesh of an entirely different sort from that which weighs us down in our present earthly state.

Compare the flesh of men even now, with the flesh of beasts, fishes, birds! Men have bodies of flesh as beasts, fishes, and birds have. But how different! And how vitally important the difference! Were my flesh now the same as that of a beast, a fish, a bird ; had I the flesh, the fleshly body, of the most perfect of these dumb denizens of earth, and sea, and air ; I could not discharge my functions, I could not vindicate and assert my place, as the intelligent worshipper of the Creator, and the lord of this created world. The hand apt to hold, the tongue apt to speak, must be mine, if my flesh is to be adapted to my position, and is to be the minister of my free soul. So, accordingly, God has ordained. The flesh in me he has moulded otherwise than in beasts, fishes, birds.

And what, then, should hinder him from moulding that same flesh otherwise than it now is in me, when he raises me from the dead ? May not the difference between what I am now, and what I am to be then, as to my body, be at least as great as the difference now between me and a beast, a fish, a bird ? If there can be flesh in common between me and a reptile now, and yet my flesh differing from its flesh, as my immortal spirit differs from its mortal life—why may there not be flesh in common between me as I am now, and me as I am to be hereafter ; yet so that my flesh then may differ from my flesh now, as my soul made perfect in holiness then, will differ from my soul now, groaning under "the body of this death ?"

There are various kinds of flesh in this present world, adapted to the nature and condition of the various tribes inhabiting it. Why may there not be other kinds of flesh in that other world beyond the resurrection, adapted to the nature and condition of those who are to inhabit it ? Cannot he who gives one kind of flesh to beasts and another to men here, give to men one kind of flesh here, and another hereafter ? There is no real difficulty, therefore, as to the bodies with which the dead, when raised up, are to come. Even limiting our view to this present world, we see enough to prove that God can give fleshly bodies of all various kinds. And from the analogy of fleshly bodies here, we may presume that, if needful, he can find a kind of flesh adapted to man raised from the dead,—although man should then be as much above what he is now, as he is now above beasts, and fishes, and birds.

But, secondly, earthly bodies, composed of flesh such as we handle in men, beasts, fishes, birds, are not the only bodies of which we have knowledge. "There are also celestial bodies, and bodies terrestrial :

but the glory of the celestial is one, and the glory of
the terrestrial is another" (verse 40). The manifold
working of the power of God is not limited to the
fashioning of flesh into the countless varieties of body
which we see on earth. There are other bodies besides
those of earth. You see them in the heavens. On
any starry night you may see them. What they are
made of—what sort of flesh, if they are made of flesh,
is theirs—what kind of matter they have, you cannot
tell. They are bodies, you see ; visible, and, as you
may fairly gather from your observation of their
movements, palpable bodies, substantial and material.
They differ in appearance and in glory from the
earthly bodies with which you are familiar. They
may differ, for anything you can tell, in the kind of
matter of which they consist. As there is one kind
of flesh of men, another flesh of beasts, another of
fishes, and another of birds ; so there is one glory of
the celestial bodies and another of the terrestrial.

If, therefore, the analogy of earthly bodies will not
content you, consult the analogy of the heavenly
bodies. If the vast variety of bodily frames into
which flesh is moulded among the bodies of earth is
not enough to satisfy you that a suitable bodily frame
may be found for the new state of the soul in heaven,
there are still other bodies to which you may be referred as proofs and instances of the exhaustless
resources of omnipotence.

You wish to know, you say, how the dead are raised up, and with what bodies they come. Well, there are various kinds of bodies within the range even of your present cognizance. Take this earth itself alone. The flesh, the fleshly matter of which its bodies are composed, is so pliant and plastic in the hand of the great Creator, that he can adapt it, in one form to the occasions of the creeping worm, and in another, to the exigencies of the highest human soul. Do you imagine that he cannot, if it be needful, adapt it also to the aspirations of that soul when it has passed into the heavens?

Do you still doubt? Are you still at a loss? Then look up. There are heavenly bodies in yonder sky, differing in glory from all you are acquainted with on earth. God gives to these multitudinous stars bodies as it has pleased him; and can he not find bodies for his saints to be raised up in? Can he not find for them bodies as much better than those they have now, as the flesh of men is better than the flesh of beasts, fishes, birds? Can he not find for them bodies differing from their present ones, as the glory of the celestial bodies in the firmament above differs from the glory of the terrestrial here below?

But even this is not all. For, thirdly, among the heavenly bodies themselves, also, there is diversity. "There is one glory of the sun, and another glory of the moon, and another glory of the stars : for one star differeth from another star in glory" (verse 41).

See what can be made of matter! You ask how material bodies can be found for glorified spirits in the heavenly places? My answer is—Have you exhausted in your inquiry—can you think that God has exhausted in his creative energy—all the forms and fashions into which matter may be cast?

I speak to you, not as learned philosophers, but as men of common sense. I address myself to your common observation of the facts of nature.

Even here on earth there are corporeities enough, physical organizations, bodily structures, with differences probably almost as great as any distinction that must separate the future bodies of the saints from those which they now possess. But if such terrestrial varieties of bodily conformation will not suffice, you may read the lesson taught by the material heavens. The Creator's power of dealing with matter so as to fit it for mind at any stage of advancement, is not to be measured merely by the forms and frames which flesh takes here. There are bodily existences, or material bodies, elsewhere, in a higher region, soaring in a purer air. The heavenly orbs move freely : would such matter as they are made of content you? Even if it would not, I do not despair of satisfying you. For I find among these celestial bodies a gradation like what I find in bodies terrestrial. I find sun, moon, stars, in the celestial world, corresponding to men, beasts, fishes, birds, in the terrestrial. Matter, I now see, is capable of indefinite elevation, not only through the several kinds of earthly flesh, but through more signal gradations of glory in the heavenly bodies. Why may it not rise higher still ?

Such, in substance, is the apostle's argument. He is dealing, let it be remembered, with the question, or objection, of those who doubt if matter can ever be so refined as to furnish material bodies fit to enter the heavenly state. He is cutting away the ground of their difficulty. He is at any rate silencing them and shutting their mouths, by an appeal to facts and phenomena which they themselves know.

It seems strange, in this view, that any should imagine the celestial bodies here meant to be the bodies which the higher heavenly intelligences may be supposed to possess now ; which must be such as the saints may suitably receive when they come to be " as the angels." An analogy of that sort is more in accordance with our modern modes of thought on these subjects than with those that prevailed of old. The subtle teachers with whom Paul had to reason would have made very light of any argument based on the corporeity of the inhabitants of the spiritual world. The assumption that angels and spirits have

material frames or bodies of a finer texture than ours,
and the inference that therefore we may hereafter
have similar bodies too, would have been scouted by
them as the baseless logic of an impossible hypothesis.
It is mere conjecture, they would say. It is a wild
imagination. But they did not deny the materiality
of the sun, moon, and stars. They admitted that
these heavenly bodies were composed of matter. And
some of them were accustomed to speculate somewhat
curiously about the nature of the matter of which they
were composed. They held it to be matter of a rarer
and purer sort than the gross and sordid dust, earth,
or ashes, of which, in this planet of ours, both inanimate stuff and animal flesh are made up. They
conceived also of differences and gradations in this
respect among the heavenly bodies themselves. In
the brighter and stiller of these luminaries they saw
matter becoming more and more unearthly, refined,
and ethereal ;—until, perhaps, in the great fiery body
of the sun itself, the brilliant orb and proud lord of
day, it reached the utmost perfection of rarity and
purity of which it could be imagined to be susceptible.

Now, to men familiar with such contemplations
as these, the apostle's argument is entirely to the
point. He answers these "fools" according to their
folly ; and he answers them well.

I. He proves to them that the resurrection body,
which the saints are to have hereafter in heaven, need

not be of the same kind with the body which dies, and is buried, and rots away here in the earth. It no more follows that what is raised from the grave is to have the same structure and organization with what is laid in the grave, than it follows that what comes up from the spot where a seed has been dropped, must possess the same bodily form and character as the seed. The fact, on the other hand, that what springs up from the " bare grain" that is sown, is so very different from the " bare grain " itself, affords a strong presumption that what is to be raised from the tomb at the resurrection may differ still more widely from what is lying there now. The " bare grain " is a body adapted to the place which it is to occupy, and the function which it is to serve, under ground. When it comes up, it is not " bare grain." It would not in that form be adapted to the place now to be occupied, and the function now to be served, not under ground, but in the bright and warm light of day. It comes up, therefore, having a body suited to this new sphere, such a body as God " is pleased to give ;" and still so that " every seed has his own body." So these material frames of ours, as they are now compacted and organized, are admirably and exquisitely adapted to the place they have to occupy, and the function they have to serve, in this lower world, which is the underground of heaven. But if they were to rise, such exactly as they are now, they

might be as ill adapted to the sunshine of that higher
heavenly region into which they are to pass, as the
"bare grain" sown, if it were to spring up "bare
grain" still, would be to the earthly sunshine into
which it has to emerge. Surely, on every ground of
rational analogy, the fair presumption is, that he who
brings up the "bare grain" that is sown, not "bare
grain" still, but that graceful, rich, and wavy stem of
ripe and yellow corn, which delights the eye and
gladdens the heart in a summer's noon-day—will
bring up the body that is now mouldering in the
dust, not such as it is now, fitted to grow up, and
flourish, and wither in a day; but such as will suit
that brighter sphere where all dissolution and decay
are unknown. Yes! It will be "beauty immortal"
that will "awake from the tomb."

II. Having thus cleared the way by establishing
the possibility and the probability of a change, and a
great change, upon our present bodies at the resurrection, the apostle next challenges the objectors to
prove that suitable bodies—bodies suitable for the
eternal state—may not be framed. Consider, he says,
the almost infinite varieties, in form, structure, and
organization, that within the range of your own
knowledge you may see this matter, of which you are
so jealous, assume;—this very matter that seems to you
so stiff, and hard, and unaccommodating. Even on
this earth, see how it is moulded, gross flesh as it is,

into a thousand different sorts and shapes, to suit all conceivable kinds of animal life. It is plastic enough to be fitly moulded for the crawling worm ; and yet, made of the same flesh, " what a piece of work is man !" Then lift up your eyes to these heavens. There, by your own acknowledgment, are bodies differing from those of earth ; bodies, too, differing from one another. Passing from star to star, you find matter still, but matter, as you yourselves believe, becoming more and more pure, more and more attenuated, more and more glorious. And is it that God who has so dealt, and is so dealing, with matter and with material bodies, now, before your very eyes, that you will not trust to fashion fitting resurrection bodies for his glorified saints ?

The apostle's reasoning, though thus far merely of a negative sort, intended to silence the objector, is yet very sublime. It carries us in its wide sweep over all the visible creation in all space and time. From the earliest organic form, emerging out of that old primeval chaos, onward and upward, through the teeming and successive tribes of being that have peopled this earth, until man is reached ; then away from earth, among the far-off splendours in the vault of heaven ;—the imagination soars, gathering accumulated evidence of the manifold power and wisdom of God. And then, piercing the veil that shrouds the unknown future, how may the devout soul image

forth to the spiritual eye countless new applications
of that wisdom and power, in forms of surpassing
beauty, fashioned for the highest sphere, and fit to
share the highest glory with which the manhood of
the risen Saviour himself can be crowned!

13

THE BODY CHANGED FROM CORRUPTION, DISHONOR AND WEAKNESS TO INCORRUPTION, GLORY AND POWER

So also is the resurrection of the dead. It is sown in corruption; it is raised in incorruption: it is sown in dishonor; it is raised in glory: it is sown in weakness; it is raised in power: it is sown a natural body; it is raised a spiritual body.
—1 Corinthians 15:42-44

THE apostle advances a step in his high argument. He has already sufficiently disposed of the question, "How are the dead raised, and with what body do they come?" He has done so negatively, as it were ; putting to silence the objector. He has been defying him to establish, in the face of obvious analogies, the impossibility of a bodily resurrection such as may satisfy the demands even of the most transcendental spirituality. There are generic varieties enough of flesh on earth ;—there are differences enough in respect of material structure between the heavenly bodies and the earthly ;—and there are varieties enough among the heavenly bodies themselves ;—to make it a plain presumption, that the author of all these physical organizations can be at no loss to find fitting bodies for immortal souls to occupy in the eternal state.

Something more like positive assertion is now, as it would seem, ventured upon ; not merely negatively to silence, but positively to inform. Three particulars are specified, in respect of which the resurrection body may be expected to differ from the present body.—" It is sown in corruption ; it is raised in incorruption : it is sown in dishonour ; it is raised in glory : it is sown in weakness ; it is raised in power." And the three particulars are then summed up in one general contrast or antithesis—" It is sown a natural body ; it is raised a spiritual body."

The contrast throughout is between two living bodies ; not between a dead body and a living one. This is often overlooked.

When we read of what is sown in corruption, in dishonour, in weakness, we are apt to think of the lifeless corpse which we consign to the cold and cheerless tomb. We sow it in corruption ; for before the burial, symptoms of decay occur. We sow it in dishonour ; for all our woful weeds and trappings of ostentatious sepulchral state are but designed to mask the creeping loathsomeness of death. We sow it in weakness ; for we yield it a prey to the weakest of reptiles, to worms of the earth. All this is true. Corruption, dishonour, weakness, are the characteristics of the dead body which we lay in the dust.

But they are so, because they are the characteristics of the body while it breathes, and lives, and
moves before our eyes. Death is not the cause of
these characteristics, but only the effect of them. It
is the occasion of their full manifestation ; it is their
worst and final development. But corruption, dishonour, weakness, are the attributes, not merely of
my body when it is dead, but of my body as it now
lives. It would be a poor thing to tell me that my
body hereafter is not to be as corrupt, as dishonoured,
as weak, as is my body when, after death, it lies
rotting in the grave. What I care for is to be assured
that, if I am to have a body at all, it shall be exempt
from those qualities, or conditions, attaching to my
present living body, which issue in that death.

Corruption, dishonour, weakness,—these are the
three capital faults of this present living body, which
at death is sown as "bare grain." And the three
faults are intimately connected and mutually related.
They fit into one another, and flow from one another.
First, corruption ; then dishonour ; lastly, weakness.

I. Corruption is liability to dissolution and decay.
The body that is to be sown in corruption is a body
capable or susceptible of decomposition. It may be
broken up. And when it is broken up, its fragments,
or fragmentary remains, may be resolved into the
constituent elements, or component particles, of which
they consist. This process may go on piecemeal even

during life. I may lose limb after limb by the cannon's shot, or the trooper's sword, or the surgeon's knife. I may be mutilated and dismembered, while still alive, until barely half a trunk and half a head of me are left. The bones of my severed legs and arms may be bleaching in the sandy desert, or they may have fed the monsters of the deep. And even what remains of my corporeal frame—scarce enough, perhaps, to allow the blood to circulate, and the heart to beat, and the brain to throb—will soon be dust. It will be scattered by the winds. It will be lost in the common earth of which all things that are born, and grow, and decay, and die, are made. Will that sort of material structure do for a resurrection body?

II. But dishonour also belongs to what is sown; to the "bare grain;" to the mortal frame. And yet how smooth and symmetrical is that "bare grain;" that exquisitely fashioned corn of wheat; so compact, so polished! Wherein lies its dishonour? What disgrace belongs to it? Alas! it is perishable. Such life or vitality as it has must die out. The fashion of it must be lost in nature's universal tomb—the all-absorbing, all-assimilating earth. Of the purest "bare grain," of the finest corn of wheat—it may be truly said that it is sown in dishonour. For corruptibility is dishonourable. What is sown in corruption is, of necessity, sown in dishonour.

Hence this corruptible body has in it essentially

a certain quality of dishonour, vileness, and shame. It is not merely that it may be prostituted to shameful purposes, and made the prey and victim of vile passions. Take it in its virgin purity, endowed with the most nervous symmetry of manly vigour,—the most flowing grace of female loveliness,—which eye has ever beheld, or fancy painted. That warm-breathing impersonation, in flesh and blood, of the very ideal of consummate beauty—is that devoid of honour, of comeliness, of glory? Has it not an honour, a comeliness and glory, that brightest angels might pause to gaze on? Yes!—were it only possible that it might have imparted to it the elixir of life!—that it might be steeped in some subtle essence of immortality, of incorruptibility!

Ah! my heart cries, were that given to thee, thou loved one, I would have thee to be ever as thou art now, the fairest of all creatures in my eyes. I covet not for thee any fairer, more honourable, or more glorious tabernacle to lodge that bright spirit of thine; any worthier casket for so pure a gem; if only thou mightest continue always as thou art now!

But I cannot be long—alas! I cannot be always —blind to what is but too visible to my aching heart. I see thee, even amid thy opening charms, shewing symptoms of disease and dissolution. In thy very growth I trace the ominous beginnings of decay. I find thy beauty made to consume away like a moth.

Under thy rich and rare clothing of joyous health, of radiant and smiling bloom, I watch the slow and secret gnawing of the insidious element of corruption that is too surely to undermine it all. The honour that is so perishable is scarcely honour at all. I would embrace thee in that other world, fair as thou art now, and comely; I scarcely wish thee fairer. But I would embrace thee no longer liable any more to be sown in dishonour, because no longer any more liable to be sown in corruption; "mortality being swallowed up of life!"

III. As corruptibility implies dishonour, so it occasions or causes weakness. It paralyzes physical strength. It paralyzes both strength of endurance, and strength for action and performance.

This firm and compact bodily organization of mine is doubtless in a measure strong. I can, by an effort, resist a large amount of force brought to bear upon me. I can put forth, upon an emergency, a power that I am myself surprised at. But how easily are men fatigued! How frequently do they need repose! How apt are they to yield to sloth! How feeble also are they when matched with the material elements of nature, or with the mechanical forces lodged in the bodies, and moved by the instincts, of the beasts that perish!

True, man wields an empire all but absolute and irresistible over material elements and the brutal tribes. In a sense, even the winds and the waves obey him. The solid iron and the subtle electric fluid are equally at his command ; he constrains them to do his bidding. The ox also knoweth his owner, and the ass his master's crib. The mouth of the horse or of the mule is held in with bit and bridle. But all this power is got and kept, not by the exertion of physical strength, but by the resources and devices of mental skill. It is the inventive soul in man, not this mortal body of his, however " fearfully and wonderfully made," that constitutes him lord in this lower world. Physically, man is among the weakest of animals.

Look at the poor seaman left alone to buffet the waves of an angry sea. Or see the hunter in stern and solitary conflict with the lion, the tiger, or whatever untamed power claims to be monarch of the scene. Physically, neither can stand his ground. The ocean overwhelms the one ; the wild beast overmasters the other. And even when inventive man asserts his most confident command over the stiffest and subtlest forces of nature, how apt is he to be crushed among the smallest wheels and pinions of his own gigantic machinery.

And then, how impotent is the human animal physically, in respect of bodily structure, to realize and act out his own ideal ! He would flee away as a bird ; he would soar heavenward as the eagle ; he would subordinate time and space to his designs! But the flesh forbids.

Why should man, with a soul whose "thoughts wander through eternity," find himself embodied in a frame and organization that yields and gives way before the pressure of mere force, mechanical, material, and brutal?—a frame and organization, moreover, that will not bear the stress and strain of his own higher aspirations and better spiritual desires? Why has he a body so unequal to the execution of the impulses of his soul? I would be lord over all material force and law. Is that always to lord it over me?

Such are the three defects of the present body. But none of them will be found in the resurrection body; neither corruption, nor dishonour, nor weakness.

I. The resurrection body is incorruptible, indestructible; not liable to decomposition and decay; not composed of earthly particles ever changing, and ultimately to be resolved into the dust from whence they were taken; but simple, we must assume, uncompounded, and therefore indissoluble. It is a material body still; visible, tangible, sentient, motive; it is seen, it is touched, it feels, it moves. But the attribute of incorruptibility belongs to it, rendering it at last a meet companion for the immaterial and immortal soul.

II. Then how fair is it, how honourable, how comely! And that not only outwardly, as often here a specious comeliness for a season decks the surface beneath which the canker of incipient rottenness is eating. Physically as well as spiritually, in respect of body as well as soul, "the king's daughter is all glorious within" (Ps. xlv. 13). Nothing that can offend the most fastidious taste ; nothing that can suggest, by the remotest hint, any thought even the slightest, any idea even the faintest, of impurity or shame ; nothing that can ever cause a blush upon the countenance ; nothing for which the conscious bosom need ever heave a sigh ; nothing to disgust ; nothing to repel ; no latent sore or sickness soon to to be too open ; no secret germ of what, when it comes out, may make the eye of tenderest love fain to look away ; nothing of all that hidden corrosive poison which mars earth's brightest beauty ;—will be found in that body which, "sown in dishonour, is raised in glory."

III. And finally, as to strength, what shall we say ? The materials and the structure of that body are to be such as no violence can either break or derange. No weapon aimed against it can hurt ; nor the fiercest blow touch it at all. Grosser matter, whether alive or dead, animate or inanimate, cannot affect it. Again, all its avenues and inlets for the entrance of sounds, sights, sensations, of all various kinds of harmony and beauty, from the outer world, are enlarged a hundred-fold. And, moreover, its capacity of bearing the mind's highest and profoundest cogitations is enhanced in some corresponding proportion. It is endowed with eagle's, with angel's wings; with eye far-ranging as the heaven-sweeping glass, and yet minute and deepsearching as never microscope could be imagined to be; with hand also that can at pleasure move and mould whatever it may choose to grasp. But we may not speculate. Enough to know that this incorruptible and glorious body is to be no clog or restraint, through its impotency, on the free soul; but apt and able, as its minister;—strong to do its pleasure.

The three particulars, in respect of which the resurrection body is to differ from our present mortal frame, are summed up, as it would seem, in one comprehensive and radical distinction; "It is sown a natural body; it is raised a spiritual body."

The distinction here asserted must be separately considered. I advert to it now merely to indicate its connection with the other distinctions which I have been attempting to trace.

The characteristics of the natural body are corruptibility, dishonour, and weakness; the characteristics of the spiritual body are incorruptibility, glory, and power. The body that is corruptible, and therefore so far void of glory and power, is the body that is fitted for the purposes and functions of the animal life. It is adapted to the actions and usages by which the natural life of man is sustained in the individual, and transmitted in the race. But man is made for a higher end. Redeemed and renewed, the believer in Christ is capable of a spiritual life. His "life is hid with Christ in God." So long as he is possessed merely of a natural body, his spiritual life depends on his "keeping under his body, and bringing it into subjection." Hence it is a continual struggle; —"The flesh lusteth against the spirit, and the spirit against the flesh, and these are contrary the one to the other." But we look forward to the possession of a body more in harmony with that spiritual life which, with our present body weighing us down to earth, we find it often so hard a task to cultivate. Let us therefore live now "by the power of the world to come." Let us seek, by the help of God, to keep ourselves, in soul, body, and spirit, pure amid earth's sins, and calm amid earth's sorrows. "For our conversation is in heaven; from whence also we look for the Saviour, the Lord Jesus Christ: who shall change our vile body, that it may be fashioned like unto his glorious body, according to the working whereby he is able even to subdue all things unto himself" (Phil. iii. 20, 21).

14

THE NATURAL BODY AND
THE SPIRITUAL BODY

It is sown a natural body; it is raised a spiritual body.
There is a natural body, and there is a spiritual body.
                                        —1 Corinthians 15:44

THE words natural and spiritual, as applied to the
body, have respect not so much to the substance of
which the body in either state is composed, as to the
uses or purposes which it is intended to serve.   There
is no occasion here for raising any subtle question of
metaphysics or psychology as to the ultimate distinction between mind and matter.   The meaning is
not that the body spoken of as spiritual partakes of
the essential nature of the spirit in man, which,
" when the dust returns to the earth as it was, returns
to God who gave it " (Eccl. xii. 7) ; but only that it is
congenial or suitable to it.

  This is plain from a consideration of the proper
import of the term " natural."   That term is connected
with the word commonly employed to denote the
principle of animal life, whatever that may be—the
vital spark, the vital force, which man has in common

with the beasts that perish. The adjective translated "natural," is not like our English adjective "natural," derived from the abstract term which would be translated "nature." It is formed from a noun which signifies, not nature, but the natural principle of life, or the principle of the natural life, whether in man, or in the inferior animals.* The noun in question is sometimes rendered "soul;" as when Paul writes: "And the very God of peace sanctify you wholly; and I pray God your whole spirit and soul and body be preserved blameless unto the coming of our Lord Jesus Christ" (1 Thess. v. 23). There, according to a view of man's entire organization or complex constitution then commonly received, "spirit, soul, and body," are specified as its constituent parts or elements. The "spirit" is that higher principle of intelligence and thought, peculiar to man alone in this world, to which we now usually restrict the name of mind or soul. The "soul" is that lower principle of animal life,—with its instincts, selfish and social, its power of voluntary motion, its strange incipient dawn of reasoning,—which, common alike to man and beast, is so great a mystery in both. The "body" is made to be the material organ and instrument of either principle, the higher or the lower. These three in one, this trinity, is our present humanity.

But now, as we are at present constituted, at any

---

* In Latin, *animalis*, from *anima;* in Greek, ψυχικὸς, from ψυχή.

rate since the fall, the two principles of which the body is the minister—the higher spirit or soul, which thinks, and that lower soul, or, as we might equally well call it, spirit or breath, which lives and moves— are not in harmony. On the contrary, they are at variance ; often at strife. And as Michael the arch- angel and the devil contended, disputing about the body of Moses (Jude 9), so these two,—the thinking spirit that allies us to the intelligences above us, and the animal soul or life that makes us companions of the dumb brute creation beneath us,—strive about the body which each claims a right to use as its own. As no man, however, can serve two masters, so neither can the body serve its two masters rightly. It is a case of divided allegiance. In such a case, when a servant has two masters to serve, he usually hates the one and loves the other ; nor is it difficult to see to which of the two masters his heart inclines. The body, as now fashioned, indicates its preference not ambiguously. It is very much in the interest of the lower principle, the animal soul. It may well be so ; for it is a natural body. It is a body adapted to the purposes of the natural life, or the natural prin- ciple of life. If we call that principle the "soul," as in the passage which has been quoted, then, to give the epithet exactly, it is a "soulish" body. It is a body of or belonging to such a soul, congenial to it, accommodated to it, in harmony and sympathy with it. To that higher spirit, or soul, or mind in man, which is "the inspiration of the Almighty giving him understanding," the present body stands far more distantly and doubtfully related. When required to serve this diviner lord,—when he would make use of it,—the body is by no means so much at home. It is not so apt, so pliant, so plastic a minister by far. Reluctantly, and as the saying is, against the grain, it submits and obeys—if it submit and obey at all.

Especially when this higher spirit in man comes in contact with a higher spirit still, the Spirit of God, —when it is thus separated more than ever from the lower animal soul or principle of mere animal life,— or rather brought into a new attitude of antagonism, —then the body's leaning to the adverse side is most clearly seen, and keenly, often painfully, felt.

The two principles within us, that of the higher intelligent, and that of the lower animal life, are not unfrequently fain to compromise the strife which they wage about the body. Of the two, the higher is, alas! the weaker; the lower is by far the stronger. Too often the stronger prevails by its mere strength, drags the body out of the hands of its feebler but more honourable competitor, and prostitutes it to its own purposes,—to those uses of the mere animal life which, when uncontrolled by the thoughtful mind, are simply mean and base. Where so complete a mastery cannot be secured, the weaker power refusing to

yield up the subject in dispute,—the physical frame,
—to be wholly the victim and the prey of the other
and stronger party, this last will consent to an accommodation. It will suffer the body to do some service
to the thinking principle. There shall be intervals
of pure and peaceful stillness when, freed from the
fumes and vapours of sense, the serene unclouded
brain shall be able to bear the stress of meditations
the most profound, investigations the most elaborate,
aspirations the most sublime ; the eye shall be clear ;
the forehead cool ; the bosom calm ; the soaring
spirit, ranging over the vast ideal universe of thought,
shall scarcely feel even its loftiest flight of fancy, or
its warmest flow of feeling, arrested or embarrassed
or chilled, by any consciousness of the infirmity of its
bodily attendant. Such concession may the lower
and stronger principle of life occasionally condescend
to make to the higher and weaker principle of thought.
But it will be sure to reclaim the body as its own ; it
will use it as its own all the more for its rival's temporary employment of it ; and that rival will find, as
things move on, the occasions on which it can command the body becoming fewer, and the service which
on these occasions it can get becoming more and more
inadequate, more and more precarious, more and more
ungracious and constrained.

So the lower principle still prevails in the strife
about the body. Nay, even if the higher principle,

putting forth unwonted energy and strength, should succeed in conquering the body for itself, the victory is unsatisfactory.

Behold the mystic, the fanatic, the ascetic, the anchorite, whether saint or sage! His body, as it would seem, is wrested from the grasp of the lower soul; violently, and often with most unnatural cruelty of self-denial and self-torture. Starved, mortified, scourged,—it is scarcely, if at all, available for the common purposes of the animal life. It is wholly at the service of his highest faculty; the faculty of life intelligent, of life spiritual, of life divine!

So it should be. But, alas! is it so? Is it not far otherwise? The lower principle, defrauded of its due, resents and avenges the wrong. It fiercely invades the territory which should be sacred to pure thought and holy musing. The chafed spirit is forced to groan under the bitter experience of intrusive animal instincts, emotions, passions, pains. Some satanic trial of carnality, some St. Anthony's temptation, some access of frenzy or of idiocy,—or, it may be, the utter break-down of all its lofty aims,—extorts the sad confession, that the body with which it is associated,—in which, and by means of which, it must for the present act out its high and perfect ideal, —is still, alas! a natural body; in the interest and on the side of the natural soul or principle of life, and sure in the long run, one way or other, to make it only too apparent—to which of its two masters it is most inclined "to hold."

But "there is a spiritual body." And for that spiritual body the spirit of the man whom the Spirit of God teaches, quietly and patiently waits, with earnest longing, with calm and confiding hope. He, too, finds the body, as it is now fashioned, more adapted to the lower principle in him than to the higher; he more than any other. For in him the higher principle, the spirit of intelligence and thought, has been elevated into fellowship with God; nay, made partaker of the divine nature. Reconciled by the blood of Christ, pardoned, accepted, justified in him; renewed by the Holy Ghost in the spirit of his mind; loving, and so knowing God who is love; pure in heart, and therefore seeing God, the Holy One, as he is; Christlike in standing; Christlike in privilege; Christlike in character; loved as Christ is loved; loving as Christ loves;—his spirit has a life to live, for whose full development a body fitted for life of a very different kind may well be felt to be insufficient and unsuitable.

But what then? Does he quarrel on that account with the body which he has now? Does he madly try to force it out of the line of its proper uses and functions,—those for which at present it is manifestly designed,—as if he could change its nature? He keeps it in subjection, indeed. He "mortifies his members which are upon the earth" (Col. iii. 5). But he no more thinks of laying a rude arrest on those processes in the animal economy, and those arrangements and combinations in the social economy, for which the body as now constituted is adapted,—as if by some desperate effort he could etherealize or spiritualize his physical as well as mental frame, and force his natural body to become a spiritual body,—than he dreams of altering the flesh of beasts, or birds, or fishes, into the flesh of men ; or turning bodies terrestrial into bodies celestial ; or one star into another star ; or the twinkling stars into the silvery moon ; or the moon herself into the glorious sun.

Still he is right glad to know that there is a spiritual body ; a body as congruous and congenial to the higher spirit of intelligence in him, that is akin to Deity, as the present body is to that lower soul, or vital energy, which assimilates and allies him to the brutal tribes.

We dare not even imagine the full meaning of this phrase—" a spiritual body." But there are three ideas in regard to it, which we may venture to indicate. We hint at three of its probable characteristics.

In the first place, it takes the impress or stamp of the higher spiritual principle of divine intelligence, or intelligence divinely enlightened and inspired, as easily and spontaneously,—as much in the way of its being a matter of course,—as naturally, in short, as the present body assumes the character, attitude, and expression, of the lower principle of mere animal life —of animal feeling and emotion. It is as good an index of what is spiritual, as the present body is of what is animal, in man.

The body which we now have is truly natural, SOULISH; congruous and congenial to the natural principle of the mere animal life; in this sense, that it is easily acted upon by that vital energy, and is the ready exponent of its various moods and movements. For expressing the appetites, passions, and affections of that sentient and active vitality which we have in common with the brutes, what more apt and habile organ, what more sensitive and true electric medium, than the human form, the human face, the human voice? Hunger, lust, rage, revenge, in all their modifications,—and with all their accompaniments of cunning, fear, jealousy, hate,—are better imaged in the look and attitude of man than in the look and attitude of any other creature. His, in this respect, is the perfection of the natural body. When there is no hypocrisy, no studied simulation or dissimulation, what a tell-tale, what a revealer of whatever is animal in me, is my countenance, air, manner—my ever varying and ever expressive habit of body! Not to speak of the leering eye, the liquorish mouth, and other similar symptoms by which the grosser and more grovelling propensities of the animal soul are betrayed—see how anger dilates the nostrils, and pride curls the lip, and shame suffuses the cheek with blushes, and terror stirs the hair, and carking care or anxious envy knits the contracted brow !

Doubtless, even in its present state, while it is still a natural body, it may bear some impress of the higher spirit that it lodges. The broad pale forehead may mark the lonely student ; a certain indescribable peaceful glow, as of universal good-will, may irradiate, as with a divine halo, the humble and loving saint. Nevertheless, it must be admitted, that whatever flavour or relish the cask may have of the purer element that is poured into it, is but slight and evanescent, in comparison with what it receives from the other element to which it is itself akin. It is the natural principle of life, in all its workings, that most easily and perfectly finds its vent, or outlet, or index, in the body—not the spiritual principle of high and holy thought.

Language itself, which is a condition of our present bodily state and bodily organization, is an additional proof of this. The faculty of articulate speech is indeed a great endowment. But inasmuch as it is a bodily faculty, depending upon the structure of the natural body which we now have, how in-adequate is it as an expression, as well as an instru-ment, of thought !

"How fleet is a glance of the mind !
　　Compared with the speed of its flight,
　　The tempest itself lags behind,
　　　And the swift-winged arrows of light."

"How fleet is a glance of the mind!" And how slow is the utterance that expresses it! Yes, and how imperfect and insufficient too! Especially when it is the spiritual mind whose fleet glance is to be traced!

It may be otherwise when there is a spiritual body. Thought may travel, not in the same mind merely, but from mind to mind, as with instantaneous, electric flash, more swiftly than words rush through ocean along the magic wire from shore to shore ; thought, moreover, conceived and conveyed with a precision and exactness, a fulness and force, of which no tongue of man on earth is capable,—in a way for which no tongue, such as man has on earth, is needed any more.

Let a condition of things be imagined, in which the higher spirit in man has a frame as expressive of itself, as the present body is of the animal soul or life, of which it is the exponent. For one thing, there is no more in that spiritual frame any tendency to express, any power of expressing, the emotions of the lower nature. It has no features, no gestures, no attitudes, no phraseology or vocabulary, for giving vent to the ideas, desires, and feelings, that relate to the functions of that animal life which is the lower nature. Nothing remains of that structure of the body which exhibits men here as having appetites and passions in common with the beasts. That is much. But more than that, far more I gain. I find myself in a body that in its new structure is the very image of my higher intellectual nature, the fitting index and expression of the spiritual life which I have in common with Christ in God. In and through that body, the glory and the beauty of that high intelligence and spiritual life of mine shine as clearly, and as conspicuously, as my lower life reveals itself in the fashion of my present frame. And at pleasure, by an act of will, I clothe my thoughts in forms more meet for them than any words my present tongue can frame. Not piecemeal and in fragments, imperfectly conceived and imperfectly conveyed,—but full and fresh, entire and whole,—my ideas, at my pleasure, pass forth from my own to other minds. The spirit in me is no longer, as it were, pent up and straitened. It has a free scope, and a large outlet, and a full utterance.

And those I live with are in the like case with myself. Transparently, translucently, in their shining frames, is the lamp of intelligent and spiritual life seen burning. Swiftly and surely do their high thoughts and holy musings pass from their minds to mine—as mine also pass from my mind to theirs.

What a fellowship of the saints is this! It is a fellowship, not dim and doubtful, hesitating and reserved, as the best saintly fellowship on earth must be. Here, our natural bodies separate us, as spiritual men, from one another. At the best, they but very imperfectly and inadequately discover us, or enable us to discover ourselves, to one another. We can only partially know one another. We can only partially trust one another. The lower life is often seen and felt to be at issue, in others and in ourselves, with the higher. The spiritual cannot break through the natural. Hence we must necessarily be cautious, and more or less constrained, in our closest Christian intercourse. The very offices and arrangements in the animal and social economy, for which the natural body is fitted, make this inevitable. But it will not be so then. Whatever in the structure of our present body is merely natural, whatever pertains to the functions of the merely animal life, is for ever laid aside. It is henceforth wholly a spiritual body.

Oh! what a barrier is now removed! How may the full tide of the spiritual life gush forth uncontrolled from every bosom! And as it freely circulates among the open and unveiled inhabitants of glory— the glory into which the hidden streams of grace have all been flowing—how, in the discovery of one another's hearts and one another's histories, may they find ever new occasion for the simultaneous burst of

loyal and grateful praise—"Thou hast redeemed us !"
Thou hast redeemed us all alike !

Are we expecting such a fellowship of the saints,
as the result of "what is sown a natural body being
raised a spiritual body?" Are we making any corresponding sort of preparation for it ? Have we any
foretaste of its blessedness in our walk together now ?

Secondly, The body is an inlet as well as an outlet. It is the index or image of what is within. But
it is also an avenue inwards for things without. It
takes the stamp or impress of the inner life, whatever
that may be, for which it is adapted. It takes the
stamp and impress also of the outer world, and conveys that stamp and impress of the outer world to
the "inner man" of the soul and spirit.

Now, as at present constituted, being a natural
body, made to minister primarily to the animal soul,
or the principle of animal life, it naturally supplies
its own master with appropriate and congenial food.
Hence the bodily senses admit the outer world into
the inner man, in the way most congenial to its
natural or animal tastes and tendencies.

Take the highest of our bodily senses—sight and
hearing. In the natural body as it now is, which of
the two living principles in us do they most readily
serve ?—the animal or the spiritual ?—the life we
share with the living creatures beneath us, or the life
we share with the living creatures,—nay, with the

living Creator, above us ? What things are we most apt to see and hear ?—to see and hear with thoroughest insight and deepest satisfaction ?

Alas! who among us will not confess, that the sights and sounds which tell most upon us, are those which appeal to sensations and associations connected with the animal life in us ; the emotional soul that thrills and beats on the impulse of the very appetites that stir the brutal tribes to passion ?

What are the paintings which are most sure to charm the eye ? Are they not those which come home to the principle of animal life ?—which bear upon the homely, natural processes of "eating and drinking, marrying and giving in marriage ? "—which portray actions embodying the most passionate energy that these animal instincts inspire ?

And what is the poetry, what the music, that fascinates the ear,—especially the unsophisticated ear ? The birth-song, the love-song, the war-song, the death-song ; any song of animal life ; any life-poem, —life-lyric, or life-epic ;—any life-poem of any sort !

What, indeed, are the fine arts, even at their best, but attempts to rectify and spiritualize what is to pass, through the medium of the eyes and ears of the body, into the chamber within, where the principle of the spiritual, as well as that of the animal life, has its seat ? Painting, poetry, music, all seek to reach through the body, not the animal soul merely, with its susceptibilities of animal sentiments and passions, but the intelligent spirit—the principle of pure thought. And in their highest efforts, they aspire to be the handmaids of the spirit of man, in its holiest communings with the Spirit of God. Hence we have devotional pictures, poems, psalms, hymns, and songs —all meant to be subservient and auxiliary to the higher spiritual life. And hence the danger, as to all of them, of their ministering chiefly to the instincts and feelings of the natural life ; and so ministering to these, that the sort of animal excitement or gratification which is occasioned, shall be mistaken for a real movement of the Spirit of God, inspiring and animating the renewed spirit in men. The sweetest music makes me, not merry, but sad,—and as it would seem devout. The finest representation, as of the child Samuel, or the Baptist, or the Saviour, solemnizes me. My Spirit in me is stirred or melted.

But the music strikes a chord in that part of me, —let it be breast, or heart, or bowels,—which animal feelings and passions move. The picture appeals to recollections and associations connected with the conditions of my animal life. I listen to the music ; it charms my ear. I gaze on the picture ; it fascinates my eye. But I feel that I must beware. The impressions which, while mine is still a natural body, my ear and my eye receive and send in, are but too apt to be such as are congenial to the lower prin-

ciple of animal life, rather than to the higher principle of spiritual thought. I cannot trust my present
bodily frame as a provider of fit materials for my
sanctified spiritual nature to feed on. I find that even
when it professes and seems to be handing in and
transmitting what is to nourish the spiritual life in
me, it is catering for the fleshly soul, and pandering
to its least offensive, perhaps, but by no means its
least dangerous, manifestations.

Thus my natural body is not only inadequate, as
representing and explaining me, so that I cannot, by
means of it, express myself as a spiritual man. It is
no less inadequate as representing and explaining the
outer world to me. I see, as through a glass, darkly.
I hear as if a chaotic babel of sound were ringing in
my ear. I cannot safely suffer my bodily senses,
even in the highest and purest exercise of them, to
minister to my spiritual life. I must regard with
jealousy what appeals to me through the eye, even
when it is rivetted on the purest heavenly ideal that
ever painter drew ; and what appeals to me through
the ear, even when it is ravished with loudest con-
cord of heavenly harmony, or softest notes of " grave,
sweet melody."

But there is a spiritual body. What its senses
are to be I cannot tell. How it is to receive impressions from without, and present these impressions
to the spirit within, I know not. But this, at least,

I may be bold to affirm. It will be true and faithful as that spirit's minister ; and it will be apt and able too. It will bring the external world to bear upon what is spiritual in me, not on what is merely sentient and sensuous. It will lay the entire universe of God under contribution, not at all, in any sense or in any measure, to the lower principle of animal life, but wholly and exclusively to the higher principle of pure intelligence and divine thought.

What a new aspect may all creation be expected to assume when thus viewed through the medium of a spiritual body ! What new mysteries of glory and beauty may break upon the astonished eye ! What new melodies and harmonies may fill the entranced and enraptured ear ! How may it then appear that there are indeed "more things in heaven and earth than are dreamed of in our philosophy !"

What a prospect for the devout student of nature, the devout lover of nature ;—the devout admirer of her beauteous forms, the devout drinker in of her sweet sounds ! Here, in the natural body, we must lay an arrest on these tastes and studies, refined and ennobling as they are. There is ever a risk of the objects with which they are conversant setting up the lower part of our nature against the higher ; stimulating rather the affections and passions of the animal soul, than the aspirations of the spiritual life. But there will be no such risk then ; no such need of caution. In that spiritual body, we may roam unchecked over all worlds, prying into all their secrets, taking our fill of all their treasures. No roving eye then to be restrained! No itching ear then to be reproved! No danger of excess in loving the creature then! Through the organs and senses of that spiritual body all created things address themselves to the spirit in us, and to that alone. They cannot, therefore, be studied, or tasted, or relished too much. They are all then felt to be congenial to our highest spiritual life. They fit into it. They are its materials. Out of them is woven the everlasting song of praise, in which the glory of creation and the glory of redemption are combined :—"Thou art worthy, O Lord, to receive glory, and honour, and power, for thou hast created all things, and for thy pleasure they are and were created. Thou art worthy, for thou wast slain, and hast redeemed us to God by thy blood. Great and marvellous are thy works, Lord God Almighty ; just and true are thy ways, thou king of saints" (Rev. iv. 11, v. 9, xv. 3).

Lastly, in the third place, besides being an index or outlet by which the spirit in man expresses itself, and an inlet or avenue by which things without reach the spirit within,—the body is an instrument by which the spirit works. The present body is so. Its various organs and members, internal and external, are the tools which the higher principle of spiritual intelligence and thought, as well as the lower principle of animal life, may and must use. The body is the spirit's engine or machine for moving the world. It is so, however, somewhat as if the higher spirit got the loan of it merely from the lower animal soul. It is to that lower animal soul that the body at present properly belongs. It is fitted for the uses of the animal life. "Be fruitful and multiply;"—"I have given you food" (Gen. i. 28, 30);—such is the original law of man's creation in the body. And for compliance with that law the natural body is constructed. Hence it is naturally at the disposal of the lower principle of mere animal life, whose pleasure it executes and whose work it does,—very much as the fleshly body of a beast, or a fish, or a bird, executes the pleasure and does the work of the vital principle or living soul that animates it. When it has to execute the pleasure and do the work of the higher principle of spiritual life, especially of the highest spiritual life,—the life of the Spirit of God in the spirit of man,—the present body is, as one might say, on foreign service.

No wonder it should be found, in such service, to be a somewhat cumbrous and clumsy instrument, an imperfect machine;—an engine apt to go wrong, to break down and need repair, in the hands of the higher master,—the mind,—which, as if by courtesy and upon sufferance, wields it. No wonder if that higher master often fails to wield it to the best purpose. All the less wonder if for such precarious use as he has of it, the higher master has to keep up a hard fight with the lower animal soul, whose servant the body, as now constituted, naturally is.

But give to the spirit in man,—the spiritual principle, which he has as redeemed by the Son and renewed by the Spirit of God,—a body that it can call its own and claim as its own,—absolutely and exclusively its own. Let it have a body with nothing at all of that organization which fits the natural body for the functions of the animal life. Let it be a body wholly formed and fashioned with an eye to the uses of the life that is spiritual and divine. How, by means of such a spiritual body, may the spirit or soul which is to live that life, be able to realize in it its own highest ideal, and even God's highest ideal, of what is great and good! Sleepless, unfatigued, needing neither food nor rest; marrying and giving in marriage no more; "made like unto the angels;"—with no animal wants to provide for, no animal passions to gratify, no animal weaknesses or wearinesses to yield to;—how may the redeemed in glory, with those glorious spiritual bodies of theirs, be ever plying the glad and busy task of acting out, in full measure, the impulses of their own spiritual nature, and doing all the pleasure of the Lord that bought them!

"Therefore are they before the throne of God, and serve him day and night in his temple; and he that sitteth on the throne shall dwell among them. They shall hunger no more, neither thirst any more; neither shall the sun light on them, nor any heat. For the Lamb which is in the midst of the throne shall feed them, and shall lead them unto living fountains of water; and God shall wipe away all tears from their eyes" (Rev. vii. 15-17).

The griefs and groans, as well as the wants and cravings, of which their natural bodies made them so sensitively susceptible, in a world of sin and sorrow, —of change and death,—are all over. No such agitations can mar their joy, or hinder their work, in that sinless, sorrowless, changeless, deathless state, where all is spiritual and all immortal!

And when all is spiritual and all immortal, what an opening is there for the spiritual and immortal soul, possessed of a kindred body and ushered into a congenial world, — *first*, to express itself in communion with all holy intelligences, unembarrassed by any perishable chains, — *secondly*, to receive pure light from the light that shines all around in "the new heavens and the new earth," and *thirdly*, to go forth, with strength proportioned to its own untiring aspirations, on errands of God's holy and righteous love, over all the realms of creation!

15

THE TWO ADAMS

And so it is written, The first man Adam was made a living soul; the last Adam was made a quickening spirit. Howbeit that was not first which is spiritual, but that which is natural; and afterward that which is spiritual. The first man is of the earth, earthy; the second man is the Lord from heaven. As is the earthy, such are they also that are earthy: and as is the heavenly, such are they also that are heavenly. And as we have borne the image of the earthy, we shall also bear the image of the heavenly. —1 Corinthians 15:45-49

THE two bodies, the natural and the spiritual, are connected with the first Adam and the second Adam respectively. That is the teaching of these verses. It is meant to strengthen the conviction that "there is a spiritual body" as well as a "natural body."

Do not imagine that the body which you are hereafter to receive is to be altogether like that which you have now ; a body adapted to the lower principle of your animal life ; fitted for animal functions, and animal sensations and sensibilities. Consider, in the first place, how reasonable a thing it is to expect that, if you are partakers of a higher principle of life,—of living intelligence and thought ;—and, above all, if you are made partakers of a principle of life higher even than that,—the spirit of life divine ; there shall be found for you a body suitable and corresponding. This is not in itself an improbable assumption. It is all the less so, if you consider, secondly, how these different sorts of life come to you ; whence they spring and flow ; from what sources or fountain-heads. The one life you have from "the first man Adam ;" the other from "the last Adam," Christ. And mark the essential difference between these two. "The first man Adam was made a living soul," So are we naturally in him. "The last Adam was made a quickening spirit." So we come to be by grace quickened in Christ.

I. "It is written, the first man Adam was made a living soul" (verse 45). The reference is to the second chapter of Genesis ; "The Lord God formed man of the dust of the ground, and breathed into his nostrils the breath of life ; and man became a living soul" (verse 7). In that chapter, a second account is given of the creation of man ; the first-being contained in the opening chapter of Genesis ;—"And God said, Let us make man in our image, after our likeness : and let them have dominion over the fish of the sea, and over the fowl of the air, and over the cattle, and over all the earth, and over every creeping thing that creepeth upon the earth" (verse 26). The two

accounts, in these two chapters, present man in two
distinct and contrasted points of view ;—in his relation to God who is to rule him, on the one hand, and
in his relation to the earth which he is to till, on
the other. The one indicates his look and tendency
upward and heavenward ; the other, his bias down-
ward and earthward. The one brings out what he
has in common with God, as being made in his image
and after his likeness ; the other, what he has in common with the inferior animals, as being made, like
them, of the dust of the ground. Formed out of such
materials, man has, like them, the breath of life
breathed into his nostrils by him who formed him.
And so he becomes, or is made, "a living soul."

The expression, therefore,—"a living soul,"—in
that second account of his creation, describes the
constitution of the first man, as to his material frame,
and as to the animal soul, or the principle of animal
life, which quickens and moves it. It indicates what
is, strictly speaking, the natural and original make
or fashion of the human animal. Like the other
animals, he is simply a piece of organized earthly
matter, animated by the mysterious breath of sentient
and motive life. His organization, it is true, is more
perfect than theirs. He has the hand that feels
and holds ; he has the mouth that speaks ; which
they have not. The instincts also of the natural
life are more akin and allied to the reasoning

faculty in him than in them; although in them
sagacity often rises well nigh into thought. Still
his nature,—as a being "which the Lord God formed
of the dust of the ground," and into whose "nostrils
he breathed the breath of life,"—is substantially
the same as theirs. He is, like them, an animal, "a
living soul." As such, he takes rank with "every
beast of the earth, and every fowl of the air, and every
thing that creepeth upon the earth, wherein is life,"
or,—for it is the same phrase that is applied to them
and to him,—"wherein is a living soul" (Gen. i. 30,
marginal reading). So far he and they alike are
"living souls."

No doubt, a higher endowment, a nobler capacity,
a better principle of life, belongs to him. He wears
the image and likeness of God. He is possessed of a
spirit, or what we now call soul, which, in respect of
knowledge, righteousness, and holiness, resembles his
great Creator. And, in a measure, his material frame
is adapted to the uses of that higher spirit and the
development of its higher life, as well as to the purposes and functions of the lower animal economy.
In body as well as in spirit, man is made capable of
glorifying and enjoying God, and rendering a perfect
obedience to his law. Nevertheless, and in entire consistency with that statement, it may be maintained
that its earthly origin and character do constitute a
deduction from the body's perfect fitness to be the

permanent or perpetual minister and companion of
the heavenly principle, the divine soul or spirit,
which is man's "glory" (Ps. xvi. 9, xxx. 12, lvii. 8).
When man, formed out of the ground and having the
breath of life breathed into his nostrils,—made, like
the other animals, "a living soul,"—is endowed with
that heavenly principle, that divine soul or spirit,
allying him to God,—it is as if something foreign and
adventitious were put upon him; as if, in a sense, it
were new wine put into an old bottle. The divine
robe of glory and beauty does not sit quite naturally
on one who is but dust and ashes. The heavenly
element does not find itself completely at home when
it has to dwell in a cottage of clay; in the "earthly
house of a tabernacle that may be dissolved" (2 Cor.
v. 1). There is felt to be a certain incongruity.

And accordingly, who can doubt that if that first
man Adam had but been faithful for a season; if he
had been true to him whose image and likeness he bore;
if he had been true to the higher spirit in life in himself;—his day of trial, his period of probation, being
well over;—he would have undergone a change in
his bodily frame that would have brought it into more
thorough harmony with his spiritual and nobler nature?
It could not be intended that, godlike in the spirit,
he should be for ever animal in the flesh. There
must have been a set time when there would have
been found for the divine spirit of life in him a bodily

instrument and companion more meet than what was first formed out of the dust of the ground; and into that changed body the breath of a more spiritual vitality would have been breathed. He would have been furnished with a frame no longer bound in any way to the functions of the animal life which he has been sharing with the brutes, but adapted exclusively to the loftiest aspirations and activities of the spiritual life which he has in fellowship with God. And so furnished, he would have passed on to a paradise of higher spiritual joy than the innocent bliss of Eden; —and to higher spiritual society there, more congenial to his better nature than the most docile of the tribes he ruled in Eden could supply.

Thus, had he not fallen, the first Adam might have fared. And thus, doubtless, in due succession, all the race would have fared. In that case, he would have become, as to his corporeity, not "a living soul," or animal,—but, as it were, a living "spirit," or spiritual;—his material frame being no longer accommodated and assimilated to the lower "soulish" principle of the animal life, but only and wholly to the higher principle of life spiritual and divine.

Even in that case, however, he would not have become a life-giving or "quickening spirit." That honour belongs to the second Adam alone. At the very best, the first Adam would have been only a receiver of that new spirituality, or spiritual vitality, in his body, which was to supersede and displace altogether its original merely animal vitality. It would have been to him personally a gift of grace. And so it would have been also to every one of his posterity partaking in the benefit. It was not his to give. He never could have received it on such a footing as to possess the power or privilege of bestowing it upon others—the power and privilege of transmitting it to his seed. What he can transmit to them as they issue out of his loins, can be nothing better than that first kind of corporeity, which alone, by the birthright of his original creation, is properly his own. And, alas! now that he has sinned and fallen, he can transmit even that only in a vitiated condition, with all that is animal in it—its animal instincts, propensities, and passions—working in antagonism to what is spiritual; infected with the malignity of sinful corruption. To him we owe, from him we inherit, those bodies that, with their animal tastes and tendencies, seem so hopelessly at variance with our higher spiritual life. And if we hold still of that first Adam, we may well despair of ever having better.

But is it so? Have we not known the Second Adam? Is not he our head now? Is it not of him that we hold? Then surely we may confidently look for all that, as regards corporeity, we can possibly desire. For—

II. "The last Adam was made," or became, "a quickening spirit" (verse 45). The antithesis is Paul's. To the statement which he quotes from Genesis concerning the first Adam, he himself appends the counterpart statement concerning the second.

1. Now here the first question that occurs is, when and how did "the second Adam" become "a quickening spirit?" Is the reference here to his incarnation? So at first sight it might seem. For does not the incarnation in his case correspond to the creation in the case of the first Adam? Does not the proper contrast lie between the first Adam, when made, being "a living soul," and the second Adam, when made flesh, being "a quickening spirit?" But on reflection, we may see cause to understand the apostle as referring rather to the resurrection of Christ than to his incarnation, as constituting him what he here calls him,—"a quickening spirit." For in fact, strictly speaking, it is only at his resurrection, and through his resurrection, that Christ becomes the second Adam. Before that event he is rather to be considered as himself connected with the first Adam ; a branch or scion of the old family, the old vine, not as yet formally and fully qualified for being the head of a new family,—himself the true branch-bearing vine.

Look for a little, in this view, at the meaning of our Lord's incarnation, and the work for which he became incarnate. He was then made, he then be-

came,—in the first Adam "as the seed of the woman,"
—simply a living soul." He was made in his incarnation what the first Adam was made in his creation.
In respect of corporeity, so far as his bodily frame
with its animal soul or principle of animal life was
concerned, he became what the first Adam was before
the fall. What as the second Adam he had to do,
was exactly what the first Adam had to do, and failed
to do. There was, indeed, something else that he had
to do. He had to undo what the first Adam did, to
expiate the guilt of the sin which the first Adam
brought into the world, and to procure the cancelling
of it for ever by his atoning death. But, along with
that, "taking upon him the form of a servant," "being
found in fashion as a man," the last Adam had to stand
the temptation which the first Adam failed to stand,
and to realise the obedience of which the first Adam
fell short. And he does all this as "a living soul;"—
made, like the first Adam, "a living soul." He takes
the first Adam's living corporeity, his bodily vitality,
as his own. As regards all that pertains to the
animal nature,—the body animated by the principle
of animal life,—he becomes precisely what the first
man Adam was when he was first made. And in
that character and capacity, he tries again the experiment in which the first Adam broke down.

Thus far, the last or second Adam is no life-giver,
no quickener. He is a life-winner, a life-conqueror.

Made, as to his organic earthly frame and the breath of life which animates it, "a living soul," like the first Adam,—like him also made pure and holy, in respect of his "spirit" or higher soul,—he has in the first instance to win back and gain the life which the first Adam forfeited. This accordingly he does, his humanity being sustained in the doing of it by his essential divine nature, as well as by the Spirit of the Father dwelling in him. So he achieves the victory. Undoing, by his atoning sufferings and death, what the first Adam had done by his sin—accomplishing and fulfilling, by his perfect obedience, that righteousness in which the first Adam failed—the last Adam comes forth at his resurrection,—and then for the first time, —in the new character of "a quickening spirit."

Thus it was at his resurrection, and in virtue of his resurrection, that "the last Adam was made a quickening spirit."

2. But now another question occurs; How is he a quickening spirit?—not quickened merely, but quickening—not living only, but life-giving—not simply himself possessing spiritual life in the body, but imparting it to others? Might it not be enough that the second Adam, risen from the dead, should take the place which the first Adam, if he had kept his integrity, would ultimately have reached? In that case, he might have received, for himself individually, a spiritual corporeity. His own physical frame might have

been refashioned or transformed, so as to be adapted
to the uses, not of the animal, but of the spiritual
economy alone.   He might thus have been himself
" quickened" in his body.   And that would have
been much.   It is probably all that the first Adam
could have gained, even if he had fulfilled the terms of
his trial.   Life spiritual, in body as well as in spirit,
he might have won for himself.   But he could not
have imparted it to others.   The utmost issue of his
success would have been the handing down of the
constitution, bodily and spiritual, which he originally
had, uncontaminated and unimpaired.   He never
could have been " a quickening spirit."

But the last Adam is so.   There is in him a life,
or principle of life, for the bodily as well as the
spiritual part of man, that was not in the first Adam,
and indeed could not be.   For the second Adam is
the Living One, "the Lord from heaven" (verse 47).
When he becomes incarnate, the spiritual nature or
life is not an endowment or attainment reached from
beneath.   It comes down in him and with him from
above.   It is not in his case one who is originally, as
to his natural origin, earth-born, or earth-made, that
is elevated by being made in the likeness of God in
heaven ; it is one who is himself God in heaven,
who stoops to be made in the likeness of men who are
of the earth.   It is the Lord of life who has a body
prepared for him in the virgin's womb.   True, it is a

body of humiliation, "vile" and mortal, so long as he lives here on the earth. In it, as a corruptible body, he obeys, and suffers, and dies. But now the worst is over. And, lo! he lives again in the body. He lives now as the second Adam. And he lives, not only to receive but to give life,—spiritual life,— spiritual life in the body. He is made, with reference to the whole nature of man, physical as well as spiritual,—"a quickening spirit." For himself, personally, he has, in his resurrection, the element or character of spirituality communicated to the lower and material, as well as the higher and mental, part of that human nature of ours which he took as his own. His natural body becomes a spiritual body. He is, as to his physical frame, quickened, as the first Adam would at some set time have been quickened had he not fallen; spiritualized, as the first Adam would have been spiritualized. But more than that; he quickens us, who are not now any longer in the first Adam, but in the second. He spiritualizes our physical frame. "He changes our vile body, that it may be fashioned like unto his glorious body." And he does so "according to the working whereby he is able even to subdue all things unto himself" (Phil. iii. 21). It is his work to make the "vile body" "glorious."

Thus, as "a quickening spirit," the second Adam, the Lord from heaven, dying and rising again, is in a position and is able to quicken spiritually our whole nature, in all its parts.

Look, then, the apostle might say, if you have still any anxiety as to your future bodily condition—if you are still uneasy as to the kind of corporeity that may consist with your perfection in the heavenly state—look to this second Adam! See him as he stands before you now, having fulfilled the conditions of life which the first Adam failed to fulfil; having also expiated the guilt and redressed the evil issue of that failure. See the risen Saviour, the man Christ Jesus, himself now possessing such a bodily nature, such a corporeal structure and organization, as the first Adam might have got had he stood the test. But not as the first Adam would have had it, does the second Adam hold it. He is not merely quickened, but quickening; he is, let it be repeated, not merely living, but life-giving. And it is with special reference to that very body of yours of which you complain as the body of this death, that "the second Adam is a quickening spirit."

Can you doubt any more that there is a spiritual as well as a natural body, when you think of the last Adam, who now stands to you in place of the first? Is it not "given" to him, as "the Son, to have life in himself?" (John v. 26). Is it not given to him also, as the Son, "to quicken whom he will?" (John v. 21). Is it not "the Father's will that he, the Son, should raise up every one whom the Father giveth him at the last day?" And does he not accordingly, with remarkable emphasis, three times over repeat the assurance "I will," yes, "I will raise him up at the last day" (John vi. 39, 40, 44, 54). He is not in the position of the first Adam, a mere creature, winning his way to life in the body. He is the Son, who liveth evermore. True; in the body he consents to pay the forfeit of that life which the first Adam lost. But he liveth still. He wins the life of which the first Adam fell short. He wins it as the living one, having life in himself, for this very end, that he may quicken whom he will.

And this quickening, is it not a quickening to spiritual life?—not to that life which consists in your performance of animal functions and your compliance with animal cravings, but to that life which is exercised in the higher fellowship of heaven, and which the atmosphere of heaven sustains? And can you doubt that it is a quickening which will pervade your whole nature; and reach your bodily frames, allied as they now are naturally to earth, as well as the spirit in you that claims kindred, through grace, with heaven? Surely, if the first Adam, "as a living soul," transmits to you that bodily frame, corrupt and perishable, which he got out of the dust of the ground of which he was formed,—the second Adam, "as a quickening spirit," may make you partakers of that living spiritual corporeity which belongs to him now, as not only having life in himself, in his entire person, but able to be author of the same life to you ;—and that too, in your entire persons also.

Thus Christ, the last Adam, the second representative and head of humanity, stands contrasted with the first, as the giver of life spiritual, and the giver of it to the whole man, to man in the body. There must, therefore, be a spiritual body. It is no devout imagination to speak of such a thing. Nay more, the apostle apparently looks upon the spiritual body as the fitting sequel, and, as it were, complement of the natural. That the natural body should, in the order of time, be first, is reasonable ; it is what might have been expected. But equally, as it would seem, might it have been anticipated that the natural would in due course rise and effloresce into the spiritual.

In the first place, it is reasonable and quite what might have been expected, that in the order of time the natural body should take precedence of the spiritual ;—"Howbeit that was not first which is spiritual, but that which is natural: and afterward that which is spiritual" (verse 46). This arrangement approves itself to the reflecting mind. It is according to the analogy of the whole procedure of God in creation and providence. The law of progress pervades and governs all divine operations. There is a true as well as a false theory of development. Consider the order in which God works as the maker of all things. Beginning with inert matter, called into being out of nothing by his word, he gives birth to successive forms of life in the vegetable and animal world, rising gradually from the lowest type of organization, each new formation being an advance upon the preceding, until at last man appears upon the stage. When he does appear, it is fitting and according to order and analogy that he should first be seen with a simply natural body ;—possessed of a material frame altogether similar to the material frames possessed by the animal tribes of which he is the crown and head. But there is something in him which indicates that such a sort of body will not suit him in perpetuity. That he should have it at first, and continue to have it for a season, is right and proper. A bodily structure with animal vitality like that of the brutes, —having superadded to it a higher spiritual principle of life,—is the right and proper kind of creature, if we may so speak, to come forth from the Creator's hand, at the precise stage of creation's progress at which man is made. But that he should have such a body for ever,—that he should never have one better, or one more suited to his higher nature,—this, even on grounds of reason, might be pronounced beforehand to be improbable. Analogy—the analogy of the law of progress and development in all the works of God —might of itself raise a brighter and higher hope.

It does so all the rather when we consider, secondly, who and what the two heads respectively are on whom, in the two states of nature and of grace, we depend, and from whom in these successive states we derive our life :—" The first man is of the earth, earthy ; the second man is the Lord from heaven " (verse 47).

Look at the first man. He appears, as it were, rising out of earth ; a living creature, like the living creatures that have sprung up before him ; fashioned out of the same dusty materials, animated by the same mysterious vital breath. In some respects he has the advantage ; in others, they. If his erect stature, apprehensive hand, and speaking mouth, raise him as an animal above them, can he match the lion in strength, the roe in speed, or the eagle winging his lofty flight in the eye of the midday sun ? At all events, like them, he is " of the earth earthy." True, he has a higher nature, allying him to God. But that comes, as one might almost say, by an after-thought ; or at least it is a graft from heaven on an earthy stem. " The first man is still of the earth, earthy." And if our only life is what we have through him, or from him, by descent from his loins,—if he is the only father that begetteth us and his the only family that we belong to,—then we could scarcely look for any other sort of bodily frame and vital breath than his. For "as is the earthy, such are they that are earthy" (verse 48).

But lo! "the second man!" Not earthborn he! Not sprung from earth! He "is the Lord from heaven!" His origin, when he appears as man, is not the dust of the ground, but the highest heavens!

But does he not, as man, take the very physical frame which the first man had? Has he not, as born of a woman, the same corporeal and animal nature that Adam originally received?

True! That he may occupy Adam's place and undo Adam's work, he must assume, for a little, Adam's earthly corporeity. But he cannot retain it; he cannot keep it long; for he is "the Lord from heaven." He may put on Adam's earthy garment of a natural body till he has redressed the wrong and repaired the evil of Adam's miserable fall. But when that end is accomplished he puts it off. He must have another sort of body to wear as "the Lord from heaven," when, his work on earth being finished, he passes into heaven again; a body, a corporeity, a living material organization, in which even "the Lord from heaven," now risen and ascended to be the Lord in heaven, may feel himself, as it were, at liberty and at home for ever!

Ah! then, if our life is got from him—if we are

begotten again in him—if we belong to the new family of which he is the head—if it be his blood that now runs in our veins and his spirit that now quickens us—can we doubt that it will be ours to share his corporeity, his bodily nature, at the last? It must be so. For "as is the heavenly, such are they also that are heavenly" (verse 48).

Yes! let us be very sure, if indeed we are in him, that, "as we have borne the image of the earthy, we shall also bear the image of the heavenly" (verse 49). He himself, for us, "bore the image of the earthy;" bore it to the utmost depths of humiliation, degradation, suffering and shame, that his bearing it could by possibility imply. But he did so that we might bear the image of the heavenly. He took that mortal frame which we derive by inheritance and by descent from Adam. He took it corruptible, dishonoured, weak, and vile. But now that he has left the tomb, in which for a time that body lay, it is no longer the same kind of body that he has. It is, it must of necessity be, a body suited to him as "the Lord from heaven;" a body fit to be worn by him in heaven for evermore. Such is his body now; and such will our bodies hereafter be. For, so surely "as we have borne the image of the earthy,"—even as surely "we shall also bear the image of the heavenly" (verse 49).

What would you have more, O ye Corinthians? What brighter hope would the most transcendental ultra-spiritualist among you desire to cherish? Is it not a better hope than the dreamy notion of a sort of incorporeal and almost impersonal immortality;—of the spiritual part in you being extricated from the material, and sublimated, as it were, into affinity with the very essence of God, nay, lost and absorbed in the Divine fulness itself? As a refuge in trouble, as a motive to action,—for assuaging the grief of parting when friends fall asleep, and nerving your whole manhood for the battle of life,—is a belief like that, impalpable and ideal,—at all to be compared with the assurance that you are yourselves,—your whole selves, —to be as Christ is? Each of you individually is to be identified as he was identified when he rose. And all of you, with as real and full separate personalities as you now have on earth, and he has in heaven, are to bear his heavenly image and behold his heavenly glory!

16

A CORRUPTABLE BODY INCOMPATIBLE WITH THE INHERITANCE OF AN INCORRUPTIBLE KINGDOM

Now this I say, brethren, that flesh and blood cannot inherit the kingdom of God; neither doth corruption inherit incorruption. Behold, I show you a mystery; we shall not all sleep, but we shall all be changed, in a moment, in the twinkling of an eye, at the last trump: for the trumpet shall sound, and the dead shall be raised incorruptible, and we shall be changed. For this corruption must put on incorruption, and this mortal must put on immortality.

—1 Corinthians 15:50-53

It may be convenient, at this stage of the argument, to recapitulate the reasoning of the apostle in answer to the question, "How are the dead raised up? and with what body do they come?" (verse 35). The question seems to assume that if saints in glory are to have a bodily nature, it must be such as that which they have now; gross, sensuous, carnal. Will that agree with the high spiritual perfection of the heavenly state? Will glorified spirits be at home in such natural bodies?

The apostle has met this question in several ways. By the analogy of seed-corn, or "bare grain," he has proved that the presumption is all in favour of the body which is buried undergoing a great change when it rises from the grave again. He has pointed out instances, among earthly and heavenly bodies, of the vast variety of forms and organizations that matter may be made to assume; to shew the unreasonableness of the idea that the great Creator, in whose hands it is seen to be so plastic, cannot mould it, in the risen bodies of his people, into harmony with their spiritual perfection and unchanging glory. He has gone farther. He has plainly drawn the contrasted pictures of the present and the future bodies ; the one corrupt, dishonoured, weak—the other incorruptible, glorious, powerful ; the one naturally adapted to the functions of the natural and animal life—the other spiritual, fitted to be the apt minister of the spiritual life, which the Spirit of God infuses into the spirit of man. "There is a natural body, and there is a spiritual body" (verse 44).

There is a natural body. "The first man Adam was made a living soul" (verse 45). Formed out of the dust of the ground and having the breath of life breathed into his nostrils, he became an animal, like the animals which the earth was commanded to bring forth before him (Gen. ii. 7). He bore indeed the image and likeness of God (Gen. i. 27). But still, so long as it was in that natural body which he shared in common with the inferior tribes that he bore it, there might seem to be something wanting to his absolute perfection. Had he stood, he might have "purchased for himself a better degree ;" the natural might have become a spiritual body. But he fell. And the animal nature which he transmits to us is not even what he originally had himself, but wholly depraved and vile. There is, however, another head and representative of humanity ; the last Adam. He, like the first Adam, appears at first " as a living soul." In his incarnation, he comes forth identically the same, as to his bodily and animal nature, with what the first Adam was when he was made. He fulfils the righteousness in which the first Adam failed. He undoes the mischief which the first Adam did. He obeys, and suffers, and dies. And rising again, he is made "a quickening spirit" (verse 45). He is now possessed, in his whole human nature,—in his body as well as in his soul,—of spiritual life. And he has this life in himself that he may quicken whom he will. He is one who quickens spiritually. And he quickens spiritually the whole man. Even the body becomes spiritual in his hands. The natural passes into the spiritual ; first in the person of the last Adam himself, the risen Saviour ; and ultimately in the persons of all that are his.

All this is in due order. The natural comes first. " The first man is of the earth earthy" (verse 47). He is earth-born and earth-like, as are the other animals. He has indeed a signal advantage over them. In respect of the image of God stamped upon him, he is a far higher specimen of the earthly. And he has moreover, in his very constitution, an earnest of the heavenly ere long superseding the earthly— the natural passing into the spiritual. But he has lost all by his sin. The "second man is different." He is "the Lord from heaven" (verse 47). The humanity which, not as being "of the earth, earthy," but as "the Lord from heaven," he in gracious conde- scension assumes,—may be for a time such, in respect of its bodily life or animal corporeity, as the first man had when he was made "a living soul." It may be so until he has finished the work which the first man's fall entailed upon him. But it cannot be so any longer. It must now be such as is meet, not for the earthly mode and manner of existence to which for a little he stooped, but for his own endless divine life and eternal heavenly home. Surely, then, it is enough for us to have the positive assurance that "as we have borne the image of the earthy, we shall also bear the image of the heavenly" (verse 49).

Nay, we may be even doubly assured on this point. Our assurance may be based, not only on the word of promise, but on the very nature and necessity of the case. For, as the apostle now goes on to show, there is an inexorable law which really ends all ques- tioning :—"Now this I say, brethren, that flesh and

blood cannot inherit the kingdom of God; neither
doth corruption inherit incorruption" (verse 50).

The two clauses of this verse are certainly parallel.
The same thought is expressed in two different ways,
according to Hebrew usage, so that the second illus-
trates or explains the first. Or if there is any shade
of difference, it can only be this, that the second
clause gives the reason of the statement in the first.
Flesh and blood is corruption; whereas the kingdom
of God is incorruption. But corruption cannot inherit incorruption. Therefore flesh and blood cannot
inherit the kingdom of God. So the argument may
be put in strict logical form.

The two main propositions, therefore, are these,
First, Flesh and Blood is corruption; Secondly, The
kingdom of God is incorruption.

I. Flesh and blood is corruption. "Corruption,"
must not be understood here in a moral or spiritual
sense. Such a sense would not be in point or to the
purpose, as regards the apostle's reasoning. To say
that bodies corrupted by sin cannot enter heaven,
would be simply an irrelevant truism, and would
be held to be so by the parties with whom Paul is
dealing. It is the admission that "flesh and blood,"
even in its best estate, is "corruption," and cannot
therefore "inherit incorruption," which alone meets
their view fairly. And it is this which lays at the
same time the foundation for the inference that

what is composed of flesh and blood must be changed into something better. The corruption, then, here spoken of, is not an evil quality, superinduced on the human frame by the fall; it is the inherent property of flesh and blood as originally made.

This interpretation may be confirmed by a survey of the passages in the New Testament in which the phrase occurs. These are four in number. (1.) Our Lord says in acknowledging Peter's prompt confession,—" Thou art the Christ, the Son of the living God,"—" Flesh and blood hath not revealed it unto thee, but my Father, which is in heaven" (Matthew xvi. 17). (2.) Paul, in support of his assertion that he did not receive the gospel at second hand, but directly from the Lord, thus speaks: " When it pleased God, who separated me from my mother's womb, and called me by his grace, to reveal his Son in me, that I might preach him among the heathen; immediately I conferred not with flesh and blood; neither went I up to Jerusalem to them which were apostles before me" (Galatians i. 16). (3.) He thus describes the Christian conflict—" We wrestle not against flesh and blood, but against principalities, against powers, against the rulers of the darkness of this world, against spiritual wickedness in high places" (Ephesians vi. 12). (4.) Referring to the human nature which Christ assumed, he says—" Forasmuch then as the children are partakers of flesh and blood, he also himself likewise took part of the same." (Hebrews ii. 14).

Such are the uses of this phrase, " flesh and blood," in the New Testament. And if we connect these uses of it with the proposition that " flesh and blood is corruption," we may be satisfied that the corruption here meant is its characteristic, not in its worst state only, but even in its best.

1. The first two passages may be taken together ; for when Paul says, " I conferred not with flesh and blood," he probably had in his mind the Lord's words to Peter, " Flesh and blood hath not revealed it unto thee, but my Father which is in heaven." On both occasions, the expression is used to disparage human nature, simply as such, and to deny its capacity of apprehending what is divine. The true knowledge of the Son of God must come, not from flesh and blood, but from the Father. Man, in his natural bodily condition, cannot originate it. Nay more. Man, in his natural bodily condition, cannot adequately comprehend or communicate it. These are two important truths ; the one implied in what the Lord says to Peter, the other in what Paul says of himself. Peter's confession, " Thou art the Christ, the Son of the living God," is the result, not of a discovery made by man on the earth, but of a revelation from his Father in heaven. Paul rejoices in his having received the same revelation, not through the inter-

vention of man, but from the Lord himself. He received it, therefore, in its divine simplicity and unity, complete and entire ;—not broken up, as it must necessarily more or less be, when the agency of men, even inspired men, is employed. " For we know in part" (1 Cor. xiii. 9). Our knowledge at the best is partial and fragmentary. We possess pieces or bits of knowledge, out of which we vainly strive to make up one whole. For this " flesh and blood" of ours, by means of whose organism, inner and outer, we receive and work up our knowledge,—is not itself one and indivisible, but made of divers particles of dust, resolvable into dust again.

2. But not only does this " flesh and blood" negatively, as it were, limit our knowledge and render it fragmentary ; it positively obstructs and hinders it. It is the antagonist of the divine life. Other and more formidable adversaries we may lay our account with having to face. But at all events, we have to " wrestle against flesh and blood." For " flesh and blood," even in its best state, is apt to be adverse to spiritual insight and spiritual advancement.

Was it not so in paradise ? Artfully reaching, through the lower tendencies of her bodily nature, her higher powers of reason,—the tempter prevailed over the innocence of our mother Eve, and awakened in her the lust of the flesh, the lust of the eye, and the pride of life. There was no taint of moral corruption in man's nature then. But his material frame was liable to dissolution. It had in it the seed of possible decay, which sin ripened into actual death. And this quality of corruption, or corruptibility, in respect of which, being composed of dust, it might return to dust again, made it possible for it to be brought, through an appeal to its animal appetite, into conflict with the spirit's pure worship of him who is a Spirit, and who must be worshipped in spirit and in truth. Even then, it might be said, man was called, in a sense, to "wrestle against flesh and blood."

So also, or rather much more, we, in our fallen state, are called to "wrestle against flesh and blood;"— against flesh and blood, simply as such. For we are not merely to keep in view, in our treatment of our body, the evil taint which our lower animal nature has got by descent from fallen parents. We are to take into account also that property, allying it to the dust of this lower earth, which is in obvious contrast to the imperishable life of heaven. It is not merely against the positively sinful movements of "flesh and blood" that we are to watch and wrestle, but "against flesh and blood" itself. It was not the workings of evil in his lower animal nature that the apostle had in his view, but that lower nature itself, when he said, "I keep under my body, and bring it into subjection ; lest that by any means, when I have preached to others, I myself should be a castaway" (1 Cor. ix. 27).

3. The last passage brings out yet a third element of incompatibility with the kingdom of God attaching to "flesh and blood." Besides being first, a disqualification for the perfect knowledge of God and the Son of God,—and secondly, the antithesis or antagonist of the higher life of the divine spirit in man,—"flesh and blood" labours under this additional disability, that it has become actually mortal. Death is not now a possible contingency that may be shunned, but a certain and inevitable fate. Remaining on the earth unchanged, "flesh and blood" is sure to decay and die. The sentence on guilty man, "dust thou art, and unto dust shalt thou return" (Gen. iii. 19), takes full and universal effect. Hence it was needful that, "as the children are partakers of flesh and blood, the Son also himself likewise should take part of the same,"—that he might be capable of dying in our stead. The living bodily frame which he assumed was identical with ours. In him, as in us, "flesh and blood" dies.

Now, put these things together, and see how thoroughly "flesh and blood" is identified with "corruption." Corruption is its characteristic; not moral pollution; but if I may so speak, physical divisibility, liability to be broken up into parts, dissolved or resolved into particles of dust. That is "corruption;" and that is "flesh and blood." And see how this characteristic of "flesh and blood" unfits it for bearing its part fully and perfectly in the higher spiritual life, to which man is meant to aspire.

Thus, in the first place, I cannot, through the loop-holes of this veil of dust, get a full sight of God. Lines and angles, as it were, I perceive here and there, as on a broken glass on which his shadow partly falls. But the circle, the full orb of his all-embracing perfection and glory, I strive in vain to see. His works, even dimly discerned, in a fragmentary way, are great and marvellous. But I feel with Job—"Lo, these are parts of his ways. But how little a portion is heard of him? The thunder of his power who can understand?" (Job xxvi. 14)

Then again, secondly, how uncertain a comrade of the spirit in me do I find this animal body of mine to be! How apt is it to become a rival or a foe! Because corruption, or liability to dissolution, is its attribute, it is incessantly demanding what may keep it from being dissolved. It asks rest, refreshment, recreation. It has a right to ask them, and it is at my peril if I refuse; it is my sin. But this very need,—or rather, the corruption, the liability to dissolution, the perishable nature of the animal body, which occasions the need,—sets up "flesh and blood" as, at the very best, an ally not to be thoroughly trusted. And it is now become an antagonist against which the spiritual man has to watch and wrestle.

Above all, thirdly, "flesh and blood" is doomed

to die. That is the fatal drawback on the happiness of the spiritual man here on the earth. For even to him death is formidable. That I have to die is ever to me a solemn thought. I might struggle on with this "flesh and blood" of mine, groping after God. I might wrestle on against this "flesh and blood" of mine, keeping it in subjection. The prolonged continuance of my present spiritual aspirations and spiritual contendings, even in my present bodily organization, might be tolerable. But corruption is certain death. And the fear of death keeps even spiritual men all their lifetime, if not "subject to bondage," yet at least "subject to vanity" (Rom. viii. 20). "Verily, every man at his best state is altogether vanity" (Ps. xxxix. 5). With the prospect of death before me, I can scarcely be said really to live. To have death always in my eye, is to have a dark shadow always lowering over the brightest light and best life of my soul.

So much for the first proposition;—Flesh and blood is corruption.

II. The second is the antithesis of it;—The kingdom of God is incorruption. It is a state of things in which there is nothing destructible, nothing perishable, no corruption. What it is positively is not here said. The kingdom of God, the heavenly world,—in a word, heaven,—is not here described. The elements which enter into its pure and holy joy are not specified. One only feature of its felicity is indicated ;—it is identified with incorruption. This is simply a negative commendation. It tells what the kingdom of God is not, rather than what it is. But how much may a mere negation imply !

Reversing the order under the previous head, let us notice three particulars comprehended in it.

1. Death is out of the question. In that kingdom of God there is nothing capable of death ; nothing liable to decay or dissolution. It is a reign of righteousness and peace that knows no change but only that of progressive advancement, without limit and without end. No abrupt shock or slow siege of the king of terrors can mar its blessed life.

2. Hence there can be no occasion for such arrangements as are here necessary to stave off death. If the kingdom of God is incorruption, in the sense of there being in it no more death, it must be so also in the sense of there being no more in it any deathward tendency, needing to be counteracted by carnal or corporeal appliances. There is therefore no room for those animal functions that are now exercised in stemming the tide, and repairing the waste, of that liability to death which characterizes all life in this present world. In that kingdom, there is no necessity to be ever using means for keeping death at arm's length.

3. Hence, farther, as there can be no death to be

held at bay by means of acts and offices not always favourable to the spiritual life, so there can be nothing to intercept, or obscure, or break in pieces, the beatific vision of God. To "see God" is the blessedness of the "pure in heart" (Matt. v. 8). To "see God as he is," is the hope of the children of God (1 John ii. 2). The perfection of that state which is called the kingdom of God, is that there we shall "know even as we are known" (1 Cor. xiii. 12). There can be nothing broken or fragmentary in our knowledge of God there ; no analysing or compounding of God ; no analysing of him, as if he were a heap or bundle of attributes to be assorted ; no compounding of him, as if he were to be made up of the materials of our own spiritual consciousness. All that sort of knowledge savours of corruption. It is partial, imperfect, like what we see when we look through, or when we look into, a broken glass. There is none of it in heaven.

Thus the kingdom of God is incorruption. It is so, in the first place, in respect of its immunity from death, and the fear of death. It is so, secondly, in respect of its independence.of those means for warding off death which a condition of mortality renders necessary. And it is so, in the third place, in respect of its adaptation for the pure and bright vision—the clear, unbroken, and unclouded sight and knowledge of the Holy One ;—not of parts of his works and ways only, but of himself and of his full-orbed glory in the face of his Son.

This last is the crowning joy and glory of heaven. And it grows out of the other two. First,—No death ; no liability to death ; no possibility of death ; no susceptibility of division, dissolution, or decay. Next,—No machinery or system of animal organism working merely to counteract the deathward tendency and keep life agoing in spite of it ; working often therefore in opposition to the higher life of the spirit. Lastly,—No looking out on God as through the clefts of a rock, or from behind a hedge, admitting only some scattered rays of his majesty. The kingdom of God knows nothing of the hindrances which mortality, and the strife or struggle against mortality, interpose in the way of a clear and calm insight into the bosom of the everlasting Father, in which the Son dwells evermore.

Thus these two things,—flesh and blood which is corruption, and the kingdom of God which is incorruption,—may be seen to be so opposed to one another that the one cannot inherit the other. The "eternal and exceeding weight of glory" which awaits us in the heavenly state, these frail and mortal bodies of ours could not sustain. Undergoing alteration every moment—wasting and having the waste repaired— subject to a constant flux and flow of the earthly particles of which they are composed—liable always and

at any time to death, and only staving off that calamity by unceasing attention to their animal wants
and unceasing care to guard them from the harm that
threatens them on every side—these material frames
would not be at home, they would be out of place, in
that heaven where no change can come,—where
eternal peace reigns. A mortal body in that immortal
world would be an incongruity, an anomaly, revolting
to all intelligences. It is, in fact, a plain contradiction in terms. It is simply impossible for flesh and
blood to inherit the kingdom of God—for corruption
to inherit incorruption.

But how then are those to enter heaven who are
found alive at the last day? That is now a natural
question; and accordingly the apostle goes on to
meet it—"Behold I show you a mystery; we shall
not all sleep, but we shall all be changed" (verse 51).

It is not a mystery, in our modern sense of the
term, that the apostle here says that he shows us. It
is a plain enough fact or doctrine that he states; easily
intelligible, and having nothing of what we would call
mysterious about it. What he means is simply that
it is a revelation; a great truth which could be known
only by a discovery or communication from above.
" I show you a mystery;" I announce to you a revelation from God; to the effect that all are not to die,
but all are to be changed. In one way or other, all

are to undergo the process needed to transform the natural body into a spiritual.

For death, with a resurrection following, is not the only way of effecting that change. Had sin not entered into our world, the change would doubtless have been otherwise brought about. Even since on account of sin death has come to be the universal law of our being, there have been signal exceptions. Enoch and Elijah were surely changed when they were translated without tasting death. They did not carry natural but spiritual bodies with them when they passed into the heavens. What happened to them will happen to the saints who are alive on the earth when the resurrection morning comes. They will not be left behind when the dead are raised ; as it were to fill the vacant graves, and crowd the world again with charnel-houses. No. The face of the earth is to be renewed. It can no longer be a " golgotha," a " place of skulls ;" a receptacle for carcasses rotting in corruption. It will have got rid of the accumulated dust of old generations to little purpose, if the dust of new generations is to mar its renovated beauty. Men cannot, therefore, be suffered to die and be buried in it any more. Even the saints of God can no longer be allowed to lay their bones in it. Earth refuses to hold any more even the monuments of the just. If they need to have their natural bodies converted into spiritual bodies, it must be by some

266 · Nature of the Future Body

other process than that of a death, a burial, and a resurrection.   And so it shall be,—" In a moment, in the twinkling of an eye, at the last trump : for the trumpet shall sound, and the dead shall be raised incorruptible, and we shall be changed" (verse 52).

Ah! what a reunion will there then be!   What a meeting between the dead who are raised and the living who are changed!   First, what a surprise for the living themselves;—for us living ones ;—as Paul naturally speaks, realizing the event as at hand.*   In a moment, in the twinkling of an eye, we find our-selves changed.   There is no long interval, in our case, between our laying down the natural body, and our resuming the spiritual body.   The process, whatever it may be, that effects the needful alteration upon our material frame, is quick as lightning.   The trumpet

---

* There is a perverse tendency in certain quarters to twist this way of speaking about the second advent into a proof that the apostles fell into a mistake on the subject,—the mistake of imagin-ing that that event was to happen in their own day.   This is a favourite theme with some who would fain convict the sacred writers of error, and so impeach their inspiration and infallibility.   Here is a point, not of secular science, but of sacred truth, and a point of some importance, in regard to which Paul laboured under a delusion, at least in the earlier part of his ministry, for they are sometimes good enough to allow that he came right before he died.   And the sole ground on which the notion rests, is Paul's speaking in the first person when he speaks of those who are to be alive at the Lord's coming, as if it would not be the most natural thing in the world for me, or for any one, to do the same at this day.   See Hackett (an American writer), on the Acts of the Apostles iii. 20.

sounds—the last trump, the last of the trumpets that indicate the judgments of God, or the critical eras of his administration. It is the signal that all is over, that the curtain is to fall on the eventful drama of redemption. What it shall be, who can tell ? And what matters it ? There is an alarm of some kind, sudden and sharp. And lo ! on the instant, we who are alive, the living members of Christ and of his church, find ourselves altogether ;—invested with bodies no longer natural, corrupt, weak, and vile,— but spiritual, incorruptible, powerful, glorious.

But quick as the transition is, we find a company assembled before us. The dead are raised incorruptible. We do not "prevent," we do not anticipate or get the start of them "that are asleep." They are raised first. Then "we which are alive and remain," being changed, " are caught up together with them in the clouds," that so we and they together may be " ever with the Lord" (1 Thess. iv. 13-18).

It is idle here, and worse than idle, to give the reins to an excited imagination, and paint an ideal representation of that glorious day. The inspired apostle has not dared to do so ; his not doing so is one of the strongest evidences of his inspiration. But surely we do not err in regarding this as the final catastrophe of the church's history on earth. It is not a mere description of successive departures or disappearances of individual men from this world, as these have been going on for ages, and may go on for ages more. The transactions here indicated are simultaneous. There is not a going away of one after another, but a coming together of all into one company. A signal of some sort, like a trumpet sound, is given. At once, the dead in Christ are raised incorruptible. We, the living, are changed. And with renovated spiritual bodies, made like his own, all of us are welcomed to the many mansions of his Father's house, in which the Lord has been preparing a place for us.

17

"FLESH AND BONES" DISTINGUISHED FROM "FLESH AND BLOOD." NEAR KINSMANSHIP OF THE RISEN SAVIOR AND HIS SAINTS

Flesh and blood cannot inherit the kingdom of God.
—1 Corinthians 15:50

For this corruptible must put on incorruption, and this mortal must put on immortality. —1 Corinthians 15:53

Handle me, and see; for a spirit hath not flesh and bones, as ye see me have. —Luke 24:39

IN connection with the announcement (verse 50) that "flesh and blood cannot inherit the kingdom of God"—with the reason implied in its being added (verse 53), "this corruptible must put on incorruption,"—a difficulty is sometimes raised. It is founded upon the supposed constitution of our Lord's corporeal nature after his resurrection, as it is seen in the interval between that event and his ascension into heaven. Did he not, during these forty days, perform acts and offices such as ordinary "flesh and blood" performs? And did he not himself appeal to the fact of his having a fleshly body, to prove that it was not a spirit or mere ghost that appeared to the disciples, but their Lord himself in person?

Now here, generally, it must be remembered that
there hangs over the risen Lord's forty days' sojourn
on the earth a veil or cloud which the Spirit has not
seen fit, by any clear revelation, to remove. Plainly,
his manner of life was peculiar, and wholly different
from what it was before his death. He did not
frequent public places of resort. He did not, as he
used to do, worship in the synagogues or in the
temple. He was not to be met with familiarly in
the common streets and highways, on the mountain
side, or by the sea shore. He did not go about doing
good. He did not even go in and out among his
chosen friends, as was his wont in the more private
hours of his previous ministry. He was not, as of
old, the welcome guest of Lazarus and his sisters in
the quiet village of Bethany. He did not live, as if
at home, among the apostles ; sharing with them
common fare and a common purse. All is changed.
He shews himself only occasionally, and indeed
rarely. And when he does shew himself, it is in a
strange, mysterious kind of way, by glimpses and
momentary flashes as it were, in brief and hurried
interviews,—like " angels' visits, few," if not " far
between." He appears and disappears, abruptly,
suddenly. He comes, they know not whence. He
goes, they know not whither. And none of them
ask him, " Where dwellest thou ?"

(John xx. 1-17). Mary Magdalene, weeping

beside the empty sepulchre, hears her name called. It is the well-known voice of love. She turns and cries, "Rabboni, which is to say, Master!" But she is not suffered to embrace her beloved.* She may not tarry to enjoy his company. A short kind message to the brethren she gets. And lo! in an instant, the interview is over.

(Luke xxiv. 13-32). Two weary travellers are wending their disconsolate way to Emmaus. One draws near, who is apparently, like themselves, a traveller. They do not at first recognise him. He is a stranger; but apparently he is a pious man, who can speak to them of the Messiah's sufferings and glory; and as such they insist on entertaining him. He blesses, in his own well-remembered form, their humble repast. Their eyes are opened;—they know him. And lo! again on the instant, he ceases to be seen of them : he vanishes out of their sight.

(John xx. 19-29). Twice, in successive weeks, on the first day of the week, the little company are gathered together. For security against intrusion, or against something worse, the doors are shut. Unexpected, unannounced, making a way into the room for himself, the Lord stands in the midst of them. They hear the customary salutation, " Peace be unto you," and are glad. They listen to the few words he has to say. But they seek not to detain him, nor

---

* See a probable explanation in the author's " Scripture characters."

does he offer to remain. He goes as strangely as he came. And whither he goeth they cannot tell.

(John xxi.) A party of them go a fishing at the sea of Tiberias, and all the night they catch nothing. As morning dawns, one who seems to be unknown to them is seen standing on the shore. " Children, have ye any meat?" he asks ; and they simply answer, " No." Try once again, is his reply. The miracle which they had seen wrought before at the same spot,—the miracle of an overwhelming draught of fish,—is repeated ;—and the beloved disciple says to Peter, " It is the Lord." A conversation thereafter ensues, when they have come on shore, more like the fellowship of former days than what any of them had had with him since he had reappeared. It is for Peter's sake ;—it is to meet the affecting case of the fallen apostle. That being done, this scene ends as unaccountably as the rest. Jesus is gone, and they are alone again.

(Luke xxiv. 50, 51). Once again he met the eleven, and as it would seem, a larger number, on Mount Olivet, near Bethany, and in the act of blessing them, was carried up into heaven.

Such is the historical evidence of the Lord's manner of existence and intercourse on earth being altogether different, after he rose, from what it was before he died. In the face of this difference, it is scarcely possible to doubt that his natural had become a spiritual body—that it had been raised "in incorruption, in glory, and in power,"—that it was no longer "flesh and blood," but that substance, whatever it may be, into which "flesh and blood" is to be altered when it is to "inherit the incorruptible kingdom of God" (1 Cor. xv. 50).

But there is one particular instance in which the Lord seems to assert the reverse of all this.

When he first stood in the midst of the disciples, his sudden and inexplicable appearance disconcerted them. "They were terrified and affrighted, and supposed that they had seen a spirit." To reassure them, the Lord simply says, "Why are ye troubled? and why do thoughts arise in your hearts? Behold my hands and my feet, that it is I myself: handle me, and see; for a spirit hath not flesh and bones, as ye see me have" (Luke xxii. 36-43).

This verse is sometimes read and commented upon, as if the risen Saviour on that occasion had used identically the same words which Paul uses, "flesh and blood;" or, as if the words which he did use, "flesh and bones," had identically the same meaning. Hence a very serious difficulty is supposed to arise.

To harmonize the saying of Christ with the doctrine of the apostle,—as they are thus respectively understood—some have felt themselves shut up to the conclusion, that our Lord's body did not undergo

the needful change from corruption to incorruption,
—that it did not become a spiritual body,—until his
ascension. Until then, in their view, his risen body
was of the same kind with his body as it hung on the
cross, and as it was laid in the grave. It was on its
going into heaven, that it was so transformed from a
natural to a spiritual body, as to be fitted for its
heavenly immortality.*

There seem to me to be insuperable objections to
this solution of the difficulty. I would not, for my
part, very willingly acquiesce in the idea of my Lord
and Saviour being different, in any material respect,
now that he has ascended into heaven, from what he
was when he shewed himself on earth after his resurrection. I would feel as if I were forced to give up
the strongest proof I have by far of his being the
same person now, in his exaltation, that he was in his
humiliation ; the same as to his entire humanity,
body as well as spirit.

Let me speak as if I were Peter, or John, or any
one of those who had been with Jesus. Let me speak,
for example, as the beloved John. And I would say
—Leave to me the impression which all that I saw
of the Lord after he rose confirms, that he is now in
heaven,—that he is to be when he comes again,—
that he shall be through all eternity,—exactly what
he was when he shewed himself to us during the

* See Dr. John Brown's Resurrection to Life, p. 211.

memorable forty days ;—and I am satisfied. I know
that, however the structure of his material frame may
have been altered at his resurrection, however it may
have been changed from a natural into a spiritual
body, it was not so metamorphosed but that I could
recognise and identify him, as the very friend on
whose bosom I leaned at the supper. And not his
spirit merely, or airy unsubstantial filmy ghost, could
I thus recognise and identify ;—but himself bodily ;
his very self ; seen and felt to be the same as when
he touched us upon the mount of glory, or wept with
us beside the grave at Bethany, or pitied us amid the
agony of the garden. If, however, you tell me that,
changed as I certainly found him to be at his resurrection, he has been still farther changed in his ascension,
—you make him, alas! an unknown friend to me. I
am to see him again, it is true. But what he may be
—what he may be like—when I see him, I cannot
guess. He may be so altered that I shall need
another Baptist to introduce me to him anew (John
i. 35-40). But it cannot be. I remember the angel's
word ; " This same Jesus, which is taken up from you
into heaven, shall so come in like manner as ye have
seen him go into heaven " (Acts i. 11). The glimpses
which I got of him when in his spiritual body he
revisited the earth for a season—glimpses necessarily
imperfect and obscure—assure me that, when I have
risen as he rose, and my body becomes spiritual like

his, we shall know one another in that kingdom of
God which flesh and blood cannot inherit ;—and shall
have fellowship in person one with another, not as
during these few weeks, only now and then, but
uninterruptedly throughout endless ages.

So John might feel! And so I cannot help feeling
too. To me, as to him, the fact of Christ's bodily
nature having undergone all the change it is ever to
undergo at the resurrection, and continuing ever since
to be such as it was shewn to be during the forty
days thereafter,—recognisably substantial, and recognisably also the same as it was before death,—is a
precious confirmation of that most blessed hope, that
in our spiritual bodies, in the heavenly state, we are
to know one another and converse with one another;
that when I and my brother meet on the resurrection
morn ; I among the living who are changed, he
among the dead who are raised ; we shall meet, not
as strangers, but as old familiar friends,—to resume
some interrupted argument, or labour, or song of love
divine,—and to start together on a new course of
study, work, and praise, in the realms of cloudless
light and everlasting bliss.

The resurrection of the Lord from the dead, therefore, and not his ascension into heaven, must surely
be held to be the turning point as regards the great
change which it was necessary should be effected
upon his bodily constitution, in order to fit it for the

heavenly and eternal state. Whatever he is, as to his entire humanity, body as well as soul, when he rises from the grave, that he continues to be,—the same thenceforth and for ever.

And yet he speaks of his having still "flesh and bones." How then, it is asked, can Paul say,—"Flesh and blood cannot inherit the kingdom of God?"

The answer is, that the expressions are not identical. Christ did not say—"A spirit hath not flesh and blood as ye see me have:" but—"A spirit hath not flesh and bones as ye see me have."

Nor is this a mere verbal or technical distinction.

The instances have been already noted in which the phrase, "flesh and blood," occurs.* It is altogether a New Testament phrase. And it has a distinct meaning. It denotes man in his present bodily state, and implies that even at his best, and when doing his utmost, he is unfit while in that state for his eternal heavenly home of light, love, and liberty.

The phrase, "flesh and bones," is quite different, and is, as if of set purpose, differently applied. It is twice used in the New Testament;—first, by the Lord on the occasion now before us—"A spirit hath not flesh and bones as ye see me have;"—and secondly, by Paul when, speaking of our oneness as believers with Christ, he says, "We are members of his body, of his flesh, and of his bones" (Ephes. v. 30).

---

* See Chapter 16.

The corresponding Hebrew phrase is used more frequently in the Old Testament, and always, as I cannot but think, with a very definite import. The following examples may suffice :—

1. Adam says of Eve, his wife, as he receives her from the Lord,—" This is now bone of my bones, and flesh of my flesh " (Gen. ii. 23). 2. Laban salutes Jacob as a kinsman, " his sister's son," when he " runs to meet him, and embraces him, and kisses him, and brings him to his house,"—" Surely thou art my bone and my flesh " (Gen. xxix. 14). 3. Abimelech, paying court to the men of Shechem, " his mother's brethren," reminds them of his relationship to them,—" Remember also that I am your bone and your flesh " (Judges ix. 2). 4. " All the tribes of Israel," coming to Hebron to make him king, claim a family interest in David,—" We are thy bone and thy flesh " (2 Sam. v. 1). It is Judah that evidently takes the lead in trying this argument. 5. David reproaches the elders of Judah, because, although they were his kindred, they were dilatory in welcoming him as he returned in triumph after Absalom's defeat and death; " Ye are my brethren, ye are my bones and my flesh ; wherefore, then, are ye the last to bring back the king ?" (2 Sam. xix. 12). 6. The king appoints Amasa to be captain of the host in the room of Joab, on the ground of relationship,—" Art thou not of my bone and of my flesh ?" (2 Sam. xix. 13).

In all these instances, the idea of affinity, of close personal union and family relationship, is implied. A certain oneness of nature is indicated. And the uniting principle or element,— the seat or tie of union,—is not blood, or "flesh and blood," but "flesh and bones."

In regard to this matter of family kinsmanship, I cannot but think that a difference is to be observed between the Scriptural or Jewish notion, and that of the Gentiles ;—with which last, that of the Gentiles, the modern notion of relationship coincides perhaps more nearly than with the other, that of the Jews and the Jewish Scriptures.

In our reckoning, community of blood, or consanguinity, is the chief connecting bond. So it was among the old Gentiles. And hence Paul, at Athens (Acts xvii. 26), speaks of God as having "made of one blood all nations of men." Such a way of expressing the unity of the race is Gentile and Grecian, not Jewish, nor according to the Jewish Scriptures. There, oneness in respect of marriage, or in respect of the unions of family and of race that flow from marriage, is expressed by a reference, not to blood, but to flesh and bones. Indeed it would almost seem as if, in this connection, the idea of the blood was studiously and of set purpose avoided.

The blood, let it be borne in mind, was understood among the Jews to be the principle of the animal

life. Thus the original prohibition of blood as food
(Gen. ix. 4) runs in this form,—"Flesh, with the life
thereof, which is the blood thereof, shall ye not eat."
So also in the Mosaic law (Lev. xvii. 14; Deut. xii. 13),
the prohibition is made to rest on the same consideration,—"The life of all flesh is the blood thereof;
therefore ye shall eat the blood of no manner of flesh."
"Be sure that thou eat not the blood; for the blood
is the life; and thou mayest not eat the life with the
flesh." The vitality of the body, as it now exists, in
its present mortal state, is held to be in the blood.
Hence, when Satan proposes that Job should be
tried by the utmost severity of infliction upon his
person that is consistent with the sparing of his
animal life, he challenges God to "touch his bone
and his flesh" (Job ii. 5). No mention is made of
his blood. Is not this significant? "His life" is to
be "saved" (verse 6); and the blood is the life. The
blood, therefore, is spared. It is the bone and the
flesh that are touched. He is to be tried in his
person, and in his tenderest personal relationships
and friendships. "But save his life," says the Lord.

If there is anything in this view, the Jewish
mode of expressing kinsmanship, by unity of flesh
and bones rather than of blood, bears the trace or
mark of a higher conception than our Gentile phraseology embodies. To say that you and I are "of one
blood," is to put our unity upon low ground; upon

the ground of our being joint partakers of the same animal nature and lower animal life,—the " life which is the blood." To say that we are " one bone and one flesh,"—that I am "bone of your bone and flesh of your flesh," or you of mine,—if the origin or original meaning of the language is realised,—is to elevate our affinity, our kinsmanship and brotherhood, into a higher region. It is to extricate it from the conditions of the lower economy, in which we are partners with the brutes which perish, and to give it a direction upwards to the state in which humanity is to be perfect, incorruptible, and immortal.

Is it not possible that the words put into the mouth of unfallen Adam on his receiving Eve, his spouse, at the hands of the Lord, may have been intended by the inspiring Spirit for this very purpose, —to place the marriage union on this higher footing? She " is now bone of my bones, and flesh of my flesh?" We are one, corporeally as well as spiritually one ; not, however, as regards our blood merely, or that lower animal life which is in the blood, but as regards the condition of our human nature which is independent of that life, and above it. And is not the apostle's argument about marriage (Eph. v. 30), in which he uses the identical words which Adam spoke concerning Eve, as applicable to the church's relation to her heavenly Spouse, somewhat remarkable in connection with our present argument? He virtually

identifies the union of Christ and his people with the
union of husband and wife. He interchanges, as it
were, or rather associates, what is spiritual in the one
with what is bodily in the other. He gives a corporeal character, in a sense, to the heavenly marriage-
union, as well as a spiritual character to the earthly.
And in doing so he adopts, surely designedly and
deliberately, and not accidentally, the same language
which Adam employs in welcoming Eve. "We are
members of his body, of his flesh, and of his bones;"
—so says the apostle of the heavenly marriage-union.
"This is now bone of my bones and flesh of my flesh;"
—so says our first father of the earthly.

Such being the use and wont, if I may so speak,
of the Holy Spirit in employing this phrase, "flesh
and bones," and such being the marked distinction
between it and the other phrase, "flesh and blood,"—
is it too much to suppose that the Lord had this very
peculiarity of meaning in view when he said,—"A
spirit hath not flesh and bones, as ye see me have?"

He vindicated his corporeity; he asserted his
manhood, his bodily manhood, as still a real bodily
manhood, after his resurrection. And God be praised
that he did so. God be praised, also, that he did so
by a more emphatic and convincing proof than his
merely partaking of human food would have implied.
He did indeed eat once before his disciples (Luke
xxiv. 43). That seems to have been the only instance

of his doing so ; for it is not said that he ate with the two brethren at Emmaus, or with those whom he met at the sea of Galilee. That he condescended, on that one occasion of his first appearance to the eleven gathered together at Jerusalem, to partake of man's ordinary diet, was a most gracious accommodation to the weak faith of his disciples. But on reflection, they might have felt that this was no more than angels, and he himself as the Angel of the Covenant, had done of old, long before the incarnation ; as when the three celestial visitors were entertained by Abraham at noon-day, and the two by Lot at night (Gen. xviii. xix.) They might be thankful for his own surer words, addressed first to them all collectively, and then to Thomas in particular ;—words most significant of continued corporeity in the resurrection state :—" Handle me and see ; for a spirit hath not flesh and bones as ye see me have ;"— " Reach hither thy finger, and behold my hands ; and reach hither thy hand, and thrust it into my side ; and be not faithless, but believing."

There is, therefore, no real inconsistency between the apostle saying " flesh and blood cannot inherit the kingdom of God," and the risen Lord saying, " I have flesh and bones." The two expressions are quite distinct. The first, " flesh and blood," denotes the human bodily nature, liable to dissolution and decay. The other, " flesh and bones," points rather to its higher spiritual development in a structure having extension and form,—bones and flesh of some sort,—but not necessarily of a sort resolvable into dust, and perishable. And when the Lord used that phrase to indicate his resumed corporeity, purposely avoiding the former, he may be understood as addressing to his disciples an affecting appeal.

You thought that I was gone and that you were never to see me more in the flesh. Now, when I appear, you take me for a spirit, from whose approach you shrink as from a strange and alarming phantom. But I have not left you, nor have I taken or received a nature in which you can claim no affinity to me, and I have no union and communion with you. My manhood is still such, that in respect of it I may be your kinsman, and you may be to me, what Eve was to Adam, "bone of my bones, and flesh of my flesh." True, you may not retain me in the body here; I cannot welcome your embraces, as I used to do when I was a sojourner among you; "I go to my Father and your Father, to my God and your God." But I go possessed of a bodily frame in which I am still one with you, and you are still one with me. We are one, as husband and wife are one, or as brethren in the flesh are one. I claim to be still one of you; of the same body and the same family with you. And I would have you to look upon yourselves as still one with me, of the same body, now spiritually quickened, and of the same family, with me ; "members of my body, of my flesh and of my bones."

We surely cannot altogether err in regarding our Lord's remarkable language, especially when interpreted by the scriptural usage, as designed to teach some such lesson as this, ultimately at least, if not immediately, to the apostles and to us. At all events, it is clear that it is no contradiction of the statement that "flesh and blood cannot inherit the kingdom of God; neither doth corruption inherit incorruption."

That statement is the ground on which the apostle rests the assurance that our bodies must and shall undergo such a change as is needful for removing the disqualifications under which they now labour. It must be so, for otherwise we could not enter heaven in the body ;—"for this corruptible must put on incorruption, and this mortal must put on immortality." It shall be so, for we are to enter heaven in the body ;—"So when this corruptible shall have put on incorruption, and this mortal shall have put on immortality, then shall be brought to pass the saying that is written, Death is swallowed up in victory."

What the change is to be, and how it is to be effected, it is needless to inquire particularly. Enough has been said already on that subject. It may be more profitable to notice some practical lessons which it suggests.

I. By an irresistible argument, *a fortiori*, it bars the door against whatever is unholy, impure, sensual, or vile. If even physical corruptibility is inadmissible in heaven, what shall we say of moral defilement? Is the body better than the spirit? If even the righteous cannot pass into these realms of light and glory with a body corruptible and mortal, how think you that you can reach them with mind, heart, and soul, polluted and unclean? How can you, who work iniquity, enter into the kingdom of God, if even sinless flesh and blood cannot inherit it?

Think of the far different doom awaiting you. You, as well as the righteous, survive death. For you, as well as for them, there is a resurrection. But in the Lord's own awful words, it is a "resurrection of damnation!" Your bodies, as well as the bodies of the righteous, will undergo a change then; a change that will make them as indestructible as your immortal spirits are. Oh! what will it be for you to meet your God on that resurrection day!—"unjust still and filthy still!"—furnished with bodies of fearfully enhanced power for evil, and intensified sensibility to pain! What will it be for you to reap in such bodies the bitter, bitter fruits of your sowing to the flesh now! And these bodies, ah! they are made to last for ever. The worm that dieth not will never eat them away. The fire that is not quenched will never consume them. That tremendous sacrifice of righteous retribution is salted with salt for its endless preservation! (Mark ix. 48-50). O ye workers of iniquity, have you no knowledge? Will you not be moved to tremble at the prospect of an eternity like that?

II. How high and holy is that fellowship with Christ into which you are brought, as "members of his body, of his flesh, and of his bones!" He took your natural body, corruptible and mortal, that you might take his spiritual body—incorruptible, immortal. In respect of your corporeal as well as your spiritual nature, you are married, you are united to Christ. You who believe are thus thoroughly, out and out, one with him. Yes! you who believe.

Oh! wondrous power of faith! How mighty a spell lies in so simple an act! Only believe, thou doubting, trembling soul. Believe! Christ is near thee saying to thee, Believe! Believe in me, as joining myself in spirit and in body to thee;—to bear thy sin, to atone for thy guilt;—to take thy place, to be thy substitute, thy surety, thine elder brother, thy kinsman-redeemer;—to obey for thee, to suffer for thee, to bring thee back to my Father and thy Father, to my God and thy God. Believe in me also as joining thee in body and in spirit to myself; espousing thee to myself; that thou mayest be a "member of my body, of my flesh, and of my bones." Believe in me as sharing with thee the very corporeity which I have myself; that I may present thee among my brethren before the Father, saying—"Behold I and the children whom thou hast given me."

Oh! wondrous power of faith, uniting thee thus to Christ! Nay rather, oh wondrous power and glory and beauty of him to whom faith unites thee! And what a union! How close, how constant, how comprehensive! Whatever it was necessary should happen to him, must happen also to thee. "The Lord from heaven" could carry to heaven nothing corruptible, nothing mortal, either in himself or in any of his members. Therefore "this corruptible must put on incorruption, and this mortal must put on immortality."

III. What a motive to be spiritually minded and heavenly minded! And to be so more and more, as our union to Christ grows closer, and the time of our being glorified with him draws nearer!

Our present bodies are corruptible and mortal. In respect of them, we are of the earth, earthy. This condition or quality which now belongs to them, calls for acts and offices which cannot be omitted with impunity. It entails upon us the necessity of dicharging the functions by which life in the individual and in the race is maintained; those functions of the animal organization and the social economy which in this world repair the waste of corruption and the ravages of death. To neglect these functions—to affect a spirituality that is above them—is folly and sin. The direst consequences have ever come of the attempt. Let it be broadly stated, that as he lives now in the body, man must obey the laws and fulfil the ends of his bodily nature and bodily condition. To do so is plainest duty. But surely it is duty that ought to occupy only a subordinate place in his esteem.

About what shall I be occupied? About things relating to my present body, corruptible and mortal? Or about things that will task to the uttermost the energy of my body, when it shall have become incorruptible and immortal? What is to engage my mind, what is to interest my heart? Is it eating and drinking—marrying and giving in marriage? These are indeed matters with which I must concern myself; for they involve the life and health of the body as it now is, and of the social state for which, as it now is, the body is adapted. But the body is not to be long what it is now; the social state for which it is now adapted is to pass away. Mortality is to be swallowed up of life. In heaven they "neither marry nor are given in marriage ; neither can they die any more ; but are equal unto the angels, and are the children of God, being the children of the resurrection" (Luke xx. 35, 36).

Surely the things which should chiefly engage my mind and interest my heart, in the view of what I am then to be, and where I am then to be,—are the pursuits for which my risen body, in that heavenly world, will be adapted, rather than those for which my natural body here on earth is fitted. Surely I should be giving myself to the acquiring of those tastes and habits that will be found to be congenial, when I am raised in Christ incorruptible, in body as well as in spirit, to be with him in glory for ever.

IV. Finally, what a reason is there, in this high hope, for patient waiting, all the days of our appointed time, till our change come. Many and bitter are the griefs occasioned by the corruptible and mortal nature of our present bodies, and the sad vicissitudes of the mortal state with which they connect us. Pain, suffering, sickness, disease, rack the limbs and waste the frame. Sorrow and trouble come, through the ravages which death works in this changing world. But courage! O child of God. It is but a little while. The Lord is about to change all things soon. "This corruptible must put on incorruption, and this mortal must put on immortality. So when this corruptible shall have put on incorruption, and this mortal shall have put on immortality, then shall be brought to pass the saying that is written, Death is swallowed up in victory." Yes! "He will swallow up death in victory, and the Lord God shall wipe away tears from off all faces" (Isa. xxv. 8).

18

THE VICTORY OVER DEATH

So when this corruptible shall have put on incorruption, and this mortal shall have put on immortality, then shall be brought to pass the saying that is written, Death is swallowed up in victory. —1 Corinthians 15:54

"DEATH is swallowed up in victory." The apostle quotes this saying, or prophetic oracle, exactly as it is written in the Old Testament (Isa. xxv. 8); excepting only that he throws it into the passive voice, to adapt it to the form of his discourse; and he makes it express time present instead of time future, to bring out more emphatically the triumph which he celebrates. What Isaiah foretold as future, —"He shall swallow up death in victory,"—is become a present reality, an accomplished fact,—"Death is swallowed up in victory."

The rendering, in our version, both of Isaiah's words and of Paul's, is exactly literal. It is true that the figurative and poetic expression—"swallow up"—may be reduced to the plain prosaic term— "destroy;" and this, accordingly, our translators have done in the verse of Isaiah's prophecy preceding that

now in our view ;—"He shall destroy,"—literally it
is, as given in the margin, "he shall swallow up, in
this mountain, the face of the covering cast over all
people, and the veil that is spread over all nations."
It is true, also, that the phrase,—"in" or into
"victory,"—is often found, in both languages, in the
Old Testament Hebrew as well as in the Septuagint
and New Testament Greek, in connections in which
it must be understood as simply equivalent to—utterly, or for ever. The apostle, therefore, might have
quoted Isaiah thus :—"Then shall be brought to pass
the saying that is written, Death is utterly destroyed ;"
or "Death is destroyed for ever." The saying would
then be virtually the same as that announcement of
John in the Revelation, "There shall be no more
death." And this, in fact, is really what is meant.
But one recoils from so tame and bald a manner of
expressing it. Surely the glowing and vivid ideal of
"death swallowed up in victory,"—is more in accordance with the enthusiasm into which the apostle
has wrought himself as he closes his lofty argument.
And there is a good exegetical reason for keeping the
higher rendering which we have got. Evidently the
apostle attached importance to the word "victory."
It is the key-note of the triumphant strain into which
he immediately bursts forth. The mention of victory,
in Isaiah's oracle, suggests the theme of that glorious
jubilee song : "O death, where is thy sting ? O grave,

where is thy victory? The sting of death is sin, and
the strength of sin is the law : but thanks be to God,
which giveth us the victory, through our Lord Jesus
Christ" (verses 55-57).

The oracle, as Isaiah gives it, points to the
heavenly state. Apart from the apostle's quotation
of it, a fair investigation of the passage in which it
occurs is sufficient to prove this.* It is not, therefore, a mere accommodation on the part of Paul,
when he applies it to the resurrection ; as if he were
borrowing Isaiah's words to express a different
thought from what Isaiah meant. The prophet and
the apostle, inspired by the same spirit, point to the
same event, when the one utters, and the other inter-
prets, that great jubilee note of triumph,—Death is
swallowed up in victory !"

Two ideas are here suggested. First, Death is
swallowed up. Second, Death is swallowed up in
victory. First, there is the event itself to be considered ; then, secondly, the manner and issue of it.

I. "Death is swallowed up." Perhaps it may
look like verbal trifling to dwell on the mere form of
expression here. And certainly it would be un-
warrantable to attempt to make much of what, after
all, is but a figure of speech, meaning, in plain
language, nothing more than that death is destroyed,
or is no more. Still the figure is a striking one.

---

* See Supplementary Discourses 1, 2.

Death, in this world, is the great devourer. He swallows up all living things. He has an insatiable stomach. No nicety of taste, no fastidious delicacy of palate, is his. Indiscriminately, promiscuously, one equally with another, his voracity swallows up all. He is a ruthless, pitiless monster of prey. Neither man nor woman nor child will his horrid appetite spare. The tender babe ; the fair youth ; the blooming maid ; the strong man in his prime ; the veteran, tough and scarred ; the feeble cripple, tottering under the weight of years ;—all come alike to him. He swallows up them all. Hungry and greedy, he prowls in all streets and lanes ; in all highways and by-paths ; in every city, village, hamlet ; throughout all houses. He has agents and purveyors by the hundred who are keenly on the scent to find him food ; insidiously and unscrupulously catering for him ; always, and in every place. Diseases, a multitude that no man can number ; accidents that no man can prevent ; wars, plagues, pestilences ; poverty and famine ; lusts, passions, sins, crimes ;—what troops of ministers has he incessantly doing his pleasure! And with all he gets he is never gorged ; he craves for more. Like the devil whom he serves, he goes about seeking whom he may devour. Bribes, entreaties, tears, alike fail to move him from his purpose. Beauty has no charm—love no spell—to mitigate his rage. Oh! how he riots as his cruel fang pierces the loveliest form, and chills the warmest heart. Power has no weapon to resist his onset. Worth has no protection against his rancour; nor wisdom against his wiles. None are humble enough to be overlooked and pitied. None are good enough to be reverenced and spared. None are high enough to bid him stand at bay. The king of terrors, formidable to all, is himself afraid of none. He seizes and swallows up remorselessly the whole family of man.

Yes! Even when there stood before him one of that family over whom he had no power; one who could say, "No man taketh my life from me"—"the prince of this world has nothing in me:" even when the Son of the Highest, "the Holy One of God," "the man Christ Jesus," "holy, harmless, undefiled, and separate from sinners," stood before him;—and when that holy one on the cross, giving himself a ransom for many, bowed his head and yielded up the ghost; —Death! hadst thou no shame, no scruple, no fear, when thou hadst to deal with him? Was there no misgiving, no relenting, when to the long list of thy victims his name was to be added, and thy mouth was opened to swallow up him?

Truly, O Death! that was thy choicest morsel!— the daintiest and rarest delicacy thou hadst ever tried to devour! But it was thy bane, thy poison, thy ruin. It was the death of thee, O Death! Thou couldst not digest that bloody prey,—that bleeding Lamb of God,—all-ravenous as thou art. Thou couldst not keep him in thy bowels ;—any more than that great fish of old could keep Jonah in its belly. The Lord spake to thee, as to that fish, and compelled thee to "vomit out" his Holy One before he could see corruption,

That was thy first disgorging ! But, O Death ! thou knowest it is not thy last !

On the very morning on which thou hadst to let him go,—the Lord's Holy One, the Lamb of God,—how many "bodies of the saints which slept arose," and left their empty graves ? (Matt. xxvii. 22, 23). These were bodies sown,—thanks to thee,—long before in corruption, but raised,—no thanks to thee,—as incorruptible as that glorious body which, to thy sore discomfiture and dismay, thou hadst then discovered, O Death, could not be "holden of thee."

And on that other morning which is soon to dawn, when the last trump sounds, what an emptying of thy foul maw awaits thee, O thou gross and wormy feeder upon carcasses and carrion !

Give up ! is then the word. And it is the voice of thy conqueror, O death !—the conqueror of him who has "the power of thee," and who wields that power to keep mankind in bondage through fear of thee. Give up my slumbering saints, as thou wast forced to give up me ! They are mine ; "members

of my body, of my flesh, and of my bones." They
are a part of me. I and they are one. While thou
keepest them swallowed up, thou keepest me swallowed up. But I cannot be holden of thee. Not, as
thou well rememberest, in my single person can I be
holden of thee. No, nor, as thou must now be made
to see, can I be holden of thee in these my members.
I have but waited until my body should be complete
in all its members ;—down to the very least of them,
the very lowest, and the very last. And it is complete now. Therefore, let it be given up. Let it go.
Yes! open thy myriad-mouthed throat, thou glutton
of many thousands of years! And from the graves
of earth and the depths of ocean, let my people's sunk
and buried bodies come. They shall come, not as thou
hast made them in thy hideous digestion of them, but
as I am able to make them, like my own body in its
glory. Give me up my mystical body, O death, as thou
wast forced to give me up my natural body. Thou
must needs give it up to me ; and give it up to me,
"the holy one of God,"—as not "suffered" now, any
more than I was "suffered" then, to "see corruption."

And now thou art emptied of all that thou hast
swallowed up since sin gave thee an entrance into
the world. Yes! thou art emptied of all. For not the
bodies of my people only must be given up to be
"fashioned like unto my glorious body ;"—but the
bodies also of those whom he who hath the power of

thee, that is the Devil, may still, alas! claim as his—
they too must be given up to me,—for judgment. What
then remains, when thou hast disgorged all thy dead,
great and small? Prepare to meet thyself the doom
which thou hast inflicted upon them. Thy turn has
come. Thou, O destroyer, art thyself destroyed.
Thou, who swallowest up, art swallowed up thyself.
Starved and lean, stripped of all thy prey, thou art
thyself an easy prey to victory!

II. Thus death, destroyed, gives place to victory.
He, or it, "is swallowed up in victory." This is the
second idea suggested by the oracle. And it admits
of being subdivided into two. First, death is swallowed up victoriously and triumphantly. Secondly,
death is swallowed up and destroyed,—merged and
lost, — in victory. In either view, victory is, as it
were, on the field; determining, on the one hand,
the manner of death's destruction, and on the other
hand, the fruit or consummation of it.

(1.) Death is swallowed up, or destroyed, in victory,
or victoriously; in the open field,—in open fight and
triumph. It is by open conquest that death's ruin is
effected, and not by stealth or by stratagem.

His own successes are mainly gained in this last
way. He got his entrance into paradise sneakingly
and fraudulently. The devil, having "the power of
death," managed to introduce him, through the medium
of sin, by a trick,—an underhand manœuvre,—a

subtle lie. Thus, serpent-like, death meanly crept and crawled into the world. And ever since he has been working for the most part under ground;—or, as it were, by secret plotting. He is everywhere and always busy among men, with his attendant train of grim and ghastly executioners. And yet men live as if there were no death, and no instrument or minister of death, anywhere in all their borders. He is bent on keeping himself and his agents out of sight and out of mind. And for the most part he succeeds only too well in doing so. He is a prince, wielding the power of him who is pre-eminently "the prince of this world." But he wields that power, as it would seem, with an awkward sense of its not being legitimate. He assumes no state ; he affects no pomp ; he ascends no throne. He worms himself insidiously, and by covert means and influences, under the highest state ; the richest pomp ; the firmest throne. He does not interrupt the bargaining of merchants with any intrusive question about " What shall it profit a man if he shall gain the whole world, and lose his own soul? " He does not startle the joyous social circle by any loud voice, or clear handwriting on the wall—" This night thy soul shall be required of thee." He goes about his work far more cunningly ; so cunningly, that men transact their business in the market-place, and take their seats at the festive board, very much as if there were no such potentate as death at all, or as if they had made " a covenant with death, and an agreement with hell," that would hold good for ever. So he entraps his victims, and swallows up his prey. Ignominiously, he ensnares and undermines the objects of his malignant wrath.

But his destruction ;—the swallowing up of death ; —will not be thus stealthy, insidious, and, as it were, underground. It is to be a public and triumphant achievement or exploit. It is to have the character, not of a secret success, but of an open victory, " Death is swallowed up victoriously."

That victorious swallowing up of death will be a terrible surprise to some. " In a moment, in the twinkling of an eye, at the last trump," they find themselves again in the body, as if death had never had any power over them ; nay, more, with the certainty that death can never come to them again. Unawares, almost, and unwittingly, they suffered themselves to fall into the arms of death. It was an easy process ; a process almost of unconscious slumber. But not thus gentle will be the awakening, when death himself is victoriously swallowed up! Abruptly, as by a thunder-clap, they are summoned, in those bodies which death then gives up, to render an account of the deeds done in them on the earth, and reap the fruit of these deeds for ever,—in " the everlasting fire prepared for the devil and his angels."

But for you who, when in death you fall asleep,

are enabled by grace to fall asleep in Jesus,—what a
prospect is yours in connection with this victorious
swallowing up of death! It would be a great matter
to be told that you were to get the better of death on
any terms. You might be well content to be assured
that you would find him gradually relaxing his hold
over you and your brethren ;—and suffering you to
steal one by one into paradise restored and regained,
with the same sort of creeping subtlety, as it were,
with which he insinuated himself into the primeval
paradise at first. To know that death would somehow
at last work himself out of the economy or system to
which you belong ; that one after another you would,
while yielding to him, elude his grasp ; and that thus
escaping, you would find yourselves alive for ever in
the spirit in some world of spirits ;—this would, even
if it were all your hope, be a hope full of immortality.
But it is not thus by flight, so to speak, or by seeming
submission, that you are to be delivered out of the
hands of death. It is not merely a part of you that
is to live on, as if by sufferance, after death has finally
swallowed up the rest of you. You are not merely to
be gathered in succession, as ghosts or spirits, into a
ghostly and spiritual world. That might imply a
limitation of the power of death ; a restriction of it to
your bodily frames. But it would be no victorious
swallowing up of death ; no doing to him as he has
done to you ; no undoing of what he has done. If

the destruction of death is to be a great crisis,—if the manner of it is to be signal and triumphant,—it can be so only when, not as regards believers departing one after another, but as regards all the saints collectively,—and as regards their bodily as well as their spiritual nature,—"this corruptible shall have put on incorruption, and this mortal shall have put on immortality." Then, and only "then, shall be brought to pass the saying that is written, Death is swallowed up in victory!"

It is good to contemplate the manner of death's ultimate overthrow, and to contrast it with the manner of his present dominion. Here and now death reigns. He reigns universally, all-subduing, all-conquering. You do well to watch this grisly king and conqueror, making his way stealthily among the families of men, and one by one picking out his victims; this cunning reaper, putting in his sickle secretly, silently, slyly, to snatch at unawares the tenderest of the grass, the finest of the wheat. Ah! he goes about his work like a coward and a spoiler; and you need to watch lest he overtake you "as a thief in the night."

But with all this wary caution against his wiles, remember what death really is to you who are in Christ Jesus. Think of him as already conquered, and doomed at last to perish ignominiously, at the first sound of the trumpet heralding the conqueror's triumph. Pay him not so great a compliment as to be any more in bondage through fear of him. Tell him, believer, when he draws near to alarm you, that you are content to let him have this corruptible and mortal body of yours ; content to let him do his worst upon it with his devouring jaws ; since you see the day already near, the bright morn already dawning, when he shall himself be swallowed up, and that victoriously, at the glorious appearing of the all-conquering King.

For (2.) As the manner of death's destruction is indicated by this phrase,—" Death is swallowed up in victory,"—so also is the fruit of it, or the consummation in which it issues. There is a victory, a glorious victory ; a victory so glorious, that in its glory the gloom of death is lost ; disappears ; vanishes ; is swallowed up. It is the victory which Isaiah saw in vision, and which, even with all the aid of the Spirit's inspiration, he could but paint inadequately in earthly colours (xxv. 6-8). It is the victory which was shewn also in figure to the beloved apostle in Patmos. The picture of it crowns and closes the book of God.

The elements of the victory are the final overthrow and utter casting out of evil ; the full fruition of the banquet of eternal life ; the city of the Lord coming down from God out of heaven, prepared as a bride adorned for her husband ; the completed marriage of

304 • Nature of the Future Body

the Lamb. The Lord then takes his long betrothed spouse to himself. He comes in person,—henceforth for ever personally to nourish and cherish the church as part of himself,—as his very self,—"the members of his body, of his flesh, and of his bones."

In that joyous consummation, in that nuptial feast, death is not. He expires in the blaze of that triumphant glory. Death yields to that victory and disappears. There is no remembrance of him any more.

O illustrious day! What day in earth's history can be a faint type of thee?

Hark! what shout is it I hear among that handful of long-beleaguered and half-famished men, and women, and children, who, for weary weeks and months, have been forced to be familiar with grim death, as their daily, hourly guest? In how many various forms has the king of terrors been among them! The brave soldier on the ramparts or in the trenches; the sick and wounded in the frail tent or the unsheltered hospital; the delicately nurtured form of beauty; the fond smile of infancy;—death has been busy with them all. It has been a terrible time. Hope deferred has been making all hearts sick. Hunger, care, disease; incessant watching, working, fighting; the enemy's uninterrupted fire; the slow wasting influence of fatigue and famine; have all been conspiring to plunge the little company into the deepest gloom of all but absolute despair. Scarcely, with all their dread of horrid usage if they yield, and all their leal and loyal confidence in the friendly power that is coming to the rescue, can they keep up one another's hearts, and nerve themselves for the endurance of the dismal extremities of distress that are oppressing them. Still they hold on. Drooping and dwindling away, they resolutely hold on, firm and dauntless, in the fierce and almost fatal struggle ; although every moment seems to be bringing them nearer to their inevitable doom. Suddenly—what sound salutes their aching ears ? It is the rattle of friendly rifles. It is the shout of friendly voices. It is the well-known martial music that stirs home memories and home longings in every bosom. The deliverer, the conqueror, is come ! On the instant all is forgotten. Their toil, their weariness, their peril ; their losses and privations ; their sufferings and sorrows ; all is lost and drowned in the glad cheer of welcome that bursts from their all but broken hearts, as with one voice they hail the triumph that sets them free ! Yes ! to them, emphatically, and in their glad experience of relief, death is swallowed up in victory !

Ah ! who may paint the swallowing up of death in victory, when He shall come,—when He draws near, —who has triumphed over all principalities and powers, and who brings to this weeping and grave-covered earth a new and imperishable spring. The groans of creation are ended. There is no more cry of distress, or bitter tear of sorrow. There is no more any memory or thought of the dismal fruits of sin that have been felt so long in the world's painful strife with vanity and corruption. The conqueror appears. All the past is forgotten; it is all lost in the glad and glorious emancipation. Yes! It is in victory that death is finally swallowed up.

But it would be presumptuous to enlarge on a theme like this. I close with one solemn question.

How do you, brother,—how do I,—stand related to this victory in which death is swallowed up? How do we stand related to Him whose victory it is?

Sinner, Godless, Christless sinner! living, dying in thy sins!—thy grave shall give thee up! Thy resurrection to an endless life, as well as that of the holiest of the saints of God, is a part of the victory of Christ in which death is swallowed up. But ah! what share hast thou in the victory and in its fruits? What but the share which the devils have in it, over whom the Lord then finally triumphs? What but a share in the "everlasting fire, prepared for the devil and his angels?"

Be not like the devils, when Christ draws near to plead with you, that, receiving him now, you may reign with him then. Say not, as they said, "Art thou come to torment us before the time?" Let him torment you now;—if it be tormenting you, to cause your sin now to find you out ;—the sad sin of your ungodliness, your unconcern, your unbelief. Put not away from you the movements of his Spirit in your consciences and hearts, "tormenting" as they may be for a time. Let the Spirit shut you up into Christ now ; into his death, as you die unto sin ; into his life, as you live unto God. Be partakers of his grace now, that you may be partakers of his glory at last.

And count it not strange, believers, that if you are to reign with Christ, sharing his crown of victory, you should have, in the meanwhile, to share his cross of shame. Be content to "suffer with him, that you may be also glorified together." Be like minded with Paul in his saying, "I reckon that the sufferings of this present time are not worthy to be compared with the glory which shall be revealed in us" (Rom. viii. 17, 18). And hear the Lord's own words, which surely, whatever application they may have to your experience on earth, point ultimately to the heavenly and eternal state : "A woman when she is in travail hath sorrow, because her hour is come : but as soon as she is delivered of the child, she remembereth no more the anguish, for joy that a man is born into the world. And ye now therefore have sorrow : but I will see you again, and your heart shall rejoice, and your joy no man taketh from you" (John xvi. 21, 22).

19

THE SONG OF VICTORY

O death, where is thy sting? O grave, where is thy victory?
The sting of death is sin; and the strength of sin is the law.
But thanks be to God, which giveth us the victory through
our Lord Jesus Christ.   —1 Corinthians 15:55, 56

THIS is a song of victory.   It is the song of those on
whose behalf is brought to pass the saying that is
written, "Death is swallowed up in victory."   It has
three parts : a confident challenge ; a humiliating
explanation ; a comprehensive thanksgiving.

The challenge is one of triumph ;—"O death,
where is thy sting ?   O grave, where is thy victory ?"
It is not the voice of one daring an assailant and
defying him to the fight,—but of one exulting over a
prostrate foe.   The explanation, again, is of the nature
of a confession : "The sting of death is sin ; and the
strength of sin is the law."   It comes in parentheti-
cally, as if to qualify and abate the lofty tone of the
triumph.   And the thanksgiving fitly crowns the
whole : "But thanks be to God, which giveth us the
victory, through our Lord Jesus Christ."   Thus death

is triumphed over; man is humbled; and the Lord alone is exalted and glorified.

1. THE TRIUMPH OVER DEATH

The most remarkable feature of this triumphant challenge is the acknowledgment of death's victory, and of the manner of it. A sting and a victory belonged to him once. But where are they now? "O death, where is thy sting? O grave, where is thy victory."*

---

* The sense here is little affected by a different reading of this clause of the verse, to which the most competent judges of manuscript authorities seem now, all but unanimously, to incline. According to that reading, there is no mention of the place, or state, denoted by the term *hades*, here translated grave; or, as it should rather be understood, the unseen world, the receptacle of spirits separated from the body. It is death itself which is apostrophised in both clauses. And the words, "sting" and "victory," are transposed. The exclamation then runs thus,—"O death, where is thy victory? O death, where is thy sting?"

Two things may account for the present reading having early crept into some copies of the text. The one is the association of death and *hades* in the Revelation ;—"I am he that liveth, and was dead; and, behold, I am alive for evermore, and have the keys of hell"—or *hades*—"and of death,"—of the invisible world, and the entrance thereto (i. 18). (See also vi. 8 ; xx. 13, 14.) The other is the notion that the apostle is quoting or referring to a prophecy of Hosea;—"O death, I will be thy plagues ; O grave," or *hades*, "I will be thy destruction" (xiii. 14). That Paul had the prophet's bold personification of "death and hades" in his mind,—and that his own still more animated language was partly suggested by it,—

Death, then, has a victory. He is a conqueror; the conqueror. All other conquerors yield to him; he yields to none. He lends his aid to other conquerors. By means of him, and his instruments of destruction, they succeed. But whatever else they may thus conquer, they cannot conquer him. He, on the contrary, vanquishes them. Neither science nor

---

is not improbable. But the two passages are quite distinct; in sense, as well as in phraseology. The apostle celebrates an altogether different deliverance from that which was contemplated by the prophet. And the sentence in which he does so is not the prophet's, but his own.

It may be remarked, indeed, that the introduction of "grave," or *hades*, as the ally of death, is not according to Paul's usual manner of speaking on the subject; nor does it fit in very well into the simple, as well as noble, strain of his note of triumph over the last enemy subdued. It brings in a new and somewhat distracting element, to which no reference has been made in the whole of the long argument that is now concluded. The repetition of the term death, on the other hand, is emphatic; as also is the transference of the term victory from the last clause of the verse to the first. This gives it the priority over sting, and brings it also into immediate connection with the victory claimed in the verse before;—"So when this corruptible shall have put on incorruption, and this mortal shall have put on immortality, then shall be brought to pass the saying that is written, Death is swallowed up in victory." Where then now, O death, is thy victory? Where, O death, is that sting of thine by which thou didst get thy victory?

The meaning, however, when this new turn is given to the verse, is substantially the same as when the old form of it is retained. And therefore, being satisfied on that point, we may continue freely to use the language that has so often thrilled and stirred our hearts: "O death, where is thy sting? O grave, where is thy victory?"

power, neither arts nor arms, can resist him. Thou art the all-conqueror, O death! And what a victory is thine! The traces of it are everywhere. They are indented deep in memory's retentive soil; and freshly furrowed on the warm bosom of love. What tears and groans attest its greatness! It is a victory over all on earth that is brightest, fairest, best. It is a victory which embitters joy, and makes hope grow pale with fear. It subdues and saddens all hearts.

For the achieving of this victory death has a sting. The weapon by which his great success is won is not loud artillery or flashing sword. It is rather like the sharp-pointed goad or prick that pierces the trembling flesh. It is like the envenomed dart which the reptile, or the insect, lances into the warm and flowing life-blood that is to carry the poison all through the system.

This is a mode of conquest neither honourable nor graceful. There is no bravery in it; no dignity; no pomp or pride. Therefore, the humiliation of the conquered is all the greater; the mortification of defeat is all the sorer. It is an ignoble victory that is gained in such a way. It is seen and keenly felt to be so. All the signs and accompaniments of it are of a nature to shock, to offend, to disgust. First, there is the body; so wasted and disfigured by loath-some disease; so shattered, shrunken, paralysed;— or so torn and mangled by horrid accident or bloody

war ;—that even affection's fond eye can scarcely
stand the ghastly sight, but is fain at each new
glance to turn aside. Then there is the mind in
ruins ; the keen eye of intellect gazing vacantly ; the
warm heart unconscious of a friend's embrace ; the
eloquent lips muttering incoherently ; the manly
soul venting its peevish complainings in feeble,
childish treble. The dreary imbecility of age ; the
frenzy of high fever ; the blank idiocy of an exhausted
brain ; the impatient and restless querulousness en-
gendered by long sickness and sore distress—Ah !
how do these, and countless other weaknesses incident
to life's closing scene, invest it with a character of
sad dishonour !—bringing down the very greatest
among men below the lowest level of humanity—

> " From Marlborough's eyes the streams of dotage flow,
> And Swift expires a driveller and a show."

Then there is the lifeless clay, when all is over :—
stiff, stark, cold. Swathe it as you may ;—embalm it
as you please with all sweet spices ;—adorn it with
all gorgeous trappings. Lay it out in state in lordly
hall, on gilded bed. You cannot make it venerable
or honourable. You cannot make it comely, or
pleasant, or lovely. It is a vile body ; a body of
humiliation. You are glad to bury it out of your
sight. So you lay it in the grave ; with ceremony
perhaps, expressive of admiring gratitude : a thronged
procession through the hushed and silent city ;—or

without ceremony, paying it the simple tribute of an honest tear. The tear and the ceremony alike bespeak your sense of the degradation which you sadly lament, or ostentatiously seek to cover. You lay the body in the grave; to be subjected there to new indignities; to undergo deeper abasement still; to be the food of worms; to rot in the corruption of its kindred earth.

Certainly death's victory, thus gained, has nothing in it, or about it, that is at all fitted to dazzle or to fascinate. There is nothing in the painful preparation for it,—there is nothing in the dread accomplishment of it,—there is nothing in the manner in which it is followed up,—of what, in other victories, tends to impose upon the judgment and inflame the imagination. The agencies of disaster and disease that open the way for it; the gloomy accompaniments of it when it comes; the dismal decay that follows; are all fitted to make the victory which death gains, as one by one he conquers the successive members of the human family, seem dark and hideous in our eyes. It is such a victory as a sting might be expected to win.

For surely a sting is a vile sort of weapon. And any victory achieved by it must be vile.

Other means by which victory is got are, as one would say, manly. The conqueror marching at the head of vast armies works, doubtless, misery enough.

His troops devastate the land; multitudes perish; heaps of dead and wounded on many a plain, and the smoking ruins of many a fair city, tell of wide and wasting havoc by fire and sword. Still, with all its horrors, the spectacle is not one of unmingled and unmitigated atrocity. It has its heroic side of glory as well as its blacker aspect of suffering, crime and shame. There are valiant deeds done, and dangers nobly braved; and hardships, trials, losses, wounds, patiently endured. There are acts also of generosity, instances of pity and of friendship, such as redeem the character of the victory, and make it not wholly and merely base. To be thus victorious is glory and fame.

But the sting is a waspish weapon. It is the instrument proper to an angry insect or poisonous worm. To be conquered by such a tool ; to be the victims of a victory which it has been sufficient to secure ; this surely is degradation indeed. The triumph of death over us has nothing in it glorious to him or grateful to us. There is no mitigation of the pain of defeat in yielding to him, as to a brave and generous foe.

Nevertheless, there is glory to be got in the strife with death. There is room for the exercise of stern fortitude, of calm patience, of lofty heroism in meeting him. Your sufferings, when he is fastening his sharp sting in your tenderest vitals, may give occasion for the display of many virtues—as your sufferings under any sting of any wasp might do. To maintain your own equanimity in the trying hour, and soothe the sorrow of friends around you; to die with decency, to die in peace ;—is a great attainment. There is a kind of glory in it; such as might almost seem to dignify your final surrender to the all-conquering power.

If it is nature that nerves you for this manner of yielding to death, natural force of character, the indomitable energy of a strong will,—and men have forced themselves thus to face death firmly,—it is nature proudly recoiling from a defeat which it feels to be ignominious; shutting out the thought of it because it feels it to be ignominious; dwelling upon ideas more flattering to self-complacency than the miserable victory which death is gaining by his sting. And, alas! too often it is nature, choosing to be insensible and blind to what is the chief element of bitterness and degradation in that victory—its being sin that is the sting by which it is gained.

If, again, it is grace which enables you to triumph over death, at the very moment of his triumph over you, "the victory which overcomes" is your "faith;" your faith appropriating life in your risen Saviour, and anticipating in his resurrection your own ;—your faith already, in the full assurance of present peace and the clear prospect of future glory, taking up the triumphant challenge, "O death, where is thy sting?

O grave, where is thy victory?" To you, death now has no victory at all. In your case he has lost the only weapon which he could ever wield to win it ;— he has lost his sting. The victory is now transferred to the other side.

No sting hast thou now, O death, for us ; and therefore no victory over us. The victory is with us ; it is not got by us, but given to us. It is not our own achievement ; it is the gift of God. We cannot spoil thee of thy victory, O death, for we cannot rob thee of thy sting. Thy sting is our sin, and our sin is too strong for us. This, with deep contrition, we confess ;—" The sting of death is sin, and the strength of sin is the law." But we willingly consent to owe all to God. We thank him who "giveth us the victory, through our Lord Jesus Christ."

2. THE HUMILIATION OF MAN

" The sting of death is sin ; and the strength of sin is the law." This confession or explanation, in one view of it, admits of a very short, simple, and summary interpretation.

Sin deserves death ; it is on account of sin that men die. Sin hath entered into the world, and death by sin. Therefore "the sting of death is sin.' But this takes place according to law ; in terms of a strictly legal procedure. It is by enactment of law that the suffering of death is annexed as the penalty to the commission of sin. Death is the consequence of sin. It is so legally. Therefore, as " the sting of death is sin "—so " the strength of sin is the law."

All this is implied in the admission. But is this all that is implied in it ? None who are familiar with Paul's other writings will be easily satisfied with such a view of his meaning here. The chain of thought— death, sin, the law—is a favourite one with this apostle. This is probably the first instance of his use of it ; for the first epistle to the Corinthians is one of his earliest compositions. But one can scarcely imagine that it is introduced in this passage without some intention of indicating the deeper spiritual con- nection among these things—death, sin, the law— which he elsewhere more fully unfolds.

Then, again, we must remember the bearing of the apostle's argument, as he introduces it in the beginning of the chapter. He has been carried some- what aside by the necessity of dealing with the question, " How are the dead raised up ? and with what body do they come ?" It is well that this break in the stream of his inspired reasoning has occurred. It has led him to open up very glorious views of the eternal state, and of our bodily condition there. But he is now brought back to the point from which originally he started. What is his great reason, as stated in the outset, for attaching importance to the doctrine of a bodily resurrection ? If the dead rise not, Christ is not risen. If Christ is not risen, ye are yet in your sins. The guilt of your sins still lies upon him,—and therefore also upon you. You are still helplessly under condemnation,—as he is, if there is no resurrection of the dead.

Plainly this implies that in the case of Christ, when he died, the sting of death was sin, in the sense of sin being not merely the cause of his death, but the characteristic of it too ; that which gave it its distinctive feature, as being strictly penal and retributive. Sin stung him in his death, as bringing upon him the doom of wrath, the curse or condemnation of the Holy God. Your sin thus stung him when he died. And thus it must for ever sting you, but for his having risen, and your believing in him as risen.

Surely therefore there is more in the confession— "The sting of death is sin,"—than the mere acknowledgment that sin is the occasion, or the cause of death. It is not said merely that the sting of death is the effect of sin ; or that sin lets in that sting of his by which death achieves his victory. Sin is that sting. He gets his power to sting through sin. He makes sin itself his sting. It is a sore and cruel sting ; piercing not the body only, but the spirit also ; inflicting a deadly wound on the whole man ; aggravating a thousandfold the bitterness and degradation of death's victory. He comes to conquer, introduced by sin. Sin treacherously throws open the gate, and allows him entrance into the city. That is saying much for the evil of sin. But that is not all; that is not the worst. Death, the conqueror, entering in through sin—through sin opening the gates for him—compels the traitor to become his tool. He takes sin along with him in carrying out his conquest. He stings on account of sin; he stings by means of sin. Sin is his weapon as well as his warrant. Literally and emphatically "the sting of death is sin."

Here then is a new element of humiliation connected with the victory of death over us, besides those already noticed. They are chiefly physical or natural; this is spiritual. They are temporary and comparatively momentary in their operation; this has issues that reach into eternity.

Ah! when viewed in this light, the victory of death is complete indeed. It is not merely the killing of our body; it is our being cast into hell. If sin is the sting he uses when he conquers us, that must be the fruit—that must be the inevitable effect of the conquest. Truly it is a fatal wound which that sting inflicts;—a wound for which, when death has triumphed by means of it, there is nowhere in all the universe,—never throughout endless ages,—any cure or palliative to be found.

O thou stern and pitiless conqueror, couldst thou not have employed some other weapon for working thy will upon us, poor children of the dust ? Couldst thou not have taken a less cruel advantage of the power which our sin gave thee over us ? Could it not content thee to fill this goodly earth with graves, but thou must people with thy victims the place of everlasting fire ? Was it not enough for thee to take the scythe of time, and with it mow down frail men like grass, but thou must wield as thine instrument that sting of sin which sends them, guilty and lost, to the torments of hell for ever ?

No ; thou repliest ; and for once, O death, thou repliest truly. Thou hadst no alternative. The weapon was not of thy seeking ; it was put into thy hands when thou hadst thy commission given thee, to go forth conquering and to conquer. Sin was then appointed to be thy sting. No other instrument was allowed to thee but sin to be thy sting. And if it is a sting of such terrible power to hurt, that is no fault of thine. Thou didst not give it that power to hurt ; but the law ; for "the sting of death is sin ; and the strength of sin is the law."

Were it not for the law,—the holy and righteous law of God,—sin, as the sting of death, might have less strength to injure the victims whom death subdues. And, for his part, death might be well satisfied to have it so. He might not be unwilling to accept a milder reign ; a triumph less disastrous to the conquered.

Nay, sometimes it might almost seem as if he did thus gently sway his sceptre. For death, twin brother of sleep,—gentle death, sweetest image of placid slumber,—has at times a winning way of his own. The grim king of terrors can assume the aspect of a babe smiling in its calm repose. To the weary, worn, wasted soldier in life's dreary battle-field, he opens his arms, inviting him to rest on his bosom, as in a mother's fond embrace.

Oh! who among us has not often felt as if he could welcome death as his best friend! When the heart is broken with sorrow, or the mind dizzied with care ; when there steals over the whole soul a bitter sense of loneliness and vanity ; when losses and dis-appointments, the malice of enemies, the ingratitude of friends, combine to make earth appear a desert, the world a desolation ; when every charm of life is gone, and I see nowhere any refuge from doubt, and dark-ness, and despair—Oh! "how still and peaceful is the grave !" Fain would I lay in it my aching head !

At such an hour death presents himself, not clothed in gloom, but seeming fair. "He that hath the power of death, that is, the Devil," is no doubt with him ; but he is transformed so as to be wearing the image of "an angel of light." The sting of death has then for me no terror. Death promises to use his weapon tenderly ; and his companion backs the promise. The fatal dart is hidden. I care not to ask what, or where, it is. I take for granted that all is well—till, hugging me in his grasp,—hark! what fiendish satanic shout is that I hear beside me? —he flings me,—with a worm in me that shall never die,—into fire that never shall be quenched!

Or perhaps on some occasion when I have to confront death face to face, the apprehension of his sting does at first give me trouble. I am afraid to die. For I know that I am a sinner;—and I dare not think of what my sin, in death's hands, as his sting, may do to me. I tremble when I call to mind what I have been told, that it has a terrible power to destroy me everlastingly.

Not so!—it is the friendly voice of death; and his accents are bland; and the same shrewd ally is with him to corroborate what he says;—Not so! Think not so badly of me as to imagine that I would wield against you a weapon so deadly. True, I am obliged to use your sin as my sting; and there has been something said about what sin deserves, and what must be its inevitable doom. But you cannot surely imagine that so kind and gracious a God,—so merciful and loving a Father,—as He is whom by your sin you have offended, will be so unrelenting as to let that sin of yours, which is my sting, put forth all its strength to condemn you evermore. If, indeed, your God and Father were to act very rigorously towards you, and visit you with the full penalty of your offences, there would undoubtedly be in your sin, as my sting, a strength, and power, and force, that must consign you to eternal ruin. But the force will be abated ; the power restrained ; the strength relaxed. You will not be treated so severely. Matters will not be pressed so hard or so far. My sting will not strike so strongly. Your sin, which is my sting, will be extenuated and softened down. "You shall not surely die ;" at least not for ever. Thus plausibly would death, and his ally or master, persuade me.

Am I tempted to listen credulously? Are their smooth prophesyings beginning to tell on me?

Let me hear another voice sounding in my ear— "the strength of sin is the law." It is the voice of God's word to me. Let it be the voice also of God's Spirit in me. It comes just in time. Let it be in time! It comes not a moment too soon!

Were it anything else that constituted "the strength of sin;" its strength to condemn, and to hand me over condemned to death ;—the second death as well as the first ;—there might be some hope of death's sting being mitigated and mollified in my favour. Were it passion in the breast of the highest,—or policy, —that made sin a capital crime in his dominions, there might be room for some proposal of adjustment that would make sin venial, and death therefore comparatively stingless and harmless. Were it even such a necessity of sequence as is observed in the natural world; did the strength of sin to condemn lie in any mere law of nature, analogous to the law that regulates the falling of solid bodies to the ground; if it were by such a law that sin got its deadly power; can we doubt that it would be as a gossamer thread in the grasp of him who, in the teeth of all such laws, walked upon the water, and gave health to the sick, and sight to the blind, and life to the dead? He certainly did not come to expiate the guilt of a breach of the law of gravitation, or of the law of health. No; nor to expiate the guilt of any breach of some supposed law of love in the higher regions of human experience that is of the same created character with these. It is no such law that is the strength of sin. If it were, we may well believe that there would be no difficulty, on the part of a gracious God, in its being so relaxed as to make sin, in the hands of death, a very gentle weapon;—a very mild and modified sting.

But it is not passion; it is not policy; it is not order; that originates and enforces this law. The law which is the strength of sin, has its origin in the very nature,—it has its enforcement in the high authority, —of the holy and righteous ruler over all. This is what makes sin, as the sting of death, strong. Passion might be pacified; an angry God might be appeased. Policy might admit of arrangement; a diplomatic expedient for accommodation might be found. The natural order and sequence in virtue of which suffering comes in the train of sin, might be superseded or suspended, ere the case became desperate. But law,—the law of which sin is the transgression,—is inexorable, inviolable. It is unchangeable as the nature and authority, the being and the throne, of God himself. And this law is the strength of that sin which is the sting of death.

Is then the law my enemy? Is it of the law that I complain when I say—" The sting of death is sin ; and the strength of sin is the law?"

God forbid! "The law is holy; and the commandment holy, and just, and good." True, I am taught that this law is the strength of sin. It is the Spirit in the word who teaches me. True, also, I am made to feel in my inmost soul that this law is the strength of sin. It is the Spirit in my conscience and heart that makes me feel it. The law comes home to me ;—" I was alive without the law once ; but when the commandment came, sin revived, and I died." " Sin, taking occasion by the commandment, deceived me, and by it slew me." Nevertheless, although thus in my experience " the strength of sin is the law,"— " I delight in the law of God after the inward man." I approve of it, I love it—even when I am deeply, nay, almost despairingly, conscious of its being to me "the law of sin and of death" (Rom. vii.)

This indeed is my misery ; this is my shame and

grief; that the good and holy law of my God,—the more I apprehend and feel its holiness and goodness, —does but strengthen all the more the sin in me which is the sting of death. The guilt of sin that is on my head and the corruption of sin that is in my heart come out only the more prominently and painfully, the more that good and holy law is put within me. The convincing Spirit humbles me in the presence of death obtaining the victory, in strict terms of law, over me, a transgressor of law. I bow in lowliest self-abasement before the holy and sovereign majesty of him whose kingdom rests on this immutable ordinance of righteousness:—"The wages of sin is death." Yes! I am constrained to justify God in my own condemnation,—accepting the punishment of my sin;— "Against thee, thee only, have I sinned, and done this evil in thy sight; that thou mightest be justified when thou speakest, and be clear when thou judgest" (Psalm li. 4).

3. THE THANKSGIVING

"But thanks be to God, which giveth us the victory through our Lord Jesus Christ." I. It is victory that is here acknowledged; not escape and deliverance merely, but victory. II. It is through our Lord Jesus Christ. And, III. It is the gift of God through him.

1. Victory is ours. " Where is thy victory, O death?" The fortune of battle is turned. We have the victory now.

And what is this victory? It is victory in an open court of law; victory in the high assize of heaven's eternal justice. No victory of any other sort would now satisfy me, if I am taught by the Spirit to reverence the government of God as a government, not of arbitrary force and mere will, but of righteousness and righteous law. Nor, indeed, would any other than a legal victory give me a right to triumph over death.

For his conquest over me is achieved by means of law, and the conditions and sanctions of law. It is by calling forth against me the sentence of the law, that death gets my sin to be his sting, and so subdues and slays me. That is his victory. Is it any victory on my part, to be set over against his, if I steal away without venturing to meet him at all ; or if I meet him anywhere else than on the floor of the law's judgment hall? Mine must be a legal, a judicial victory over death. It must be as unchallengeable in law as is death's victory over me.

But mark a signal difference here between our victory over death and his victory over us. How does the honourable character of the one contrast with the underhand manner of the other!

For how does death prevail in making good his

victory? He goes to work according to law. But he goes to work stealthily and slily. He gets us to commit sin. How? It is by telling us a lie; availing himself of the lie of Satan—"Ye shall not surely die." He thus cheats us into sin; and our sin, to which the law gives a condemning strength, becomes immediately his sting. By means of it death keeps us, " through fear of him, all our lifetime subject unto bondage." " Sin, taking occasion by the commandment, deceives us, and by it slays us." Such are death's tactics; such is his victory.

No such tactics, no such victory, will now satisfy our conscience, or meet our case. We will not consent, any more than Paul would consent (Acts xvi. 37), to be let out of prison and get off privily, as it were,—by sufferance and by stealth. Our discharge must be in the face of day, and in terms of law,—of law openly "magnified and made honourable." Otherwise it is really no victory at all. It may be a flight, or an evasion, or a compromise; it may be a feigned truce; it is no true triumph.

II. It must necessarily be victory that is ours, " through our Lord Jesus Christ." It is he who undertakes to deal, on our behalf, with death the conqueror. And how does he deal with him?

He fully acknowledges death's victory. Nay, more, he acknowledges its legitimacy or lawfulness. Thou hast conquered, O death. Thou hast conquered

by an adroit and dexterous misuse of law. The law
has been so presented to men as to irritate and offend.
It has been made to appear harsh and stern. Feelings
of jealousy have been awakened. The pride of inde-
pendence has been appealed to. Desires, impatient
of subjection to mere arbitrary will and power, have
been called into violent exercise. Thus thou hast
got men,—or Satan thy master has got men,—to rebel
and commit sin.—And their sin is thy sting.—And
by it thou conquerest. It is all according to law ;
strictly according to law. It is a cruelly unscrupulous
way of applying law :—to irritate, to deceive, and
then to slay. Still it is all strictly legal. And now
since the thing is done, and so done,—and thou art
thus victorious, O death,—he who encounters thee as
our champion will meet thee on thine own ground,
with all the advantage on thy side which the law
thou hast so cunningly worked allows thee.

Come, then, O death ! Put forth thy sting, with
all the strength the law can give it. Here is one
inviting, courting the infliction ; waiting for it ;
" straitened until it be accomplished." Spare him
not, O death. Thou hast a hold over him, such as
thou never hadst over any other of the race of man.
Sin is upon him ; more sin than millions of the
human family have to answer for. He is made sin
for us—for us, countless myriads of miserable sinners.
There is a sting for thee to use—sin, all the sin that

he made his own. And thou needst not fear lest its strength should be weakened, or its power to condemn relaxed. The law is firm. The lawgiver is firm. "Awake, O sword, against my shepherd, against the man that is my fellow, saith the Lord of hosts!" The cup cannot pass from him!

It is done! Thy sting is sheathed in the bleeding body, in the agonized soul, of Emmanuel. Death! thou hast triumphed. Thou hast darted thy sting into the highest and noblest victim thou couldst ever have. But it is a triumph involving infinite hazard for thee. For if he can survive the stroke, then for him, and for all that are his, thy sting is exhausted. And where, O death, is thy victory then?

He does survive the stroke. Your sins, O my brother sinner, and my sins, numerous, heinous, aggravated,—the accumulated and concentrated venom of the guilt of all the sins of all his people ;—which was the sting that pierced him when he voluntarily yielded himself up to death ;—could not destroy that divine and holy one. It pierced him sore, that sting. It wrung from his body the bloody sweat, and from his soul the cry of agony ; "My God, my God, why hast thou forsaken me !"———

Oh! that all careless sinners were moved to ask themselves how they are to endure in their own persons, and through a long eternity, without relief, or remedy, or alleviation, that burning sting of sin which cost the Lord such tears and groans !———

But now sin, the sting of death, has done its worst. The cup of wrath which it filled with its own poison is drained. And lo! that crucified one lives. He lives again in the body, in his manhood, complete and entire ; as free as if the grave clothes had never bound him ; as pure and spotless as if sin had never touched him ; living as if death's dart had never drawn his blood ; glorious in his righteousness ; mighty to save ; having life in himself, and quickening whom he will. And he wills,—does he not ?—to quicken thee, brother, and thanks be to his name, to quicken also me!

Death! Hast thou any other sting to try on this man, who is the Lord from heaven ? Go, ask the law which is the strength of sin,—of the sin which is thy sting. Once the law strengthened and sharpened thy sting; made it quick and powerful, and oh, how keen! —dipped it in the dark and pestilential fiery flood of hell ; gave it into thy hands, and bade thee do thy worst with it upon "the man Christ Jesus." Go back now to that law, O death, and tell the issue. Thy sting was thrust sore and deep into the bosom of that holy one, and yet thy victim liveth. Will the law, will the lawgiver, allow thee to have another chance ? Will it put into thy hands another sting to supply the place of the one that has been spent and is now gone? Can sin be twice visited;—punished a second time in the same person, in the same sufferer? Shall not the judge of all the earth do right? The vindicated and satisfied law will strengthen and sharpen no sting for thee now to use any more against the risen, righteous Lord.

Then where, O death, is the victory now? Confess; it is not with thee, but with him; it is his. And confess, too, that he has gotten it fairly. Legitimately, lawfully it is his, as lawfully as ever it was thine. There has been no advantage taken in the fight; there was no favour shewn to him; there was no relaxation of the conditions, no abatement of the rigour, of that bitter encounter, that he might be spared. The furnace was heated seven times for him. The sword was freshly whetted when it awoke against him. Death, armed with sin as his sting, and backed by the law which is the strength of sin, had fair play and full scope. The victor triumphs righteously, and is crowned lawfully. Therefore the victory is glorious.

III. And is that victory ours?— Is it yours, O believer, yours and mine? Even so. "Thanks be to God who giveth us the victory;"—the very victory his Son has got. Yes, it is ours; freely given to us of God, if we will but receive it as his free gift, "through our Lord Jesus Christ."

Ah! it was no free gift to him. This victory was not freely given to him. Sore and sad was that travail of soul by which he had to win it. Great, infinitely great, the price he had to pay for it, the price of his own blood ; his own endurance of the curse, the condemnation, due to our sin. Fierce and terrible was the agony of that hour of darkness. Truly it was a costly victory to him.

And is it to cost us nothing to make it ours ? Are we to have it "without money and without price?" Have we no work to do for it, no term to serve for it, no condition to fulfil for it, no blood to shed for it, no law to obey for it, no expiating pain or penance to endure for it?

Oh ! "thanks be to God who giveth us the victory through our Lord Jesus Christ !" Thanks to him for this, that it is his good pleasure to give it to us in free gift. For never otherwise could it be ours. We could never merit it ; we could never earn it ; we could never win it by any suffering. That sting of death, which is sin, sharpened and strengthened by the law, must ever prove too powerful for us.

Have you not experimentally found it so ? Have you not tried and failed ? I speak to you who know the law ; who know it by the Spirit bringing it home to your conscience and your heart, and causing you to apprehend its holy, heart-searching spirituality, as it is ever urging against you its condemning sentence. You have known sin by the law ; you have known its sting, and the strength of it. You have been involved in that struggle of an awakened conscience with a heart reconciled to the authority of the law, which brings out the innate and inveterate power of indwelling corruption ; the evil in you,—the heart-sin of ungodly and unholy desire,—which, resisting all your attempts to subdue it, and baffling your utmost energy of will, stings you the more keenly the more closely you grapple with it, and sinks you ever deeper and deeper in helpless guilt and hopeless condemnation.

Yes! And have you not known, will you not now consent to know, the relief, the gladness, the blessedness, of trying a more excellent way ? Reduced to utter straits, forced to cry out in bitterness of spirit, as your case seems to be getting worse, the more you try to better it,—" O wretched man that I am! who shall deliver me from the body of this death ?"—will you not be persuaded, instead of painfully working for deliverance yourselves, to accept victory as the free gift of God? It is not far off, long to wait for, far to seek ; this deliverance which you need ; this victory ; full, complete, secure. It is yours now in Christ ; yours for the taking ; yours if you will but have it to be yours. Yes! " there is now no condemnation to them that are in Christ Jesus." To you in Christ the law is no more the strength of sin ; for it is satisfied ; Christ in your stead has fulfilled all its righteousness and endured all its curse. Sin therefore

has no more power to condemn you, or to reign over
you. You are emancipated and free ; free, as accepted
in the beloved, and quickened in him to newness of
life ; free to " walk not after the flesh but after the
spirit." Well may we now exclaim, " I thank God,
through Jesus Christ our Lord." " Thanks be unto
God who giveth us the victory through Jesus Christ
our Lord." " Thanks be unto God for his unspeakable gift."

Thus gracious, thus glorious, is the victory which
God giveth us through Jesus Christ our Lord, in its
very commencement ; in the first experience of the
believer ; when he finds the dark and malignant
strength of sin broken ; and light, liberty, enlarge-
ment, beginning to break in upon his soul ; through
his simply receiving and resting on the Lord Jesus
Christ, as meeting and answering the law's demands
in his stead, and·so becoming to him the author of
eternal salvation.

And if it be so in its very commencement, what
may it be expected to be in its subsequent progress,
and in its consummation !

Ah ! it is a victory that is ever brightening as we
press on in our christian course and calling ! The
security of it is ever more and more distinctly seen.
The peace of it is ever more and more deeply felt.
The high hope which it animates is ever more and

more eagerly grasping the fulness of its everlasting heavenly joy. It is a victory which, as we gather the fruits of it in our daily walk with God ;—walking at liberty, and having respect to all his commandments ;—gives forth more and more of its grace and its glory ;—its grace as won for us by Christ, its glory as realised by us in Christ. Until at last the full and final triumph comes, in that day when the body, as well as the soul, is made partaker of it ; when this corruptible puts on incorruption, and this mortal puts on immortality, and the saying is brought to pass which is written, Death is swallowed up in victory !

20

STEADFASTNESS IN THE FAITH
OF THE RESURRECTION

Therefore, my beloved brethren, be ye steadfast, unmovable. —1 Corinthians 15:58

THE argument for a future state and a bodily resurrection which the apostle has been so nobly maintaining, settles down into a very simple, but very earnest and affectionate, practical appeal. It is an appeal which joins together hope and work ; the hope of future glory, and the present duty of work. And it does so through the medium of faith.

For the exhortation, "be ye steadfast, unmovable," has respect to faith. It is an exhortation to a rooted and unshaken firmness of adherence to the belief of the truth. But the faith is to be active and operative; "always abounding in the work of the Lord." It is to be so because it works and labours in hope—"forasmuch as ye know that your labour is not in vain in the Lord." On the ground of all that this lofty argument proves, faith may well be firm. In the view of all that it opens up, hope may well be bright, and therefore work may well be abundant.

First, then, let the exhortation to constancy in the faith be duly weighed :—"Therefore, my beloved brethren, be ye steadfast, unmovable."

These words, "steadfast and unmovable," have substantially the same meaning, but with some difference of shade. If, speaking of a building, we call it steadfast, the idea suggested is, that it is a work of strong masonry, standing firm on a solid foundation. To say of it that it is immovable, is to call attention to its being proof against wild storms and violent assaults. The two thoughts are intimately connected. It is its being steadfast that renders the fabric immovable. It is immovable, because it is steadfast.

It is evidently in the belief of the resurrection of the body that we are to be thus steadfast ; having a well-grounded conviction of the truth of the doctrine, and a strong sense of its importance. For it is our sense of its importance that will lead us, when thoroughly satisfied as to its truth, to be very firm and tenacious in keeping hold of it. Let us, with a view to this, recapitulate the grounds on which the apostle rests his own impression of its being a vital question that is at issue.

I. It touches the credibility of those on whose testimony our faith rests (ver. 15). This is surely a very serious consideration. For if the apostles of the Lord are not to be believed, when they tell us that they saw him alive in the body, after he was dead and buried,—and when they appeal for corroboration of what they tell to some five hundred brethren, most of whom are still alive ;—the very apostles, upon the foundation of whose testimony we, as believers, are built ;—where is the proof of Jesus Christ himself being the head corner-stone ? The divine mission of Christ is no longer certain. For if the reality of the bodily resurrection of Christ is called in question,—as it must be if you listen to those transcendental spiritualists who scout the idea of there being any bodily resurrection in connection with the life to come,—the integrity, not to say the authority, of the apostles, as Christ's witnesses, is overthrown ; and as a necessary consequence, their whole testimony and teaching concerning our blessed Lord is cut up by the roots.

II. But not only generally is the Lord's divine authority thus involved in the question of the resurrection ;—the reality, in particular, of his great work of propitiation is at stake.

Here let two questions be plainly faced. First, is death the penalty of sin ? Secondly, is it from the penalty of sin that Christ redeems us ?

First, is death the penalty of sin ? I do not enter into any consideration of death, as the law or condition of being among those tribes of animals that are not appointed to live for ever. There may have been, there certainly was, a reign of death over the reptile and monster races that peopled earth and ocean for ages before the birth of man. For anything that Scripture says, even if man had never sinned, death might have continued to prevail among the creatures made for man, and placed under man's dominion. It may be a universal law of this lower creation of God, that the brutes, not having immortality, must perish successively by death. I see nothing in the Bible against that view.

But it is a very different thing when there appears on earth, among these brutal tribes, a being of a higher order ;—fashioned partly like them, but endowed with that high gift of intelligent and spiritual life which they have not. Here is a family, not merely designed for prolonged existence as a race whose individual members perish,—but every one of whose members is destined to live for ever. Such a being, such a family, cannot well be subject to death, by anything like the same kind of natural law as that which takes effect on the successive generations of the lower animals. It may be the design of their Creator, that after due probation, the individual members of this new family shall undergo, one by one, some change, transforming their natural bodies into spiritual bodies, and shall so pass, one by one, into some higher and more spiritual and perfect state of being, for which their material frames may thus be adapted. But whatever provision may be made for their undergoing such a change and passing into such a state, it cannot be at all analogous to what happens to the brutes when they die. For in the case of the brutes, death is a provision, not for their passing into another state of existence, but for their perishing finally. If man is appointed to die, as they die, it must be in virtue of some other sort of law than that physical or natural law which ordains their death. And so, accordingly, it is. Not by the necessity of any physical or natural law, originally imposed upon him at his creation, but by the sentence of an authoritative moral law, which he subsequently chose to violate, man is doomed to die. Death is not to him the law of his constitution,—operating, as other laws of nature do, by a force and in a manner of which no other account can be given than simply that things are so ordered. It is the judicial and retributive punishment of the sin which he committed in voluntarily transgressing the holy and good law of his God. Death, in his case, is not the ordinance or arrangement of the Creator ;—it is the verdict and award of the Judge. It is not as a creature, but as a criminal, that man dies. No other death on earth is like his. Such is the uniform testimony of Scripture, in passages far too numerous to be quoted.

It is not meant, of course, that man's being made subject to death, in common with the other animals, is the whole of the penalty of his sin. When he was sentenced after his fall, he was doomed to undergo many evils in this life preliminary to death ; shame, remorse, fear, sorrow, suffering, toil ;—expulsion from Eden, with the necessity of cultivating, instead of a teeming garden, a comparatively barren waste ;—the loss of his Maker's love, and the helpless dread of his Maker's righteous wrath. Then there is the state into which death ushers the guilty soul ;—passing, as one says, " denuded of all but conscience, into the open presence of the Holy One ; "—and that other state which is to begin, when " all that are in their graves shall hear the voice of the Son of God ; " " and they that have done evil shall come forth to the resurrection of damnation."

Still, of all these terrible inflictions, death, with sin as its sting, is, as it were, the index and type. They are all summed up in death ;—the subjection of a rational and imperishable being, conscious of guilt, to the ordinance of death ;—and that by the just sentence of a judge, authoritatively enforcing the sanctions of statutory law. Hence, while death, as a law of their nature, sits light on the unthinking brutes that perish,—to man death is bitter, as the wages and the punishment of sin.

But now, secondly, Is it from the penalty of sin, —is it from death as the penalty of sin,—that Christ redeems us ? It cannot be, if there is no resurrection, and if consequently Christ is not risen.

This is so very clear, that such reasoners as I have now in view—and they are to be found in the modern as well as in the ancient church—would scarcely think it worth their while to question it. They do not contend for anything like a literal redemption of guilty men by Christ; his literally giving himself a ransom for them; taking their place, as criminals, condemned by a legal and judicial sentence to a penal death; and by his endurance of that death in their stead delivering them. Death, in fact, according to them, was not really a penal infliction upon Christ at all. It could not be so. For it is not really a penal infliction upon the sinners whom he came to save. Hence his death was not vicarious; it was not his endurance of the penalty of the law in the room of those who had incurred that penalty. He was not in any such sense " a propitiation for our sins." That he came in our nature,—and lived, laboured, suffered, and died on our behalf,—these persons admit and strongly hold. He came to be our brother; and as our brother, to go through all the experience through which we have to pass. It is an experience having in it many elements and ingredients of trial and pain;—including the dissolution, by suffering and decay, of this corruptible mortal frame, that our better part may survive and live. Christ, uniting himself as a loving brother to us, went through it all; carrying us, in some mysterious way, along with him. And we, united to him as brethren, are enabled to go through it all as he did, and so to reach in him perfection.

Such seems to be their idea of the Son's work of mediation and atonement. And, indeed, it is the only sort of idea of it which they can well have, so long as they do not recognise,—either the penal character generally of the death which sinners have to die ; or the penal character in particular of the death which Christ, as bearing sin, died. In their view there is no occasion, and indeed no room, for Christ in his death being really the substitute of sinners. Sinners, in fact, need no substitute ; they can have none. A companion they may have ; an example ; a sympathising brother ; a leader and captain ; a representative also, in some sense and to some effects ;—but not a substitute. There can be nothing in Christ's death, any more than in their own, beyond the operation of an ordinary law of nature ; nothing indicating the sentence of a higher law of an altogether different sort ; nothing, therefore, demanding such assurance of that sentence being reversed as a resurrection alone can give. They, accordingly, who conceive thus of man's mortality and of Christ's mediation, can afford to look with a large amount of indifference on the doctrine of the resurrection—Christ's resurrection and their own. With them the question as to a real bodily resurrection has little or no bearing on the redemption of the world by Christ; or on man's hope in Christ for eternity.

But it must be otherwise with us who own the condemning power of sin. Death is not, in our view, a debt of nature. It is a debt of law; a legal punishment; a judicial infliction. It has a strictly penal, a deeply penal, character. We die by sentence of law. That is the character of our death. That is the character and meaning of the death which Christ dies on our account. Will it do, will it suffice, if he thus die for us and rise not again? We believe that the death from which he has to redeem us is a penal death. We believe that he has to redeem us from it vicariously; by a vicarious substitution of himself in our room and stead. Is the redemption complete—is there any redemption at all—if he still underlies that penal death?—if he has not broken its bands, and come forth anew into a life to which the legal penalty of death can attach itself no more for ever?

"Therefore be ye steadfast and unmovable." Those who seek to move you from your settled faith on this subject can afford to be moved from it themselves. They do not take the views which you take of sin, and what sin deserves; of death, and what death involves. But sin to you is deadly. And death by sin is eternal ruin. How can any redeemer who dies for you, and does not rise again, meet your case? If he really dies for you, it is a penal death that he dies. He dies by sentence of law. And if he does not rise again, he is still under that sentence of law by which he died. There is no reversal of it, for him, or for you. If your sin has brought upon you the flood of judicial wrath,—and if Christ is to be your Redeemer, by plunging himself into that flood, and letting its stormy waves go over his head instead of yours,—the sacrifice is vain unless he himself first emerge and come out from among the billows. Without the resurrection of Christ there is really no redemption. "Be ye therefore steadfast, unmoveable," in this firm faith that the dead rise,—that Christ is risen.

III. Our standing as believers, our justification, our peace, is intimately connected with the doctrine of the resurrection. It is a doctrine as essential to our completeness in Christ, as it is to his completeness for us.

The new life which believers have in Christ, if it is to be worthy of the name, must be the reverse or counterpart of the old death which he dies for them. If that old death is by sentence of law, so also must the new life be by sentence of law. If the death is a death of conviction by law, the life is a life of acquittal by law. If the death is condemnation, the life is justification and peace.

But all this is inseparably bound up with the belief of the resurrection. A resurrection, and nothing but a resurrection, can prove that the old penal death of condemnation is undone. A resurrection, and that alone, can give assurance of the new life of acquittal and acceptance being legitimately begun. Therefore, as Christ "died for our sins," so he "rose again for our justification." His rising again is the proof that his dying for our sins was a full atonement for them ; that it exhausted the legal sentence, in terms of which death is inflicted as the punishment of transgression. And well it might, considering who the victim was, and how willingly, in love, he gave himself up. But his rising again is more than that. It is his making good a legal claim to life, as the reward and acknowledgment of righteousness.

Here, then, is another reason for being steadfast in adhering to the great doctrine of the resurrection ; unmoved by any plausible special pleading that would deny it, or evade it, or refine upon it and explain it away ;—or that would represent it as a matter of minor importance ;—interesting, perhaps, and entertaining, for the speculations to which it may give rise as to the nature of the happiness to be enjoyed hereafter,—but having little or no practical bearing on the present spiritual life. Its bearing upon the present spiritual life is direct and strong ;— at least if it is to be a life that stands on the footing of a legal acquittal and justification.

If, indeed, we are indifferent to that consideration,

—if we can be satisfied with the notion of God's dealing with us in some other way than according to law, giving us mere impunity and indulgence, letting us alone, letting us off,—if such a life, if such a hope will content us, we can afford to let the resurrection go ; we can do without it ; we can do, in fact, without any gospel, or any faith. Or if we can imagine that God deals with us according to some sort of self-acting principle of love, working itself out in Christ's history, and in ours, without respect to the claims and sanctions of sovereign authority and a government by moral law,—if we conceive of God as acting towards us exclusively in the character of a gracious paternal disciplinarian, and not in the character of a ruler and judge,—then in that case also, we may fail to see how the belief of the resurrection so nearly concerns our standing before God, and our peace with God. But if I am taught by the Spirit, neither of these suppositions describes my state of mind. I am anxious, not merely about my ultimate escape from wrath, but about my present enjoyment of the divine favour. I desire not merely to be on terms of compromise, or a sort of decent understanding with my God, but to be on terms of clearest, closest, fullest reconciliation. I feel that this can be the result only of a judicial act; an act of legal justification. For the law, imposing death as the penalty of sin, and demanding righteousness as the condition of life, has taken hold upon me.

The Spirit has brought it home to me. I perceive that God must treat me, and ought to treat me, according to that law. It must be so, and I would have it so. An illegal, or extra-legal, or as it were extra-judicial settlement of the controversy between my God and me, would not be enough for me. I know it to be impossible. But even if it were possible, I feel that it would be unsatisfying. I must get rid of that death which the law imposes as the penalty of sin. I must get possession of that righteousness which the law requires as the condition of life. An act of amnesty will not now do. It must be an act of acquittal, of acceptance, of justification. Hence he who would save me by taking my place, must be one who not only bears for me the penal death, but brings in for me a justifying righteousness. Such a Saviour is Christ, the risen Lord. And he is so only as the risen Lord.

IV. For its bearing upon our holiness of character, and our diligence in duty, we do well to be steadfast and immovable in our belief of this doctrine of the resurrection.

It is that belief which identifies to us the life that now is, and the life that is to come. They are no more twain, but one. They may seem to be separated by an intervening gulf or space. There is an interval, it may be of ages, during which the soul or spirit dwells apart in rest and blessedness, while the body, its companion and minister, lies in the silent tomb. What that intermediate state is—how the spirit, absent from the body and present with the Lord, lives there—what are its consciousnesses, what its experiences, what its activities—we cannot tell. There is no express revelation to enlighten us on the subject; and analogy or inference, founded on parables or visions, may deceive us. It is enough to know that "to depart is to be with Christ." It is enough to hear the voice of Jesus, as the spirit wings hence its heavenward flight, "To-day shalt thou be with me in paradise."

But if we dwell much in thought on that purely spiritual or incorporeal mode of being, do we not find ourselves apt to sever it, in our musings, from the ongoings of this present every-day working world? In measure, that may be good. These musings may minister to a sort of sabbatic stillness,—making a seasonable break and solemn pause in the whirl of "the crowd's ignoble strife."

The intermediate state itself may be designed to serve some such purpose in the case of those who fall asleep in Jesus. It may be, and probably will be, one of seclusion, and, as regards the outer world, one of repose. "The blessed dead who die in the Lord rest from their labours." Their earthly toils and troubles are at an end. And for a season, it may be, they are in the bosom of God, with his beloved Son, enjoying holy fellowship with the Father and the Son, in the Holy Spirit, undistracted,—shall I say?—and undisturbed, by former earthly memories, and not yet introduced to the new occupations of the eternal world. It is to their spirits a holy sabbath of rest; fitly preparing them for what is yet before them.

So also to us now, frequent meditation on the intermediate state may, within due limits, be a profitable as well as a placid and peaceful exercise of soul. But if we continue long to make it our exclusive subject of meditation, are we not tempted to lapse into an ideal, unreal, visionary mood? And is it not the tendency of our indulging such a mood, to foster the too common habit of divorcing spiritual thought and feeling from the ordinary business of life? Religion becomes a sentiment to be caressed and fondled in the hours of secluded contemplation and devotion; not a principle that is to rough it amid the wear and tear of the world's throngest thoroughfares and busiest market-places and fairs.

If it were to serve no other purpose than that of counteracting any leaning to such a habit of mind, a steadfast and immovable grasp of the resurrection and the resurrection-life is all important. For it is the hope of the resurrection that stamps a character of sacred importance on all that we now think, and say, and do, in the body. It is that prospect which identifies the pursuits and habits of time with the pursuits and habits of eternity, and makes us practically realize the great truth, that what we are making ourselves now, by the things we are now doing in the body,—that we must be then, and must continue to be, in the same body, through everlasting ages.

A belief which has such bearings as those now suggested ;—touching, first, the testimony of the apostles and the divine authority of the Lord,—secondly, his great work of propitiation,—thirdly, the standing of the believer as justified in the sight of God,—and fourthly, the sanctification of our whole nature and our whole earthly condition ;—that, surely, is not a belief to be easily let go. It is the sheet-anchor of our faith, and holiness, and hope. Well may we be exhorted to be " steadfast and immovable" in it ; refusing to be carried away from it by crude speculations, however seemingly spiritual and saintly, that make void the atonement of our Lord, and explain away the final judgment and the eternal state of retribution and reward. Let us rather seek, as being " rooted and grounded " in the faith of the resurrection, to " abound always in the work of the Lord, inasmuch as we know that," upon that footing, " our labour is not in vain in the Lord."

21

DUTY OF ABOUNDING IN
THE WORK OF THE LORD

Always abounding in the work of the Lord.
—1 Corinthians 15:58

THIS is a description, either of what we must be, if we are to be steadfast and immovable; or of what we will be, if we are steadfast and immovable. It may be taken either way. You cannot otherwise be steadfast and immovable than as you are always abounding in the work of the Lord. That is one reading of the exhortation. Being steadfast and immovable, you will certainly abound always in the work of the Lord. That is another. The difference is not material. In either view, there is a practical duty connected with our being steadfast and immovable in the faith of the resurrection. It is,—I. To be about "the work of the Lord,"—II. To "abound in" it,—and III. To abound in it "always."

I. We are to be about "the work of the Lord;" to be occupied in it; to make it our work.

"What shall we do," said the Jews on one occasion to Jesus, "that we might work the works of God?" His reply is remarkable, "This is the work of God, that ye believe on him whom he has sent" (John vi.

28, 29). From what follows, it is plain that this means our receiving Christ as the true bread from heaven, given to us by his Father ; the bread of God coming down from heaven and giving life to the world ;—" I am the bread of life ; he that cometh unto me shall never hunger ; and he that believeth on me shall never thirst." It is our coming to him as the bread of life, on the faith of his twofold assurance : first, " Him that cometh to me I will in no wise cast out ;" and secondly, " I came down from heaven, not to do mine own will, but the will of him that sent me ;—and this is the Father's will which hath sent me, that of all which he hath given me I should lose nothing, but should raise it up again at the last day ;—and this is the will of him that sent me, that every one which seeth the Son and believeth on him may have everlasting life, and I will raise him up at the last day " (38-40). This last statement assures us of the Son's faithfulness to his Father, as the former assures us of his love to us. And on the faith of both assurances, we are to believe on him as the Saviour in whom we have everlasting life ; who can lose nothing of all which the Father hath given him ; who will raise us up at the last day. "This," then, " is the work of God," our thus " believing on him whom God hath sent."

And indeed, rightly considered and fully realised, this is the whole work of God. For it is not merely a single isolated act ; or an act repeated at intervals as occasion requires. In one view it is so. In our distress of conscience we come to Christ at first. The Holy Spirit opens our eyes to behold him, as " the Lamb of God that taketh away the sin of the world." We believe, the Lord helping our unbelief ; and we have peace in believing. So also afterwards, under the pressure of the fresh guilt which we are ever contracting and the indwelling sin that is ever vexing us, how often are we driven to do again the first work ; fain to cling, as at the first, to that gracious word of promise : " Him that cometh unto me I will in no wise cast out." This must be the frequent acting of our faith. But this is not its only acting. This is not the whole work of faith ;—of that faith which, appropriating Christ as ours, unites us to Christ as his. The work of God which we work, when we believe on him whom he has sent, is our identifying ourselves with Christ ; and that too, with reference to whatever his being " sent by God " implies ;—with reference especially to all that " doing of the will of him that sent him," for which " he came down from heaven."

And what is that will of him that sent him ? It has respect to " all that the Father hath given him." And it comprehends whatever is needed to secure that " of all which the Father hath given him, he shall lose nothing, but shall raise it up again at the last day." As sent by his Father and doing his Father's will, he must see to it, on the one hand, that of all that the Father giveth him, none shall be lost ; and on the other hand, that they shall all be ripened for resurrection at the last day. Is not this Christ's whole work on earth, in its principle and its actual realization ?

First, there is the great ruling principle or master motive ;—obedience to the Father. He comes " not to do his own will, but the will of him that sent him." Nothing that he undertakes is at his own hand, or upon any mere impulse of his own, however disinterested and generous. It is all obedience ; not a spontaneous outburst of feeling, but a simple service of duty. True, it is a service for which he volunteers himself ;—" Lo, I come to do thy will, O God !" But it is a service nevertheless ; and nothing more ; nothing else. He is " obedient even unto death." His death itself is obedience.

Next, under the constraining power of that ruling principle or master motive ;—in obedience to the Father, and as doing the Father's will ;—he cares for those for whom the Father cares ; that through no fault or failure of his, any of them may be lost ; that by his means all of them may attain to life now, and to resurrection at the last day. This was to him " the work of the Lord ;" a service of loyalty to God, first and primarily,—but at the same time a service of love to man.

And is not "the work of the Lord" the same to us? What is our calling in Christ? Is it not, in the first place, to make a surrender of ourselves to God, and become obedient; ready, as sent by him, to do his will? And under that high aim, is it not to see to it that none of his little ones suffer damage or loss through us; nay, to see to it that through us they are helped on to glory? Is it not to that sort of life that we are summoned as fellow-labourers with Christ? Is it not thus that we must be giving ourselves to "the work of the Lord?"

II. In this "work of the Lord" we are to "abound." It is a work in which we may abound with all safety, even to overflowing, or as it were to excess. For the expression in the original is a strong one. It suggests the idea almost of surplusage·or superfluity;—our not merely coming up to the amount or quantity required, but even actually going beyond it.

But what? is there then, after all, such a thing as a work of supererogation? May I so abound in the work of the Lord, as not only to do what is ·barely sufficient to enable me to pass muster as not a defaulter, but to do more than that;—to add what may enable me to accumulate a stock of merit, available for myself if I should afterwards fall short, or for others for whom, if suitably importuned, I may choose to intercede?

There may be room for this notion, if, in doing the

work of the Lord, I consider myself to be profiting or obliging him ;—or if my service is of the nature of a mercenary bargain, or a compact for hire, in terms of which I am bound to do a certain amount of work for him who hires me, and am at liberty, that being done, to work for myself. In that case, if of my own accord I still offer, as a volunteer, to go on working for him, doing more than is stipulated for in the bond, —I establish a claim of merit, and treasure up a store of superfluous good desert on which I may at another time draw. But that is not the footing on which I am engaged in the work of the Lord. It is not the footing on which he who is at once my substitute and my example was himself engaged in it.

For, first, when he took upon himself the form of a servant, he did not simply agree to render in our stead a certain limited measure of obedience to the Father, such as might occupy only a portion of his time and strength ; leaving him the option of devoting the rest, as it might please him, to the doing either of his own will or of the Father's ; and so giving him the opportunity, if he still chose to do the Father's will, when he might have been doing his own, of acquiring even a higher degree of merit than was needed to meet the case. That is not the manner of Christ ; it is not thus that he serves the Father. There is nothing of the nature of supererogation in any part of the work which he does. It is indeed, in

one view, all a work of supererogation together, not
required from him on his own account, and therefore
all available for us. But it is as one whole that it is
thus available for us. It is not his undertaking to
give so much obedience, and no more, that saves us,
but his becoming obedient. It was not at any point
at which he might arrive during his life, in the course
of his doing the will of him that sent him,—it was
not till that life was closing,—that he was to be in a
condition to say conclusively, concerning the work
given him to do, "It is finished."

If, therefore, he abounded in the work of the Lord,
it was still as a servant; yes, and in the strictest
sense, "an unprofitable servant;" not going beyond
what might be required of him as a servant, but
simply "doing that which it was his duty to do"
(Luke xvii. 10). For in his voluntarily assumed
position of a servant, even the Son must have felt,
and did feel, as the Psalmist felt when he exclaimed,
"O my soul, thou hast said unto the Lord, Thou art
my Lord; my goodness extendeth not to thee"
(Psalm xvi. 2). It is no profit to thee. It is no
more than the payment of a debt, the fulfilment of an
obligation, the rendering of what is due.

If it be so even in his case, how much more in
ours? For "the disciple is not above his master."
With the master, every disciple may and must acknowledge;—and that, too, not on the ground of short-

coming, but even on the supposition of perfection ;—
—when " he has done all those things which are commanded him ;"—"I am an unprofitable servant ; I
have done that which it was my duty to do ;" that,
and no more. " Thou art my Lord ; my goodness
extendeth not to thee." " To the saints that are in
the earth, and to the excellent, in whom is all my
delight" (Psalm xvi. 3), my goodness may in a measure reach. I may have the satisfaction of thinking
that I benefit or profit them ; not restricting my
good offices to what they might be held entitled
peremptorily to demand, but giving full scope to the
overflowing of my good will. So may one feel who
is " abounding in the work of the Lord." It is a
feeling, however, which must be kept in check, lest
it tempt him to think too much of his own generosity, and too little of his neighbour's just rights.
In the bosom of Christ alone, it might have place,
unchecked. To men on the earth, his goodness is all
matter of grace ; not matter of debt at all. Still,
even he, however he may abound in the Father's
work, cannot say to him,—" It is a gift whereby
thou art profited by me." No ; it is no more than
the work given me to do,—it is no more than I became bound and obliged to do, when I said, " Lo I
come to do thy will, O God."

That being Christ's attitude in doing the work of
the Lord—we, as one with him, must realize it as

ours. We do the Lord's work as servants. But though we do it as servants, it is not in a servile, grudging spirit that we do it. We do it heartily, lovingly, honourably, liberally. It is not eye-service; nor is it bond-service. " O Lord, truly I am thy servant; I am thy servant, and the son of thine handmaid : thou hast loosed my bonds ;"—that is the spirit in which we serve, not a master whom we dread and with whom we try to make terms, but a Father whom we love, and who has made us free. We may well, therefore, " abound" in his work.

Especially we may do so when we consider, secondly, what that work is. It is our entering into the work of the Son. It is our doing all we can to prevent loss or damage to any of those given to him by the Father ;—our doing all we can to advance their spiritual life now, and their preparation for the life to which they are to be raised at the last day.

In such a work, undertaken in obedience to such a Lord, we cannot abound too much. We cannot go too far in any sacrifices we may make, any toil and trouble we may undergo, any pains we may take ;— on the one hand, to avoid all causes of offence and remove all stumbling-blocks out of the way ; and on the other hand, to bring all holy and loving in-fluences of all sorts to bear on all sorts of men, if by any means sinners may be won to accept grace, and saints may be animated on their way to glory.

We cannot be too busy or too active,—we cannot be too zealous or too abundant,—in such "work of the Lord;"—if only we make conscience of abounding in it simply as servants. For surely we must be more and more deeply feeling that we never can go beyond what we owe to him whom we serve. Do what we may, we must still say, when all is done, "we are unprofitable servants, we have done that which was our duty to do." That only; nay, rather less than that;—less by far than might well be expected of us, to whom so much has been given, and of whom, reasonably and righteously, so much might be required. In this spirit of honourable loyalty and ardent love, let us be "abounding in the work of the Lord."

III. We are to abound in the work of the Lord "always;" at all times, and in all circumstances.

To be abounding in it only occasionally,—at intervals, or by fits and starts,—may be consistent with that mode of service which proceeds upon the idea of our somehow profiting God; our being somehow in a condition to make a merit of what we do, or to make our own terms in doing it. We rouse ourselves for a great exertion in the good cause. We are determined to do some great thing; to occupy a foremost rank among those who cleave to Christ's person and espouse his cause. There is enthusiasm in our devotions; and no end to our activities, our liberalities, our charities,

Alas! it is but for a season. The excitement wears off. We grow listless and weary. Surely we may allow ourselves a little repose and relaxation. So we may be tempted to think and feel, if, while we are abounding in the work of the Lord, we are abounding in it rather as ultroneous benefactors, than as loyal servants; doing our own will, at least as much as the will of him who sends us. Our "abounding" is apt to be fitful and capricious, not steady, uniform, and constant. Insensibly we are tempted to take credit for it, and presume upon it, as giving us some title, now and then, to use liberties, and follow our own way.

But surely this is not being "steadfast and unmovable." It infers vacillation in principle as well as in practice; in doctrine as well as in duty. There is at the bottom of it a secret, lurking, self-righteous tendency, to make occasional fits of "abounding in the work of the Lord" compensate for long intervals, and large measures, of remissness and indecision. Yes! indecision is the fatal snare. Indecision is the cause of our either not abounding in the work of the Lord at all,—or abounding in it wilfully or waywardly. We treat it as if it were our own work, which we may take up and lay down at pleasure. But it is not so. It is the work of the Lord. It is the work of Christ, our Lord; as much as his work was to him the work of his Lord, his God and Father in heaven.

Let us feel it to be so, and let us abound in it

accordingly "always." It is the work of the Lord; and therefore we may abound in it always. If it were any other work than the work of the Lord, we could not do so. The work of the most gifted of workmen on earth,—the work of the most successful merchant, or of the most brilliant scholar, or of the most valiant soldier,—is not a work in which one can abound always. In any of these works, or such works as these, we may abound sometimes. But there is not one of them whose most zealous votary would desire to be abounding in it always. Seasons of relief from it,—seasons when it may be suspended, and all thought about it may be held in abeyance,— are indispensable to the healthy action of all the bodily and mental powers.

It is the distinctive character,—the criterion and test,—the glory,—of "the work of the Lord," that it is the work in which we may "abound always." For it is not, like these other works, only occasionally in season. To one who abounds in it, it is always seasonable. It admits of all varieties of adaptation. It can accommodate itself to all circumstances, and fit into any kind of work we can lawfully have on hand. In everything we do, we may be keeping steadily before our eyes the end of our calling, as fellow-labourers with the Lord;—with him who came "to do the Father's will, that of all whom the Father giveth him, none may be lost, but all may be raised up at the last day." This sense of our fellowship with the Lord, in his great and blessed work of saving, and sanctifying, and glorifying, all whom the Father hath given him, may enter into everything we think, and say, and do. Therefore, it is possible; and, if possible, it is surely right ;—to be " always abounding in the work of the Lord."

Such then is the duty to which we are called; a duty intimately connected with our being " steadfast and unmovable" in the faith of the resurrection, and of all that the resurrection involves. Our union to the risen Saviour binds us to be about the business in which he was occupied when he was on earth; to be about it with abundance of zeal and love; and to be about it continually. And it fits us for the work to which it binds us ; as the Lord himself has said : "He that abideth in me, and I in him, the same bringeth forth much fruit;" and "herein is my Father glorified, that ye bear much fruit; so shall ye be my disciples" (John xv. 5 and 8).

22

THE MOTIVE FOR ABOUNDING IN
THE WORK OF THE LORD

*Forasmuch as ye know that your labor is not in vain in the
Lord.* —1 Corinthians 15:58

It is "in the Lord" that our labour is not in vain;—
empty, or void of result and issue. We enter into
the work of the Lord, as the Lord himself entered into
the work given him to do. We abound in that work
of the Lord, knowing that our labour in it is not, as
it were, a busy idleness, or a spending of our strength
for nought. For the work is his. It concerns him,
therefore, to see to it that our labour in it shall not
be in vain.

He is in a position to see to this. But he is
so only in virtue of the resurrection; his resurrection
for us, and ours in him.

It was thus only that his own labour in his
Father's work was not in vain. Were there no resurrection, it would have been in vain. For to what
purpose did he labour, if there was to be no resurrection to attest the complete success of his labour, and
to gather its blessed fruit?

He takes our nature, its bodily as well as its spiritual part. He extricates one part of it, the spiritual, and carries it into some unknown spiritual home. Thereafter he carries us home, one by one,—that is, the spiritual part of each one of us which is set free at death,—to be with him there. But the bodily part ours and his, is lost. If there be no resurrection, that is all. But if that is all, what is it? It is no triumph ; no victory. It is, at the best, a compromise ; a dividing of the spoil with the other party in the strife. And it fixes a great gulph between the Lord's temporary human life on earth and his subsequent human life of immortality in heaven. The line or thread of continuity between his history on earth and his occupation in heaven is fatally broken. His occupation in heaven is no longer that of a ministry of intercession and government, connected, by the consciousness of thorough personal identity, with the history of a ministry of obedience and sacrifice on earth. He is not now, in heaven, the same man Christ Jesus that he was on earth. There is nothing now in him, or about him, of what allied him to earth. It is an escape, and not a redemption, that he has effected. He has eliminated and drawn forth a subtle and ethereal spiritual element of immortality, out of the gross matter of which this earth and its animals are composed. He has done so, by leaving, as regards himself and his redeemed, the earthly state and the

corporeal life to perish hopelessly,—to perish altogether and for ever.

Surely, one would say, a salvation like that might
have been accomplished without such travail of soul
as the Redeemer had to bear. It is a salvation which
implies no expiation of guilt; no endurance of its
penalty; no reversal of its sentence. It is simply the
extrication of the better part of Christ's human
nature, and of ours in him, from that material portion
of it which perishes, and from the material earth in
which it perishes. It is the transference and transla-
tion of that better part to some sphere, or some state,
into which nothing of the material earth or of the
material body may intrude.

If that is all, I repeat that to a large extent Christ
has lived, and laboured, and died in vain. There
was no need of such toil as he had to undergo;
and there is now no proper fruit of it. He is not
now, in that body in which he bled, within the veil.
He is not, bodily, at the right hand of God. What
motive, then, had he to labour as he did, bodily,
in the work and business of his Father, "to endure
the cross, despising the shame?" Where, in connection with all that, is "the joy set before him,"
if it is nothing more than the passing of his pure
spirit into his Father's hands, leaving all that is
earthly and bodily behind for ever? That might
be a relief; an escape. It could be no recompense;

no reward. It would be oblivion of labour,—not requital.

But his labour was not thus in vain. His work followed him. He resumed it when he rose from the dead. He not merely received an acknowledgment of the work; he resumed the very work itself. He might have received an acknowledgment of the work, altogether apart from any resuming of the work itself; —his human spirit being, in consequence of it, blessed in some spiritual region, in which there could be nothing in common with what he had done or suffered in the body. In some such way he might have been the better for his labour in that work; the better able to save. But his labour itself would have perished and been in vain. There would have been a new thread of existence to him; not the taking up of the old. It is his bodily resurrection that links and fastens on Christ's life in heaven now to his former life on earth; and makes it plain that his labour during that former life, in the work of his Father, has not been in vain.

For, in the first place, he has gone,—the same man precisely that he was on earth,—the same man complete,—to present himself before the Father, whose will he has done and whose work he has finished. He carries to the presence-chamber, the judgment-hall, of his righteous Father, the body which the Father prepared for him, and his whole labour and travail of soul in that body. And he asks sentence to be passed on himself in that body, and on what he has done and suffered in that body. He asks for a judicial award. The mere bettering of his condition, as a natural consequence and gracious owning of his past history, will not suffice. He asks for a verdict on that history, as a history, not buried in oblivion's indulgent tomb, but raised for righteous judgment.

Thy will was done ; was it well done ? Thy work was finished ; was it finished satisfactorily ? I stand, —the very person who did thy will and finished thy work,—I stand for judgment. It is not a part of me, my spirit escaped out of my body, that craves a stealthy and unchallenged passage to some refuge or receptacle of shivering naked souls. It is I myself, whole and entire, in the body in which I did thy will and finished thy work, who stand for open judgment.

And then again, secondly, not only does he, in his risen body, challenge judgment upon himself and his work ;—he takes the work up, and follows it out. He carries on in heaven the business which he had on hand when he was on earth. In one sense, indeed, his work was finished here. It was finished as to all its toil and pain. But

> " He who for men their surety stood,
>   And pour'd on earth his precious blood,
>   Pursues in heaven his mighty plan,
>   The Saviour and the friend of man."

This then was the Lord's high motive and encouragement for abounding always in the work of his Father. He abounded in it even to tears, and blood, and death ; and he did so for this "joy that was set before him,"—this double joy. First, he is to rise again, that he himself in the body, and his labour in the body in the Father's work, may be judged and justified. Secondly, he is to rise again, that he may resume the work. He resumes it, with all the sympathies and sensibilities of the human nature which he had on earth entire and unchanged. In his ministry of intercession, in his sending the Comforter, in his ruling over all, in his preparing a place for us in his Father's house, and in his coming again to receive us to himself,—he resumes the work which he finished, as to its earthly part, when he died. He resumes it that he may carry it out to its endless issues of blessedness and glory, in the new heavens and the new earth wherein dwelleth righteousness. Thus, for this double reason, the Lord's labour in the work given him to do is not in vain. It is so in virtue of his resurrection, and in virtue of that alone.

For the same twofold reason, our labour is not in vain, in him.

In the first place, we ourselves, personally, and our labour in the work of the Lord, are openly judged and finally justified. The judgment is by works ;— or rather the judgment is of works. We are judged by our works ; that is, our works are judged ; our abundant labour in the work of the Lord. That day will test and try the labour of every man ; of what sort, and of what worth, it has been.

"All things here are full of labour ; man cannot utter it : the eye is not satisfied with seeing, nor the ear filled with hearing" (Eccl. i. 8). Sometimes, even in this world, the labour is felt to be very wearisome and, alas, very vain ; and one is forced to say : "I hated life ; because the work that is wrought under the sun is grievous unto me ; for all is vanity and vexation of spirit. Yea, I hated all my labour which I had laboured under the sun. For what hath man of all his labour, and of the vexation of his heart, wherein he has laboured under the sun?" (Eccl. ii. 17-22). Still the labour goes on. And alas! for the most part, whatever complaints may fall from them in seasons of despondency, it is not in the present life that men fully discover how utterly their labour is in vain. It would be better for them if it were ;—better now, than in that judgment of the resurrection-day.

In what work is our labour expended? In what work, or in whose, is it abundant? In our own? or the world's? or the devil's? Is it in the work of heaping up riches, or winning renown, or pleasing men, or gratifying our own lusts, our own tastes, our own feelings,—that our labour is abundant? Will our labour in any work like these, be owned by the

Judge in that day? Will he acknowledge it as having any thing in common with his own labour; that labour of his which his resurrection attested and crowned?

It is only "in the Lord," that any labour can then be owned and acknowledged as "not in vain." And in that view, let us bear in mind that there may be labour even of a better sort that will not stand the test. Our labour may be abundant even in a good work;—the work of beneficence; or the work of religion. And yet it may not be labour that can be accepted, as "not in vain in the Lord." For it may be labour in a good work, as a work of self-righteousness, or a work of self-pleasing; a work of penance, or a work of merit; a work of party; a work of the church; a work of our own. If so, it is not labour in that good work, as "the work of the Lord."

To whom did ye do it?—will be the question then. Did ye do it unto me?

For we may be very sure, that what is done unto the Lord cannot be in vain in the Lord. Nothing of all that is given to him,—or done in his name,—or suffered, or sacrificed, or surrendered for his sake,— can ever be lost. Be the gift ever so small,—the widow's mite cast into the treasury, or the cup of cold water held out to one of Christ's little ones; be the deed ever so humble,—ministering to a poor saint or a perishing sinner,—washing the feet of a disciple,—

speaking a word in season to a weary soul; be the suffering, the sacrifice, the surrender, ever so trifling, —petty persecution meekly endured,—" a soft answer turning away wrath,"—a domestic trial of temper patiently and kindly met,—our own will given up to please a brother for the Lord's sake;—nothing given, or done, or suffered for the Lord, for the love which we bear to him, for the love wherewith he loveth us, can fail of its reward in that day.

And, how bright and blessed the reward! To hear the Lord before all angels and all men, bringing to our remembrance long-forgotten passages in our lowly walk of faith on the earth!—recounting, to our surprise, instances of love and labour in his work, which we deemed unworthy of notice and remembrance! With what adoring wonder shall we then discover the full meaning of that gracious assurance, " God is not unrighteous to forget your work and labour of love." But this is not all. For

Secondly, we are raised up at the last day that we may resume our labour in the work of the Lord, in which here we are to abound always. We resume it in circumstances widely different from the present. It will not be the same kind of labour. But it will be labour in the work of the Lord; labour without fatigue or failure; without groans and tears.

When the Lord himself took up again in heaven the work which he had finished on earth, and as to its earthly conditions,—it was in a new sphere, and under new conditions. His labour here in that work was a labour of humiliation, suffering, and shame. It is not so now. It is in glory that he takes it up and follows it out ; not with visage marred, and having no form or comeliness ; despised and rejected of men ; stricken, smitten of God, and afflicted ; but owned and honoured as the Son of God with power, by God himself and all his holy ones. It is not as a lowly servant ; a doomed criminal ; a dying victim ; but as the king reigning in righteousness, that he carries on that work in heaven.

And we are to reign with him. We are to be with him where he is. We are to behold his glory ; the glory which the Father giveth him, for the love wherewith he loved him before the world was. Our labour in the work of the Lord, when we thus resume it in the Lord, will take its character from the position of him in whom we resume it. And therefore it will be in many respects different from what it is now. But the spirit of it will be the same. The same loyalty, the same love, the same alacrity, and activity, and overflowing zeal,—which now find scope in the work of the Lord, as now we abound in it, amid much tribulation, and many disappointments, persecutions, and heart-breaking anxieties and fears, —will be called into exercise in the work of the Lord then ;—only it will be under happier auspices, and with more satisfying issues. Yes! we may rely on it, that no habit of obedience, which we are now cultivating, as we seek to abound in the work of the Lord, will then be found to have been cultivated in vain.

If indeed we were not to live again in the body; if our final and ultimate perfection were the unbroken rest of our soul in the bosom of God; the repose of the absorption, as it were, of our spirit into the great Spirit that fills the universe; then much of our labour here in the work of the Lord might seem to be thrown away. In such a future, there would be no call or occasion, no room indeed, for many of those qualities that are exercised now, amid the activities of our bodily state and our earthly service. But that is not the future before us. New heavens and a new earth are coming. And we are to serve God there in the body; abounding there, as here, in the work of the Lord.

These, then, are the two objects on which, in looking forward to the resurrection, the eye of faith should rest; the final judgment and the eternal state.

I. We rise in the body, to give account of the deeds done in the body. It is the day of dread disclosure,—of a fiery trial of discovery. "Absent from the body and present with the Lord,"—our spirits have been resting in holy and happy complacency, with no consciousness, probably, and no thought, of things past or of things without. Now all comes back again. Our earthly and bodily history is brought up once more; brought up to be judged. Will it stand the judgment? Ah! how much of it will stand the judgment? How many things in it,—how many of its works,—will then appear to be as wood, hay, stubble,—fit only to be burned!

It was a good prayer that Paul offered for Onesiphorus,—the best return for all his "refreshing" kindness,—"The Lord grant unto him that he may find mercy of the Lord in that day" (2 Tim. i. 18). It will be mercy that I need then as now. It will be as a debtor to mercy that I pass through that ordeal; feeling myself anew to be a debtor to mercy; only then, for the first time, beginning to apprehend how deep my obligation to mercy is!

But the mercy which I pray the Lord that I may find in that day, is mercy reigning in righteousness. I humbly look for a sentence of acquittal and justification. My hope is, that when he in whom I believe as my Saviour now, and who is to sit as my judge then, calls me before him in the body, he may see in me, and in my works;—in me, for "by his grace I am what I am"—in my works, for "it is he that worketh in me both to will and to do;"—that which he may acknowledge, before men and angels, as attesting the uprightness of my faith, and entitling me to a gracious reward.

Then, if that be my hope, let me give good heed to my life and my doings now. Let me make conscience of my inner life and my outer doings being more and more such as I would have to follow me to the judgment of the great day. Let me, with a holy ambition, strive to win the blessed sentence of warm welcome and approval—" Well done, good and faithful servant ; thou hast been faithful over a few things, I will make thee ruler over many."

II. We rise to enter, in the body, into the eternal state ; and into the eternal state our works follow us. The risen believer carries his earthly doings with him into his everlasting habitation and home.

What differences of employment there may be, it would be vain and presumptuous to conjecture. Possibly there may be a closer analogy than many suppose between the future and the present. Of this at least we may be sure, that no pure taste cultivated here will want its appropriate food there ; no high and holy faculty exercised here will be without its congenial field of labour there. All the powers, whether of intellect or of feeling, which the soul exerts here, by means of the body,—all its sensibilities and activities,—will assuredly, in the eternal world, find room enough for their renewed and enhanced energy. Thus the works begun on earth, may be taken up again, and carried on in heaven. Inquiries which the saint, when called suddenly away, left unfinished, or but just begun, he may prosecute again, after an interval of holy seclusion and blessed rest; and prosecute, ah! how differently! For then, the soul that has been alone with God, reunited with the body that has cast off the corruption of sin and of the tomb, will be in a condition to range through all space with untiring wing; to ransack the secrets and solve the mysteries of eternity. The duties also, which the servant of God delighted to discharge on earth, amid pains, privations, and trials manifold—from which, nevertheless, he felt reluctant to be summoned by death away—he will in happier circumstances resume. For he will stand evermore beside the throne on high; his eye intent to catch the first indication of his Father's will; his ear quick to learn the first tidings of any work anywhere to be done; his loins girt— his feet swift—to run on any errand to creation's utmost verge;—and his tongue, familiar with the melody of praise on earth, making heaven's arch ring with the song of Moses and of the Lamb.

SUPPLEMENTARY DISCOURSES

1

THE VICTORY OF THE CHURCH IN HER HEAD; ITS PROGRESS AND CONSUMATION (ISAIAH 24:1—26:8)

He will swallow up death in victory.　　　　—Isaiah 25:8

THIS prophetic oracle occurs in the bosom of what is admitted to be one continuous prophecy, embracing four chapters,—the twenty-fourth to the twenty-seventh inclusive. The first portion, reaching from the beginning of the twenty-fourth chapter to the eighth verse of the twenty-sixth, is that which it is chiefly necessary to study, with a view to the right understanding of the oracle.

But while generally agreed in regarding these chapters as one entire prophetic poem, complete in itself, interpreters differ widely as to its application. Every crisis in Jewish history, from Isaiah's time downwards, has been pressed into the service. The captivity at Babylon, with its issue ; the persecution under Antiochus Epiphanes, and the wars of the Maccabees ; the overthrow of Jerusalem, and the dispersion of the Jews by the Romans ; as well as other far less memorable eras ;—have been singled out as fulfilling, and even exhausting the prediction. Events, also, in modern European annals, have been laid hold of, often strangely enough ;—as if this oracular word of God were like a drifting ship at sea, fain to take refuge in any harbour, let it be the narrowest of all German creeks ; or else, like a gallant vessel on a shoreless and chartless ocean, making an adventurous voyage to one knows not what millennial Arcadias and Paradisiacal isles of the blessed.

A prophecy so plastic might seem fitted only to tantalize, were it not for the consideration that this very feature of it, its capacity of being adapted to so many, and such different, catastrophes in the divine government, shews it to have been intended to bring out rather the general principles of that government than any particular details. It is not the aim of this prophecy,—or indeed of prophecy in general,—to write history beforehand. Its aim rather is to give the key to all history. True ; it has its special historical allusions ;—and much of this particular prediction may have been already historically fulfilled, perhaps more than once ;—as in the two dispersions, the Babylonian and the Roman. It was suggested also by the state of matters in Judah at the time. It was meant to be an encouragement and directory to the Jewish people in the calamity then immediately impending, and in the deliverance from it which they were taught to expect. But it was meant, moreover, to be an encouragement and directory to them in all subsequent calamities and deliverances; and not to them only, but to the Christian church as well; down to the end of time.

Hence it is cast into a mould that will more or less closely fit different successive movements in the march of providence. Ultimately, in fact, the prophet's eye is gazing on a far more awful crisis, and a far more glorious consummation, than either Jewish or Gentile history has ever brought forth out of the womb of time. It is in the light of the great spectacle of the end of the world that he views all intervening events. He sees them bathed in the effulgence of that full discovery of himself, and that complete vindication and explanation of his ways, which, in fierce wrath and in richest love, the Lord is then to give. He sees them all, therefore, shaped after the same fashion and tinged with the same hue. The vision is thus one. It is a vision of the kingdom of God,—the kingdom of heaven upon earth.

Let the successive scenes in this shifting panorama be surveyed as they pass before the prophet's eye.

I. The first scene occupies the first twelve verses of the twenty-fourth chapter.

In the first place, it shews a territory empty and waste (ver. 1-4). The land,—for it seems to be a particular country that is here meant, and not the whole earth,—has been turned upside down ; it has, as it were, spilt and "scattered abroad its inhabitants" of all ranks and classes,—of all conditions and callings.

In the second place, the character of the inhabitants is described (ver. 5). They have been in "covenant" with God, placed under his "laws" and "ordinance." But they have not only "transgressed the laws ;" they have deliberately tampered with and "changed the ordinance," and "broken the everlasting covenant." They have made void the word of God by their traditions. Therefore the very soil which they tread is " defiled."

In the third place, the disastrous issue is set forth at large (ver. 6-11). "The curse devours" the land. A blight seizes its fruits. Revelry and "mirth cease." War and famine come. There is a confused noise in the city. A brief, desperate struggle ensues ; the weary and wounded "crying" in vain "in the streets for wine." Presently all is over. The stillness of utter ruin reigns. "In the city is left desolation, and the gate is smitten with destruction."

II. The second scene is painted in the four verses

which follow (13-16). It exhibits a remnant " as the shaking of an olive tree," or " as gleaning grapes after the vintage." There is a handful of survivors scattered far and near, to the "fiery" east, and to the western "isles." They are nobly praising the Lord God, and "glorifying his name," in the countries of their dispersion. It looks as if they were leavening the whole earth with the true faith, making all lands resound with loud " songs for the majesty of the Lord." Through their wide-spread testimony, the wide world seems about to become the Lord's in truth. "From the uttermost part of the earth have we heard songs, even glory to the righteous." But alas! " the treacherous dealers have dealt very treacherously." Amid all this bright prospect, something sadly smites the seer's heart ; a sense of hollowness and unreality; a feeling of dissatisfaction ; a sort of impression that the world's treacherous dealing is still proving too strong. Fair as is the picture, and full of promise,—good the song if only it be sung truly,—some sign warns him not to let appearances deceive him. The full and final triumph of the Lord's cause is not yet. The world's falsehood must be purged by judgment.

III. The third scene, accordingly, as we have it in the next seven verses (17-23), opens with a spectacle of terror, on a large scale, extending over all the world. For it seems now to be the earth that is meant, the entire prophetic earth. This is usually to be considered as identical with the nations which have the church, or the truth of God, brought more or less into contact with them, from age to age. At any rate, the havoc of the third scene is far more widely spread than that of the first. There, it was a single, isolated country that was in extremity ; here, it is the world throughout whose borders the remnant, saved out of the former wreck, have been sounding the praises of the Lord ;—with apparent success for a time, but with insidious elements of evil, preparing the way for a second, and a worse, outbreak.

This scene, therefore, is of wide extent. It assumes the partial judgment described in the first scene, and the diffusion of light and love exhibited in the second scene,—as well as the baneful influence of the worm of treachery there also indicated. And it discloses the wide ruin which this wide abuse of the widely offered good entails on the whole earth.

On all sides, "earth's inhabitants" are in consternation. It is the consternation of a sudden and universal panic. Instruments of capture, weapons of destruction, are among them everywhere. Alarming sights and sounds are driving them distractedly to and fro. They "flee from the noise of the fear," only to "fall into the pit." They "escape the pit," only to be "taken in the snare." Meanwhile, above them, "heaven's windows" of fiery indignation are "opened."

Beneath them, the very earth is " shaken to its founda-
tions ; " " broken ; " " melted." It staggers, " like a
drunkard," under the weight of its own transgression ;
it yields, like a frail " cottage," to the pelting of the
pitiless storm. Then earth's " high ones and kings "
are smitten ; they become " prisoners in a loathsome
pit," not to be " visited for many days." The very
orbs of heaven share the consternation ; " the moon
is confounded, and the sun ashamed." It is darkness
all ; dismal darkness and fright.

But when the gloom is thickest, the dawn of glory
breaks the sky. Whèn things are at the worst ; no
light of hope anywhere ;—lo ! a blessed surprise is
near !

IV. For the fourth scene, which is spread over a
large space (from xxiv. 23 to xxvi. 8), opens with an
abrupt discovery of the majesty of Jehovah, victorious
and triumphant ;—" The Lord of hosts rèigns in
Mount Zion, and in Jerusalem, and before his ancients
gloriously ! " (xxiv. 23). And at the sight the
prophet is more than satisfied ; his heart is relieved ;
he breaks out in a strain of joyous thanksgiving :—
" O Lord, thou art my God ; I will exalt thee, I will
praise thy name." All is now to be right. Jehovah's
name is to be praised. " I will praise thy name, for
thou hast done wonderful things ; thy counsels of old
are faithfulness and truth" (xxv. 1).

But, not content with a general expression of his

satisfaction, the prophet goes on to paint the several sections or groupings which combine to fill up the bright picture now before him. For this fourth scene is complex. Under the bright overshadowing canopy of Jehovah reigning gloriously, the eye beholds three distinct objects of intense and vivid interest.

1. Here, on one side of the canvas, is " a city in ruins " (2-5). It was once a great and goodly city. But " strangers " had become its owners. It had got into the hands of a people, not loyal, but hostile and rebellious. They had fenced and fortified it as a stronghold. They had splendidly adorned it as a palace. They were a people strong and " terrible " in their rebellion. They had oppressed the Lord's " poor and needy " ones. " Their blast " swept as " a storm against the wall." But the Lord had been mindful of his own. He had been their " strength " in persecution ; and in him they had found " a refuge and a shadow " amid the fiery " storm." And now at last they are avenged. " The city is a heap ; " " its defences a ruin ; " its " palace " pomp exchanged for utter vacancy. The " noisy " pride of the apostate crew is " brought down." Their persecuting fires disappear in the smoke of their own citadels. The terrible oppressor is as a broken and withered " branch." A strong voice is heard crying mightily : Joy! joy! For " the city is fallen, is fallen ! "

" Great and marvellous are thy works, Lord God

Almighty;"—so sing the saints, triumphant over the beast in the Revelation (Rev. xv. 3). "Thou hast done wonderful things;"—so sings the liberated church here. "Just and true are all thy ways, O thou King of Saints;"—such is the response in the one song. "Thy counsels of old are faithfulness and truth;"—that is the reply in the other.

2. Not far from the ruined city appears a mountain (6-12); evidently the mountain which is the seat of Jehovah's reign; Mount Zion (xxiv. 23). There the Lord of hosts himself is welcoming the multitude of all nations to whom the fall of the tyrant city has been a glad jubilee. "A feast" is made for them; a feast, large, generous, free; open "to all people;" rich with choicest dainties; a feast of light and liberty, of life and victory. No more darkness; no more death; no more weeping; no more shame. So the Lord, the maker of the feast, ordains. The guests sit down, saying gratefully an appropriate grace: "Lo, this is our God; we have waited for him, and he will save us: this is the Lord; we have waited for him, we will be glad and rejoice in his salvation." Nor is their joy marred by fear of any foe. The table is prepared for them in the presence of their enemies; not by stealth, as if in dread of them; but openly, in defiance of them all. Not the nearest and most bitter of them,—not "Moab" himself,—is formidable now. "The Lord's hand rests in this mountain." And,

"trodden down under him," Moab is seen writhing and floundering—

> "Like some strong swimmer in his agony,"

while the "high fort of his walls is brought down, laid low, and levelled to the dust."

3. But what is that which meets the eye, crowning the mountain's lofty brow?—A city again,—another city,—and a crowd rushing in, singing a right joyous song (xxvi. 1-8).

Looking down on the black mass of the strange city's ruins below, a "city" of another sort stands. It is "strong;" its "walls and bulwarks are salvation." A nation is before it; all the people who have been feasted, now become one nation; "the righteous nation," for which, as such, entrance and free admission into the city is claimed. It is a nation entitled to be called righteous, because "it keepeth the truth." Its people have not yielded to those "treacherous dealings" which, in a former scene, so sadly pained the prophet. They have not trafficked with those who traffic deceitfully in the things of the Lord. Nor, as a condition of liberty to traffic, have they received in their hands, or on their foreheads, any false mark. As a loyal people, they hear the order given, "Open ye the gates, that the righteous nation, which keepeth the truth, may enter in" (2). And they sing, as they enter in, a song of praise. First, they sing the praise of faith;—"Thou wilt keep him in perfect peace, whose mind is stayed on thee; because he trusteth in thee. Trust ye in the Lord for ever; for in the Lord Jehovah is everlasting strength" (3, 4). And well may they so sing; for "their faith hath saved them." They enter into the city, calling loudly for a universal faith in God. Next, they celebrate the Lord's righteousness in executing judgment;—"For he bringeth down them that dwell on high; the lofty city, he layeth it low; he layeth it low, even to the ground; he bringeth it even to the dust. The foot shall tread it down, even the feet of the poor, and the steps of the needy" (5, 6). As they pass through the gates of the strong city, with its walls and bulwarks of salvation, they cannot but cast a glance down on the ruins of that other city, once so bold against him and so cruel to them,—upon which, in the Lord's righteous name, they now victoriously trample. Lastly, they tell of the kind consideration with which the Lord always treats his people;—"The way of the just is uprightness; thou, most upright, dost weigh the path of the just. Yea, in the way of thy judgments, O Lord, have we waited for thee: the desire of our soul is to thy name, and to the remembrance of thee" (7, 8). If through grace, their way has been upright with him, much more has his way been upright with them. True, they have had to wait for him. They have had to wait for him moreover in the way of his judgments;—for when he did arise, it was by "terrible things in righteousness that he answered them." But they have found it to be "the right way" after all by which he has been "leading" them,—the way most glorifying to him to whose name and remembrance the desire of their soul steadfastly and immovably inclines.

Such is this scene of Jehovah reigning in Zion. There are presented to our view, on one side, the strange city in its ruins ; on the other side, rising on the mountain's brow, the strong city in its beauty ;—and the sumptuous mountain feast between.

Now passing in review the four scenes which have been sketched, what do we seem to see ?

I. A city and community long in covenant with the Lord ; becoming hopelessly apostate ; visited with terrible calamities ; at last, after many warnings, their "house left unto them desolate."

II. A small and feeble band, emerging out of the wreck; dispersing themselves everywhere, and everywhere praising God ; changing the entire face of society ; spreading among all men the knowledge and worship of Jehovah ;—until, as it might seem, earth is about to become the garden of the Lord ;—save only that a discerning eye sees a treacherous conspiracy sapping the vitals of truth, and entrenching itself in some gorgeous palace and fortified stronghold of error.

III. A convulsed and panic-stricken world; "upon the earth distress of all nations, with perplexity;" the earth itself dissolving; "the sea and the waves roaring;" "men's hearts failing them for fear, and for looking after those things that are coming on the earth;" "the powers of heaven shaken."

IV. Jehovah reigning gloriously in Mount Zion, with these accompanying signs of victory;—1. A false city, the haunt and home of a party estranged from him and terrible to his poor ones, at last overthrown and fallen;—2. The emancipated nations feasted on the mountain-side by the Lord; their scanty fare of a few loaves and fishes converted into an abundance of fat viands and rich wines; their blindness cured; their diseases healed; death itself conquered; and all their tears wiped away;—and, 3. A second city, diverse from the other, set on the hill, strong and fair; "the nations of them that are saved walking in the light of it;" the gates thrown open to "the righteous nation."

One can scarcely help recognising here a cycle of frequent recurrence in the history of the Church. There is a local or partial desolation somewhere; a judicial dealing with some guilty church or nation. This causes a broadcast sowing of the seed of the word, and a goodly promise of harvest;—with a sad root of bitterness, however, discernible by the spiritual eye. Such a state of things leads to wide disorder and dismay. Until, at last, suddenly as it seems, the Lord is seen to reign gloriously:—with these three accompaniments—a strange or hostile city overthrown ; the liberated people fed, enlightened, revived and comforted ; and the gates of a strong city opened to all who have been waiting for the Lord. This, in fact, might almost be regarded as the law of the Church's development. Its history runs in a sort of oscillating, yet still onward, course, like that which Isaiah's prophecy sets before us. And indeed the conditions of its existence and progress in this fallen world are such that it could scarcely be otherwise.

The divine and heavenly stream issues from the bosom of eternal love. It has to make its way to the everlasting ocean, which that love seeks by means of it to fill. But it has to do so, not over a pure and smiling plain, in which it may flow gently, equably, and smoothly on, in an ever-deepening and ever-widening tide of joy and peace. It moves through a region wild and barren, rough with rocks, foul and tangled with weedy swamps and forests. Not with calm and placid current, but fitfully, violently, noisily; turbidly often, and tumultuously ;—it has to force a passage through opposing barriers. There are reaches, more or less frequent, of quiet water, like a peaceful lake. But even in these the stream is only gathering force for new torrents and eddying falls ;—until the strife at last is ended in the glad rush of its entrance into the broad and open sea.

So the church advances, through alternations of trouble and prosperity ;—first to her millennial, and then to her eternal glory. Corruption grows to such a height as to demand the avenging stroke,—but yet also to admit of the lesson of mercy, remembered in the midst of wrath. The lesson is carried abroad, by an elect and dispersed remnant ; wherever they go they spread the truth ; there is a gracious revival,—so general and so marked, that it may almost pass for the promised reign of righteousness. But alas ! the leaven of unrighteousness and hypocrisy is at work.— Hence, new outbreaks of evil ; new visitations of wrath come.—Yet again, at the critical hour it is seen, it is felt that the Lord reigneth ; to lay low the rebellious and proud citadel of error ; to refresh, enlighten, revive, and comfort the people, poor and weary ; and to open to them the gates of a strong city, in which they may dwell securely, and sing for joy.

2

The Victory of the Church in Her Head; the Scene of Consumation and Triumph, the Scene of Preparation and Trial (Isaiah 24:13-16, 24:23—26:9)

He will swallow up death in victory.   —Isaiah 25:8

Of the four scenes which we have seen passing before our eyes, in the prophet's moving panorama, the first and third represent the Lord's judicial visitations of wrath, partial or general, preliminary or final, upon the earth ; the second and fourth exhibit the church, as she appears, either in the intervals between these visitations, or at the close of them. The second scene paints chiefly the church of the present ; the fourth, the church of the future. In the former, the church is seen in the aspect she usually wears during seasons of suspended judgment, when the Lord is exercising forbearance ; in the latter, she shines forth triumphant after judgment is past, either in her eternal glory, or in some earnest of it granted by way of foretaste in time. Reversing the order, it may be interesting to consider, first, the high hope set before the church in the prophet's fourth scene of triumph ; and, secondly, the church's ordinary present experience, as depicted in the second scene of preparation and trial, to which her higher hope may well reconcile her.

I. The last of the four scenes (xxiv. 23—xxvi. 8) may be regarded as shadowing forth, more or less perfectly, those more signal seasons of deliverance in the church's history which wear the character, not so much of preparation, as of consummation; in which there is not merely a wide scattering of good seed, as in the second scene (xxiv. 13-16), but a universal reaping of the fruit. In its full and true significancy, it can represent only the heavenly state. In that state alone, when the earth is renewed—as we are taught to believe it is to be renewed—to be the central home of Christ and his saints for ever; when the new heavens and the new earth come, wherein dwelleth righteousness; then and there alone can the glorious things here spoken of the people and city of God be realized. Then and there alone is the ruin of the apostate city final (xxv. 1-5). Then and there alone is the vail thoroughly removed; death utterly destroyed; all tears for ever wiped away; glory fully given; and the table spread that is never to be withdrawn for any enemy (6-12). Then and there alone is the holy city, the New Jerusalem, descending out of heaven from God, to be set up on the earth (xxvi. 1-8); the city in which the Lord's servants are to see his face and reign for ever. It is ultimately to the heavenly and eternal state, and to that alone, that the glowing brightness of this picture can fully and fairly apply. (Compare Rev. xxi. 1 ; xxii. 4, 5.)

But, as coming events cast their shadows before, so there are rehearsals, as it were, in time, of what awaits the church beyond time. In a lesser and lower measure, therefore, this fourth scene may be regarded as bringing out the features of the millennial reign of grace;—features essentially analogous to those of the eternal reign of glory. For, indeed, all grace bestowed in time, whether on individual believers or on the church at large, is substantially identical in character with the glory hereafter to be revealed in eternity ; and the more triumphantly grace reigns, the more conspicuously does its identity with glory shine forth. Hence the millennial reign of grace is really a reign of great glory.

Like all preceding seasons of spiritual prosperity in the church,—from which it differs, not in the nature of its holy blessedness, but in the extent and degree of it, and in the length of years through which it is to last,—this golden age is to end abruptly,—so we are led to anticipate,—in a fresh outburst of unprecedented wickedness and violence on earth, to be met by one last deluge of fiery judgment from heaven. That millennium therefore is not the ultimate hope of the church. Nor is it in it that the Lord's kingdom or reign is to take its ultimate and perfect glory.

Still, during its continuance, it will partake largely of the elements that enter into the prophetic outline of heavenly glory which Isaiah paints for us.

For one thing, the great enemy is worsted; his great Babylon fallen; himself bound. Then, again, the once down-trodden saints of God are raised to honour and pre-eminence; richly fed; enlightened; set free from fear of injury or death; their shame turned into beauty. And, more than that, they have a strong city. Salvation is appointed for walls and bulwarks. God is their salvation and their strength. It is a happy time for the true church and people of God. Iniquity, as ashamed, hides its face. Everywhere godliness prevails and prospers.

But, alas! there is a worm gnawing at the root of the gourd; there is a latent dead fly in the ointment. The church is not yet moored in her heavenly harbour. The law of her earthly condition and progress still holds. There must be one more adverse swing in the oscillations of her history: a terrible outbreak of evil at the close of that millennium of good. Then, at last, all is well. And all is well—for ever!

Thus this scene depicts, first and fully, the church's eternal state of gracious glory; secondly, and more imperfectly, the church's millennial state of glorious grace;—for so perhaps the two states may be distinguished from one another.

And as it thus applies to these two stages of the

church's ultimate prosperity, so it may be taken to be descriptive also of some of those better times, those times of refreshing and revival, which the Lord now and then, here and there, grants to her by way of foretaste. At such times, some great deliverance being wrought out for them, and the Spirit being largely poured out upon them, the people of God have been made to feel as if all that this scene paints were already realised in their surprised and ravished experience. The Lord turns again their captivity ; they are like men that dream ; their mouth is filled with laughter, and their tongue with melody.

So it may have been in the Alpine valleys long ago, when, after years of bloody persecution, God avenged his slaughtered saints; and there came for the exiled remnant that joyous return. It is to a full feast, a rich spiritual banquet, that they sit down in their mountain fastnesses. And as they partake of it, a glad light breaks upon their dreary darkness. Death no longer stares them in the face. Weeping is forgotten. All their shame is over. And their place of defence is the munitions of their own rocks.

So also in our own Scottish hills and glens there have been blessed seasons when, rescued from maddening oppression and visited with gracious showers from on high, the Lord's covenanted servants have had a goodly entertainment; lightened as they looked unto him ; quickened and revived; comforted and enlarged; their faces not ashamed any more; their eyes seeing Jerusalem, after many troubles, a safe and quiet habitation at last.

Nor need the application of the scene, in this secondary sense, be restricted to the church at large, or to communities. As individual believers, we may have the benefit of it. We may take the whole picture home to ourselves, as bringing out what our experience may be, and ought to be. It shews us how God is willing, ready, anxious, to deal with us. What a table does he prepare before us in the presence of our enemies! He invests us with a title to it which they cannot challenge; his own free and sovereign gift of grace;—for if "it is God that justifieth, who is he that condemneth?" He endows us with strength for it which they cannot touch;—for "who can separate us from the love of Christ?" And then, he covers it for us with food and wine : the food and wine of love, and holy joy, and perfect peace. Nor is this all. For as we freely eat and drink abundantly, he enlightens our darkness, as Jonathan's eyes were enlightened when he partook of the honey ; and so doing, he is to us life from the dead. He dries also all the tears of our sorrow. He covers with his own beauty the shame of our nakedness. He becomes himself our rock, our fortress, our strong tower. All this and more we may gather from the picture, as shewing what God has in store for us even now ;

what treatment we may meet with at his hands ; if only we will taste and see how good he is,—being not faithless but believing.

And yet, when all this is exhausted, and we have reached the full scope of these glorious prophetic utterances, so far as the joy of them can be fulfilled here, in time,—Oh! what a thought is this,—that it is all as nothing compared to what we are to be in that eternal world, in which, when "this corruptible shall have put on incorruption, and this mortal shall have put on immortality," there shall be really and fully "brought to pass the saying which is written, Death is swallowed up in victory !"

II. But, in the prospect of this fourth scene of consummation and triumph, it is the second scene, the scene of preparation and trial (xxiv. 13-16),—with its wide-spread testimony and its latent "treacherous dealing,"—that most fitly symbolizes the ordinary experience of the church militant in the world.

In a large view, indeed, the entire interval of time, between Jerusalem's overthrow,—the critical era of trial,—and the thousand years' reign of the saints,— the beginning and prelude of triumph,—is covered by this description of a scattered remnant ;—the gleanings, as it were, of the olive and the grape ;—causing songs of glory to the Righteous One to be heard from the uttermost parts of the earth. And whatever partial, or local, or personal revivals may have occurred, at sundry times and in divers manners, to serve as pledges and earnests of good things to come, the church's normal condition is that which is thus delineated. She must lay her account with being, not a perfect olive-tree or vine, but as it were, scattered droppings, driven and dispersed abroad by the rude winds. But these droppings are seeds of life and fruitfulness. Christ's members, carried hither and thither in the turmoil of an agitated world, make conscience of " glorifying " everywhere " the Lord in the fires," or fiery climes, " even the name of the Lord God of Israel in the isles of the sea " (xxiv. 13-15).

How thoroughly is the church thus thrown into a missionary attitude ; not as the result of policy, or calculation, or reasoning, on her part ; but as a necessity of her position ; by the irrepressible instinct of her scattered members,—scattered over all the earth.

For surely,—all calm philosophic speculation and calculation of consequences apart,—Christ's people, dispersed among the nations, see enough in the foul dishonour done to their God, in cities and countries wholly given to idolatry, to rouse and stir their spirit to the utmost ; and enough in the vile abominations practised for worship by the blinded victims of superstition, to awaken the liveliest concern for their deliverance from the wrath to come. It is indeed a blessed office that these men of God are moved by a Divine impulse to discharge, dispersed as they are over

all the world, from the fiery east to the breezy isles
and continents of the west. And, whatever drawback
of latent treachery there may be, it is blessed fruit that
comes of it. To lift up the voice for the majesty of
the Lord, and cry aloud for the glory of his name ; to
put into the mouths of men, instead of songs of blasphemy and ribaldry, pure hymns of praise to the
Most High ; to win honour for the righteous, where,
till now, only wickedness has been extolled ; who can
over-estimate the obligation of a work like that ? If
the condemnation of the whole world, but for grace,
is a reality ; if the universal corruption of mankind
is a great fact ; if there is a law in men's consciences
that makes them, even in the darkest ignorance,
responsible for their crimes ;—and if there is but one
name given under heaven whereby men may be
saved ;—by every consideration of zeal for God and
kindness to men, the saints of God, wherever scattered, are bound to do all that may be done in this
great cause of spreading abroad the seed of the word
in which that name is revealed ; "sowing beside all
waters" (Isaiah xxxii. 20).

It may be that, after all, the sowing is in the
meanwhile sparse ; and there may be tares secretly
springing up. It may be but rare and small strains
of praise that, at the best, reach the ear from the
uttermost parts of the earth. Few, and faint, and far
between, may be the aggressions made, in the interest

of God and truth, upon the vast territories where the Father of lies holds all but universal sway. Vital godliness, spiritual christianity, may seem to make but little head; and even where it prevails, there may be but too good cause for the church, as well as the prophet, to cry, "My leanness, my leanness!" and to anticipate the pouring out of wrath from on high. But "who may despise the day of small things?" Rather let us make full proof of present duty being done—and done promptly—in this intermediate and transition state, ere the judgments of God come on the nations of the earth. And let us encourage ourselves by looking forward, beyond these judgments, to the reign of righteousness and peace that is at last to be established over all the earth,—when "the Lord of hosts, in his holy mountain, shall make unto all people a feast of fat things, a feast of wines on the lees; of fat things full of marrow, of wines on the lees well refined." Then "he will swallow up death in victory; and the Lord God will wipe away tears from off all faces; and the rebuke of his people shall he take away from off all the earth; for the Lord hath spoken it."

3

CHRIST THE RESURRECTION AND THE LIFE; THE BELIEVER DEAD, YET LIVING

Jesus said unto her, I am the resurrection, and the life: he that believeth in me, though he were dead, yet shall he live: and whosoever liveth and believeth in me shall never die.
—John 11: 25, 26

THE Lord here identifies himself with an event,— "the resurrection;" and a state,—"the life." The event and the state are intimately connected; the one takes its character from the other; according to what the life is, so is the resurrection. If it is life in the sense in which all men on the earth live,—if it is the life that is here and now common to all the race,—then the resurrection is a mere resuscitation. It is simply a return to this present world, under the ordinary conditions of man's present occupancy of it; such a return to life as actually took place in the case of Lazarus, and of others whom our Lord and his apostles raised from the dead. But if it is life in a higher sense that is meant—life in the favour and fellowship of God—the resurrection must obviously be of a sort corresponding to the life.

That this last is the life meant is evident, for it is associated with faith. It is the life which those have who believe in Jesus. Of this life it is said, on the one hand, that it overcomes, or, as it were, undoes and reverses death ; and, on the other hand, that it abolishes death, or renders it impossible. In the one view, the believer in Jesus may die, or be dead, yet with the certainty that he shall live. In the other view, he is never to die at all.

In either view, the life is in Jesus. He is the life. And in order to his being the life, he is the resurrection. For he was dead. But, in the first place, when he died, it might be said of him, "though he were dead, yet shall he live." There is to be for him a resurrection. And now, secondly, it may be said of him that he "liveth," and so liveth that "he shall never die." Hence he himself says, "I am he that liveth and was dead, and behold I am alive for evermore, Amen ; and have the keys of hell (or *hades*) and of death ;"—of the unseen world and of the entrance thereto (Rev. i. 18). And hence also to those who, believing, are one with him, he is the resurrection and the life. He is their life, and in order to his being so, he is their resurrection. In a double sense he is their life ; inasmuch as, first, in him, though they die, they shall yet live ; and inasmuch as, secondly, living now in him, they shall never die.

Thus there are two ways of considering the Lord's

saying, " I am the resurrection and the life." On the one hand, it may be considered in connection with the admission that the believer has to face death ; according to the promise in the twenty-fifth verse,— " He that believeth in me, though he were dead, yet shall he live." On the other hand, it may be considered in the light of the assurance that to the believer there is properly no death ; according to the promise in the twenty-sixth verse,—" Whosoever liveth, and believeth in me, shall never die."

It would seem to be admitted, in the first instance, that one who believes in Jesus, as the resurrection and the life, may die. " Though he were dead," the Lord says ; though he die ; though he be dead.

In a literal sense, this was an admission obviously demanded by the fact that Lazarus was dead. It would have been difficult to persuade Martha that a believer in Jesus was never to die when her brother Lazarus was dead. Yes, there is death. My brother is gone. The arm that used to embrace me so tenderly, the eye that so often met mine so lovingly, the manly frame I was so apt only too proudly to admire,—all is mouldering in the dark grave. But out of that death there is life. " I am the resurrection and the life ; he that believeth in me, though he were dead, yet shall he live."

The life, therefore, which a believer has in Jesus,

as the resurrection and the life, is not incompatible with death. Nay, it implies death. It is the antithesis or antagonism of death. The glory of it lies in this very concession ;—"though he were dead, yet shall he live."

Nor is it merely to the death which Lazarus had just died, that this admission applies. Death, in a far deeper sense, is comprehended in it. The expression—"though he were dead"—will cover, not merely such a death as Lazarus had died, but such a death also as Christ himself died. Nay, it must comprehend and cover that death, if he is the resurrection and the life, and if it is as one with him in that character, that he who believeth in him, though he were dead, shall yet live.

Need I say what death that was? The death which Christ had to die ; the death with reference to which it might be said of him, "though he were dead, yet shall he live ;" what death was that? A death of cruelty ; a death of agony ; a death of shame. More than that. A death of condemnation ; a death of wrath ; a penal death ; "the cursed death of the cross." He was to die, bearing the guilt and suffering the punishment of sin ; exhausting the sentence of the violated law. That was the bitterness of his death. Thus he was appointed to die. Thus he actually died.

But though he was thus to die, yet he was to live.

Even before he gave up the ghost, he was to be in a position to say, "It is finished;" "Father, into thy hands I commend my spirit." And on the third day thereafter he was to be "declared to be the Son of God, with power, according to the Spirit of holiness, by the resurrection from the dead" (Rom. i. 4).

Jesus then might truly say of himself, Though I were dead, yet shall I live. And it is because he can say this of himself, that he can say also of every one who believeth in him, Though he were dead, yet shall he live. He may have to die, not merely as Lazarus has died, but as I am to die. He may have to be a partaker, not in the first place, at least, with Lazarus in his death, but before that, with me in mine. Nay, it must be so, if he believes in me.

For, if we believe, we must enter into Christ's death, and make it our own. There must be realised in our experience an actual personal dying with Christ. There must be wrought in us by the Holy Spirit some real apprehension of a dealing with us for our sins on the part of God, the righteous Judge, exactly similar to his dealing with Christ, when he bore our sins in his own body on the cross. It may be a dealing fatal, for the time, to our peace; remorselessly destructive of any life we may once have thought we had,—any life we may once have hoped to make good, —before our God. There may be darkness above and all around. There may be a rending of the rocky heart within. There may be a sharp sword of wrath piercing us ; and a heavy sense of guilt oppressing us ; and the cry as of one forsaken of God, may be wrung from us ; "woe is me ! for I am undone." Still let us not shrink from the hour ; let us accept the punishment of our sin ; let God smite us even to the dust, till all idea of our having any life of our own is gone, and we fall at his feet as dead. Only let us believe in Jesus ; embrace him as dying for us ; consent to be dead in him. And let us lay hold of that assurance of his, concerning every one who believeth in him ;—"Though he were dead, yet shall he live."

Yes ! In spite of this death we live. Nay, more. Through this death we live. For now, believing, we are accounted one, because we are really one, with Christ in his death. His death is reckoned to be ours ; in the eye of the law, it is equivalent to ours. Because Christ is dead, the law regards us as dead. Christ, in his death, has endured and exhausted the penalty of the law ; and we who are one with him, have endured and exhausted it in him. Its condemning sentence has no more hold over him ; nor over us who are in him.

Such is the efficacy of his death ; such its legal force and import. And such is the virtue of that real and vital union which the Spirit, by means of faith, effects between Christ and us. We die with Christ ; we die in Christ. Now, "he that is dead is freed

from sin " (Rom. vi. 7) ; from sin's curse or condemnation by the law. The law has done its worst. That
penal death being over,—first as regards Christ and
then as regards us who are in Christ,—he lives, and
we live along with him. So Paul testifies ; " If we be
dead with Christ, we believe that we shall also live
with him : knowing that Christ, being raised from the
dead, dieth no more; death hath no more dominion
over him. For in that he died, he died unto sin once :
but in that he liveth, he liveth unto God. Likewise
reckon ye also yourselves to be dead indeed unto sin,
but alive unto God through Jesus Christ our Lord "
(Rom. vi. 8-11).

Is there yet awaiting us another death ? Believing in Jesus, and being partakers with him in the
death which he died, have we still, even after that, to be
partakers of the death which Lazarus died ? Then is
not the Lord's assurance as applicable to this death in
prospect, as to the death that is past ?

Nay, much more. For this death before us is less
formidable by far, than the death from which we are
already delivered. It need not have in it,—it should
not have in it,—if we really believe it cannot have
in it,—those elements of guilt and wrath that filled
the cup which our Saviour had to drink, and which
we drink with him when we are "crucified with him."
The experience of our dying hour is not to be like
that which smites us when, under a sense of sin and

of the law's curse, we die now. The Spirit,—causing us to enter into the death of Christ now, giving us an insight into his cross,—slays us once for all ; empties us of all conceit of life ; makes us own and feel ourselves to be dead. But that death we survive. From that death we are raised. Though we were thus dead, we live. What remains is not death. It is a falling asleep in Jesus.

When that hour comes, believer! the Spirit, bringing to thy remembrance what Christ hath said, will cause thee to hear these gracious words, "I am the resurrection and the life." Thou seest the heavens opened, and Jesus standing at the right hand of God. It is as raised from the dead that he stands there. And thou too art raised from the dead in him. Dying as thou art, "thy life is hid with Christ in God." Thy life is bound up in the life of thy risen Lord. He, as the resurrection and the life, has already brought thee through a worse death than thou hast to die now. He will bring thee through this death also. He will bring thee through it completely,—thy body as well as thy soul. Though thou hast to die, yet shalt thou live. Ah! then, thy end may well be peace. Yes ; though it be even amid a shower of stones that thou art perishing, the stormy tumult of angry passions raging all around ; gazing still on thy risen Saviour thou shalt say, "Lord Jesus, receive my spirit !" And breathing the prayer of charity, "Lord, lay not this sin to their charge," quietly, in the arms of thy risen Lord, thou shalt fall asleep.

This first view of the gracious assurance before us may suggest some practical thoughts.

I. In how emphatic a sense is that saying of the Lord true, " He that loveth his life shall lose it " (John xii. 25). He says this with reference to his own dark death, viewed as the condition of his life and glory ;—" Except a corn of wheat fall into the ground and die, it abideth alone ; but if it die, it bringeth forth much fruit."

And yet the love of life is inherent in man. All men cleave to life. Nor is it merely to the natural life which finds its congenial home in this warm-breathing world that men cling. To life in a higher sense they cling ; to the idea of some spiritual life which they may have, as being at all events not utterly and hopelessly condemned in the judgment of God. It is of that life chiefly that the Lord speaks when he says, " he that loveth his life shall lose it."

Are you in this sense " loving your life "—clinging still to the imagination of your not being, after all, so very guilty, so very destitute of all title to favour with God, as his whole word proclaims you to be? Are you still going about to establish a righteousness of your own,—striving to satisfy, or silence, conscience by the common pleas of worldly self-justification ?   I beseech you to consider that, as certainly as there is a God of Judgment, so certainly must that life of yours issue ere long in the discovery that all is lost ! Before the awful throne, the books of reckoning are opened. Your sins are set out before you. And your virtues, your pieties and charities. The heartlessness of your whole way of dealing with God is exposed. And the heavy sentence of his holy law of love crushes you,—unholy and unloving,—in ruin that admits of no retrieval. Love not a life like that. Rather now, in the day of grace, let that self-righteous life of yours be hated, disowned, renounced, finally and for ever. Let it go ; you are well rid of it. For " He that hateth his life in this world shall keep it unto life eternal " (John xii. 25).

II. " The corn of wheat " falls into the ground and dies. And he carries you with him. You are in him as he lies in the grave ; crucified with him ; buried with him. That old life of yours, with all its sins and all its righteousnesses, is buried with him ; never again to come up, either to tempt you again to trust in it, or to torment you with any feeling of its worthlessness. There, in the grave of that crucified one, you lie buried, as to all your guilt, your condemnation, your liability to wrath and judgment. Surely it is a blessed thing thus to die.

III. It is so, because the life that issues out of this death is very blessed indeed. " The corn of wheat," when it dies, "bringeth forth much fruit." You, believing, are among the "much fruit;"—being raised from the death of guilt and condemnation to a life of acceptance and peace. You live now, in and with Christ. His life,—his risen life,—is yours; as truly as your death,—your penal death,—was his. You are in the same position in which you would be, if you had yourselves personally died the very death which Christ died when he fully expiated guilt, and had thereafter risen again as he rose,—undergoing the very resurrection by which he was "declared to be the Son of God with power."

How complete then is your deliverance from the fear of death, and from the bondage in which the fear of death keeps you. How strong is the obligation under which you lie, as dead with Christ, "to crucify the flesh, with its affections and lusts;" and as risen with Christ, to "seek the things which are above, where he sitteth at the right hand of God." For thus you realize your fellowship with him, first in his death, and then in his resurrection and life as consequent upon his death. He is thus, through his death, and your participation in his death by faith, the resurrection and the life to you. Thus, "though you die, yet you live."

And though you have another death still before you, it is not that "second death" which awaits the ungodly. Your second death is your quietly falling asleep in Jesus. That once over, you are alive in him for evermore. You are at home with him immediately in your emancipated spirits; as the apostle Paul longed to be at home with him when he said—" To me to live is Christ and to die is gain. But if I live in the flesh, this is the fruit of my labour : yet what I shall choose I wot not. For I am in a strait betwixt two, having a desire to depart, and to be with Christ ; which is far better : nevertheless to abide in the flesh is more needful for you" (Philipp. i. 21-24). And ere long, in your glorified bodies also, you are to be for ever at home with him, according to his own blessed parting promise to his disciples ; " In my Father's house are many mansions ; if it were not so, I would have told you. I go to prepare a place for you. And if I go and prepare a place for you, I will come again, and receive you unto myself ; that where I am, there you may be also" (John xiv. 2, 3).

Surely "having this hope in Christ," we do well to "purify ourselves as God is pure," and to remember always that "our conversation is in heaven ; from whence also we look for the Saviour, the Lord Jesus Christ : who shall change our vile body, that it may be fashioned like unto his glorious body, according to the working whereby he is able even to subdue all things unto himself" (Philipp. iii. 20, 21).

4

CHRIST THE RESURRECTION AND THE LIFE; THE BELIEVER, LIVING, NEVER DIES

Jesus said unto her, I am the resurrection, and the life: he that believeth in me, though he were dead, yet shall he live; and whosoever liveth and believeth in me shall never die.
—John 11:25, 26

WHILE in one view it is admitted that "he that believeth" in Jesus as "the resurrection and the life" may die, when it is said, "though he were dead, yet shall he live;" in another view the opposite seems to be implied, when it is added, "whosoever liveth and believeth in me shall never die."

The life which he has through believing in Jesus as "the resurrection and the life," is unbroken and continuous. It admits of stages of progress and advancement, but not of interruption. From its first commencement, onward through eternal ages, it stretches its unsevered line, its uncut thread. And it is one and the same throughout. It is life in Christ; and in Christ considered as "the resurrection and the life." It is a state, reached through an event; a state of life, reached through the event of a resurrection. The event is identified with Christ;—"I am the resurrection." So also is the state;—"I am the life." When we believe in him, the event and the state become ours as well as his;—ours, in the very sense in which they are his. Being one with him as "the resurrection," we become one with him as "the life." This is the law or condition of that life which knows no death. And it is so in reference to all its stages of development; initial here; and hereafter—first intermediate, and then final.

I. Take this new life in its initial stage of development, as it begins and makes progress in this world. It is a state reached through an event. It is life springing out of a resurrection from death. And the resurrection is one which, as originating the life, Christ identifies with himself personally when he says, "I am the resurrection and the life."

The expression is figurative. But viewed in the light of the occasion, it is not obscure. Martha has been looking to the future, probably the remote future, thinking of some far distant day when she may embrace her brother in the flesh again. Jesus would recall her to the present. The resurrection to which you thought I was referring when I said, "Thy brother shall rise again," may, in one view of it, be far off. But in another view it is near; it is here; it is in me, it is in my person. For it is a resurrection which must first be realised in me personally, in order that it may then be realized also in him who, through grace, believes in me.

How is this resurrection realised in the person of Christ himself? As realised in his person, what is involved in it?

Guided by the fuller teaching of the apostles on this subject, and especially by what is written in the Epistle to the Ephesians (i. 19, 20, and ii. 5, 6), we may partly trace the meaning of that great transaction. Paul represents believers (ii. 5, 6) as, in the first place, "quickened with Christ;" in the second place, "raised up together with Christ;" and in the third place, "made to sit together with Christ in the heavenly places." He thus identifies their position with that of Christ himself (i. 19, 20), when "God raised him from the dead, and set him at his own right hand in the heavenly places."

Now the position of Christ, as thus raised, has in it the three elements of power, grace, and glory;—power, reversing the sentence of death; grace, conveying a sentence of life; and glory, crowning the conqueror with meet reward.

In the first place, in his resurrection, Christ is fully and finally delivered from death;—from the death he consented to die when he "gave his life a ransom for many." Resurrection is to him the removal or reversal of the divine sentence under which he suffered. It is the proof that, with reference to him, that sentence is exhausted. He ceases to lie under any of the penal consequences of that guilt of ours which was imputed to him, when he died. In so far as these consequences affected his soul, he was rid of them when he cried, "It is finished." But that was not enough. So long as they continued to touch his body,—so long as he suffered the separation of his soul from his body,—so long as the penal death he died had hold of him by any part of his human nature,—he was still really bearing the doom of sin, as one condemned. But there was no more condemnation when he rose from the dead.

In the second place, in his resurrection, Christ not only ceases to be dead, or to lie under the sentence of death ; he begins to live anew ; he receives the sentence of life. Not only is he absolved from the condemnation that was upon him, as "made a curse" for us ; he is judicially acquitted ; accepted as righteous ; in a word, justified. And the justification is complete. For he has brought in an everlasting righteousness ; he has rendered a perfect obedience. He has endured and exhausted the penalty of the violated law. But he has done more. Made under the law, he has honoured it by his holy, spotless, sinless compliance with its demands. As the Father's righteous servant he has done the Father's will. And his resurrection is the Father's significant approval of him, in that character, and on that account.

Thirdly, in his resurrection, Christ is set at the right hand of the Father. His seat now, as the risen Saviour,—his home,—is in "the heavenly places," beside the Father. This is his life, following from his resurrection. It is the life upon which, being man as well as God, he enters,—when he passes from the cross and the grave into "the heavenly places."

How he there dwells with the Father; how his human soul is filled with overflowing communications of the Father's love; how, as to his human nature as well as his divine, he is with the Father, being daily his delight, rejoicing always before him; how his affections are ravished there; what are his activities there; tongue cannot tell, nor heart conceive. Enough to know that our risen Lord is at home with the Father in "the heavenly places!"

Such is the resurrection, as realised in the person of Christ, and such the life which it originates.

Now it is this very resurrection that Christ becomes to us, and this very life, when we believe in him. Resurrection, as realised in us, is identical with what it is, as realised in him. First, we are quickened together with Christ. Secondly, we are raised up together with him. And, thirdly, we are made to sit with him in "the heavenly places." Thus his resurrection, and consequently his life, become ours.

There is an act of power here. There is the exercise of "the exceeding greatness of the power of God, according to the working of his mighty power, which he wrought in Christ when he raised him from the dead and set him at his own right hand in the heavenly places" (Eph. i. 19, 20). It is power, however, exercised in a peculiar manner. It is omnipotence; but it is omnipotence acting in terms of law; and that law, the moral law; the law of love and duty, which can neither be forced nor evaded, but must be honoured and obeyed.

Look again at the Lord Jesus Christ in his death. See him as his body lies in the tomb. What obstacles stand in the way of his resurrection?

Some obstacles there are, which a mere and simple exertion of divine power may remove. The stone can thus be rolled away from the mouth of the sepulchre; and the breath of life can thus be made to reanimate the clay-cold corpse. There might thus be a resurrection effected by the mere fiat of Omnipotence. The Father speaks and it is done;—"Let the grave be opened;—let the principle of vitality again possess that body;—let the disembodied spirit return to it." There is a resurrection thus effected. The dead Christ no doubt is raised.

But he is raised only to be what he was before. He is raised to resume his old life in the flesh,—under the old terms and conditions; the old obligations, responsibilities, and liabilities. He is raised, to be

again made under the law ;—under its authority, and
under its curse. A resurrection, in the case of Christ,
effected by a mere act of power, might have done that ;
it could do no more than that. It could not have
brought him into a position in which he might be
" the resurrection and the life " to us. It would have
been merely and simply a return to the old life ;—
not a resurrection to a new life.

His resurrection, if it is to be available as a
source of life to us, must be a judicial act, as well as
an act of power. Omnipotence effects it ; but I
repeat, it is Omnipotence acting according to law. It
is the Almighty One speaking, and it is done. But
it is at the same time the Righteous One saying—
It is enough ; the judgment is over ; the punishment
has been borne. The surety, when he is raised and
revived, rises and lives upon a new footing. And
therefore, on that new footing, he is in a position to
be " the resurrection and the life " to us, when we believe in him as thus risen and thus living.

There is therefore a twofold divine act in that event
of our history,—that crisis in our experience,—that
change in our spiritual state,—which is implied in
Christ being " the resurrection and the life" to us ; or
in other words, in our being " raised with him to newness of life."

First, there is an act of power ; an operation of
the Almighty Spirit. The sealed stone at the mouth

of Christ's sepulchre, the perfect deadness of his bodily frame, its utter incapacity for originating life or motion ;—these are but faint types of the obstacles, external and internal, which have to be dealt with and overcome, before one who is dead in sin can rise and live. The immediate and direct touch of Omnipotence, and that alone, can meet the case. To roll away the stone,—the hard and heavy stone,—of careless unconcern and carnal security, with which the world, and the world's prince, contrive to close the way of access into the heart and conscience ; and then, to impart vitality ;—so that the smitten conscience may mourn and the broken heart give forth its tears ;—that is the Spirit's work of power.

But, secondly, the Spirit works in harmony with that judicial resurrection-act, apart from which even a real spiritual resurrection would be in vain. For of what avail would it be to have fresh vitality imparted to the soul ; to have the conscience and the heart quickened into new sensibility, as regards the claims of God and the guilt of sin ; if it were to issue merely in our being put again where we were before,—and set again to the old task of working out a righteousness or resurrection, and a life or justification, for ourselves ? Quickened thus in conscience and in heart,—with conscience keenly sensitive and heart affectionate and warm,—we would only aim the higher in our attempt to satisfy God's law of love,—

and sink the deeper under a bitter sense of failure
and defeat,—of condemnation and of wrath!

To recal Christ again, by a resurrection of mere
power, to the state in which he was before he died,—
to place him again under law as he was then,—to
impose upon him a second time the obligations and
responsibilities which he had already so fully met,—
this would have appeared, in the eyes of all intelligences, intolerable severity. And yet he could have
stood the ordeal! He could have passed again un-
scathed through the furnace heated seven times!
But for us to be spiritually quickened in heart, and
soul, and conscience ;—and at the same time left in
the state in which we are by nature, as regards our
relation to God and our standing in his sight ;—to
be put, as it were, again upon our probation ;—to
have simply another opportunity given to us of trying
how we may right ourselves with God ;—and that,
too, with an altogether new sense of holiness and of
sin ;—such procedure on the part of God towards us
would be a sort of mockery. It would be as if God
had given Adam a second chance in the garden of
Eden ; as if reinstating him there, with the knowledge
he had got of good and evil,—of unattainable good
and inevitable evil,—God had simply proposed to
him, as if in irony, a repetition of the experiment of
the forbidden tree !

That, however, is not the manner of God. When

Christ is raised, there is an act of power; rolling away the stone and causing the buried body again to breathe. But along with that, there is a judicial act; removing the condemnation,—passing a sentence of acquittal and acceptance,—admitting him who had died a criminal to a prince's seat on the king's throne, —and to a son's place in the Father's heart. Even so, when Christ is made of God to us "the resurrection and the life," there is an act of power. The door of that heart of ours, which is a very sepulchre,— whited, perhaps, but still a sepulchre,—is broken open;—often violently, with much force of awakening and conviction, a sort of earthquake shaking us with great terror;—sometimes, however, more gently, as if an angel's hand were touching the stone very tenderly. The dead bones within are stirred to life. The Spirit breathes on them. Stupid, carnal unconcern gives place to earnest, anxious, inquiring sensibility. Thus far there is an act of power;—issuing in the cry, "What must I do to be saved?" But is that enough? Is that all? No. Along with that, there is a judicial act. We hear the call, "Believe in the Lord Jesus Christ, and thou shalt be saved." We hear; and hearing, through grace we believe. And now, first of all, we are delivered from death; for "there is no condemnation to them that are in Christ Jesus" (Rom. viii. 1). Nay, more; in the second place, we are judicially acquitted and accepted as righteous; we are raised to life in the beloved. Nay, more still; in the third place, we are made to sit with him, as adopted children, partakers of his filial rank and filial nature, in "the heavenly places." We have a life, whose seat, and centre, and home is the bosom of the Everlasting Father, where the Son himself dwells for evermore.

Thus, with reference to our experience in this world, Christ is to us "the resurrection and the life." Through union and participation with him in his resurrection, we come to have union and participation with him in his life. Believing in him, we live; absolved, justified, adopted ; and so live that we shall never die. Such a life, thus reached by such a resurrection, has no liability to death in it or about it,—no possibility of death. It is not, and cannot be, subject to death, or the risk of death. From its very nature and origin, it is unbroken in its continuity. When once begun, it must go on uninterruptedly. The act of divine power,—and the judicial act, or sentence of divine law,—concurring in the resurrection which originates the life, secure its continuing for ever ; and its continuing for ever, always the same. Living and believing in Jesus, we never die.

II. But our life, realised through faith in Jesus as "the resurrection and the life,"—our life in the risen Saviour,—has its eras. It has its eras even here in

428 • Supplementary Discourses

this world; its dates or times of progress and advancement. And in reference to the world to come, it has at all events these two;—death and the resurrection.

Death, in this view, is not really death; it is a step in the march of that life which knows no death. It is, in fact, our second resurrection. When we fall asleep in Christ, he is even then to us "the resurrection and the life." He is so, in a new sense, and to a new effect. For he then severs completely the ties that bind us to the past and present here, and throws us wholly on the future elsewhere.

In our conversion,—when we believe in Christ now and here,—he is to us " the resurrection and the life." Spiritually and by faith, we rise from the death of guilt and apostacy and pass with him into "the heavenly places." And there we "sit with him at the right hand of God." This we realise by faith;— often by an effort of faith by no means easy. Our aspirations after the resurrection-life now,—our endeavours to enter into it and carry it out,—are hindered by our present worldly condition, and our present bodily frame. Both are unfavourable to its development. The world is adverse, and the world's prince. And " the flesh lusteth against the Spirit."

At death, these obstacles are taken out of the way. The world is left behind, and the prince of the world. The flesh is cast off. Emancipated from all earthly ties, disencumbered of all fleshly desires, we depart to be with Christ. Absent from the body, we are present with the Lord. Is it not a step in advance? It is virtually our entering, through a new resurrection, into a new life. The new resurrection is the escape which the soul, perfected in holiness, makes from the world and the body ;—from the world lying in wickedness, and from the "vile body" that is corrupting and corruptible. The new life is the rapturous communion with the risen Saviour which the soul, thus delivered, may enjoy. No outward object distracts ; no burden of flesh depresses. Away from the world of sense, abstracted from things external,—all carnal tastes and tendencies cast off,—we are at home with Christ in God. And it is with Christ as risen, that we are at home in God ;—in his favour, fellowship, and love. Leaving this earth, and the body which is mouldering in its dust,—with no thought of either any more,—we pass into the august presence in which our risen Lord has his home. And we are one with him there ; our disenthralled and disencumbered spirit is one with him there ; one with him in the life which in his human nature he reached when, on the very day of the crucifixion, he himself,—carrying the spirit of the dying penitent along with him,—passed into paradise.

Is he not then to us—is he not then pre-eminently, "the resurrection and the life?" Our death, thus

viewed, is no interruption of our resurrection-life, but
the lifting of it up, as by a new resurrection, to a
higher stage and platform, on which it may be
realized and unfolded more fully than it can be now.
Surely, one might be inclined to say, this is the consummation of the blessedness to which we may aspire,
as "living and believing in Christ."

Nay; it is not, it cannot be. For this unearthly
and incorporeal life has its drawbacks. It is an advance on what goes before undoubtedly. But the very
circumstances in respect of which it is so, constitute
its imperfection. In the step taken at death, the external world and the material body are cast off; and
the soul emerges bare and naked, to find its home
with Christ in God. This, I repeat again, is a step
in advance; it may be said to be a second resurrection. Here, on the earth, when Christ becomes to us
"the resurrection and the life," the utmost we can
look for, as regards the world and the flesh, is that
we may be in a position, and may have power, to
overcome the world and mortify the flesh. At death
we cease to have any connection with a world needing
to be overcome, and with flesh needing to be mortified. It is a great and blessed emancipation.

And yet there may be a more excellent way.
Absence from the world and the flesh,—exemption
from what is here the needful task of overcoming the
world and mortifying the flesh,—is not the perfection

of our being. It is not the perfection of Christ's. If there can be a world that does not require to be overcome, and flesh that does not require to be mortified;—if we can resume our worldly condition and our bodily frame, not only without the necessity of constant war against them in the spirit, but with the certainty of their ministering to our holiness and joy ; —if we can return to this earth, or such an earth as this, renewed and purified, and return to it with bodies incorruptible, spiritual, and immortal ;—is not this a higher hope than the other ? And is not this our full and final hope in him who, as "the resurrection and the life," calls us, in and with himself, to "inherit all things ?"

He has himself a glorified body ; he is coming to possess a renovated earth. And we, seeing him as he is, are to be like him. We are to reign with him, sharing his throne and crown. Our life, begun now in him as made of God to us "the resurrection and the life," is to have its perfection of holiness and happiness then ; for "when he who is our life shall appear, then shall we also appear with him in glory " (Colos. iii. 4).

Several important lessons of a practical nature may be drawn from the views now submitted.

I. As originally uttered, in his conversation with Martha, this statement of the Lord,—" I am the resur-

rection and the life ; he that believeth in me, though
he were dead, yet shall he live ; and whosoever liveth
and believeth in me shall never die,"—was fitted, and
probably intended, to throw light on what, to believers under the Old Testament dispensation, seems
to have been a dark object of contemplation—the
intermediate spiritual state that comes in between
death and the resurrection.

Of the resurrection itself they had a firm per-
suasion and bright prospect. It was "the hope of
Israel ;" "the hope of the promise made of God unto
the Fathers." Their views as to the nature of that
world into which the resurrection was to usher them,
may have been inadequate, and more or less carnal.
But when it is testified of them that they "walked as
strangers and pilgrims in the earth, declaring plainly
that they sought a country," "a better country,"
"a heavenly country,"—it is undeniable that they
looked for an inheritance to be reached by a resurrection.

A cloud, however, as it would appear, hung over
the blank space in front of that event. It was felt to
be a dreary void ;—that vast unseen region in space,
that blank interval in time, wherein flesh and blood
are not.

Hence, probably, the excessive shrinking, sometimes amounting almost to horror, which holy men
of old manifested, when they were standing on the

threshold of that unknown eternity. They express themselves almost as if it were annihilation that they feared. And hence the passionate, and, as we might be apt to think, even unbecoming eagerness, with which such men as David and Hezekiah cling to this earthly state, and deprecate removal from it, as if it were of all calamities the greatest. The gloom which appalled them rested mainly, I am persuaded, not on the territory beyond the resurrection—for that might admit of a well-defined embodiment in the imagination—but on the awful vacancy before it.

This word of the Lord to Martha is perhaps the first distinct sound given by the trumpet to chase these dark doubts away. "He that believeth in me, though he were dead, yet shall he live," is a promise that might point to the resurrection. But what follows, "Whosoever liveth and believeth in me shall never die,"—must embrace the intermediate state. And when connected with the intimation,—"I am the resurrection and the life,"—it conveyed unequivocally the bright hope, that "to be absent from the body" would be to be "present with the Lord." It is the same hope that the Lord gives, when he says to his fellow-sufferer on the cross, "To-day shalt thou be with me in Paradise." It is the hope which enables New Testament believers to look steadfastly, as they depart, into the opened heavens, and seeing their Lord there, "the resurrection and the life," to say, as Stephen said, falling asleep in him, "Lord Jesus, receive my spirit!"

II. Still the hope of Israel is the resurrection. The belief of the resurrection,—first, of Christ's resurrection for us, and then of ours in him,—is the indispensable condition of our hope, whether in time or for eternity. Take that away, and we are indeed of all men most miserable. We may well give up our baptism for the dead, our hourly jeopardy, our daily death, our fighting with wild beasts at Ephesus. To what purpose should we commit ourselves to a course of self-denial, taking up the cross and following Jesus? Better far abandon that dream of a higher life altogether, and make the most of the world as it is. "Let us eat and drink, for to-morrow we die."

Resurrection is the only way to life—Christ's resurrection, and ours in him. No otherwise than by death, and resurrection from death, can the curse of sin, and its accompanying corruption, be shaken off. A resurrection-life alone can meet our case. It is as risen with Christ that, in the first place, we live, and, in the second place, living, shall never die.

1. The beginning of this life, in our experience, is and must be a resurrection—a resurrection, in our case, corresponding to the resurrection that there was in the case of Christ. In order to this, as we have seen, two acts of God must concur and conspire—an act of power, restoring the vital principle; and a

judicial act, placing us, with our restored vitality, on a right footing with God, the righteous judge. Regeneration, in short, and justification, meet in this resurrection, and the two together are essential to its completeness. There must be a new birth, a new creation, effected by divine omnipotence. And along with that, and coincident with it, there must be the cancelling of the sentence of condemnation against us, and the passing in our favour of a sentence of acquittal and acceptance. It is thus that we are risen with Christ, quickened with him, justified in him.

2. As it is a resurrection-life in its commencement, so it is a resurrection-life throughout;—now in this present world; after death in the world of spirits; and after the resurrection, through all eternity, in "the new heavens and the new earth, wherein dwelleth righteousness."

How completely does this consideration identify the life that now is and the life that is to come! They are no more twain, but "one spirit." It is throughout one spirit that is the breath of this life; —the Spirit of life in Christ Jesus. It is the one Holy Spirit;—making us, in successive stages, more and more partakers of the resurrection-life of Christ.

Ah! how calm and holy is this progressive life! It knows no violent breaks. Even death and the resurrection are not interruptions of it. Its changeless stream flows ever equably on. Through the portals of the tomb it enters a purer, but a narrower, channel. At the opening of the doors for the King of Glory at the last, it issues forth,—a broad river of joy and love,—rolling its ceaseless tide among the islands of the blessed for ever. From the first, throughout, its essential character is the same. It has the same taste, the same colour, the same tendency. The life which we now live in the flesh, is the same as the life which we are to live when we depart to be with Christ. It is the same, as to all that constitutes its real nature, with the life which we are to live after the Lord has come to "change our vile body that it may be fashioned like unto his own glorious body," and to say "Come, ye blessed of my Father, inherit the kingdom prepared for you from the foundation of the world."

For, finally, the life is Christ throughout. He is "the resurrection and the life." He is so now; "to me to live is Christ." He is so at death; "I depart to be with Christ," "absent from the body I am present with the Lord." He is so at the resurrection; "I shall then bear the image of the heavenly." So Christ may be regarded as teaching in this great promise of eternal blessedness and glory. I am now; I shall be when I take you hence; I shall be still more when I return hither, bringing you with me again;—I am always, evermore, "the resurrection and the life." All is in me and of me; for I am all in all; the alpha and the omega; the first and the last; the living one; the same yesterday, to-day, and for ever!

Is not this your consolation, O believers? Is not this your hope? When your tears flow fresh for your loved and lost ones, you think of them as they are now, far away from you;—and for that you mourn. But you think of them as being with Christ;—and so you are comforted for them. When, again and again, the thought of their separation from you rushes back to afflict you, you think of them as coming with Christ to meet you;—and so you are comforted for yourselves. It is their being with Christ that comforts you for them;—it is their coming with Christ that comforts you for yourselves. And when your own dissolution is present to your mind, and the eternal state is in solemn prospect before you; on what do you fasten as your hope? Is it not on the assurance that when you leave the body you go to Christ,—and that when you resume the body again it is to be with him where he is;—to "behold his glory, the glory which the Father hath given him," for "the love with which he loved him before the world was?"